YOUR SPIRIT CALLS

IN SEARCH OF

Your Spiritual Voice

SECOND EDITION
REVISED

WARREN ZIEGLER

ENSPIRITING PRESS, LLC

PUBLISHED BY
Enspiriting Press, LLC
3384 S. Valentia Ct.
Denver, Colorado 80231 USA
www.enspiritingpress.com

Second Edition, Revised
Copyright © 2009 Enspiriting Press, LLC

First Printing
Copyright © 2001 by Warren Ziegler

EDITOR
Dorsey Moore

COVER DESIGN/BOOK PRODUCTION
Sheila J. Hentges, *Hentges Design, Inc.*

INDEX
Madge Walls, *All Sky Indexing*

Library of Congress Control Number: 2 0 0 8 9 3 9 3 1 7

ISBN: 9 7 8 0 6 1 5 2 2 7 6 7 2

SAN: 8 5 7 - 4 1 9 7

PRINTED IN CANADA
The text has been printed on chlorine free paper made with 100% post-consumer waste.

All knowledge is for the sake of action.
All action is for the sake of friendship.
ARISTOTLE

Contents

PART TWO

PART THREE

Introduction

by Mandy Ziegler

Passion for his work, compassion for people, love of earth and all inhabitants shines through these pages. Warren Ziegler tapped into the spiritual realm and discovered nine archetypes of human endeavor. Beyond personality or behavior, *When Your Spirit Calls* speaks to the overarching desire for spiritual fulfillment and satisfaction.

Warren spent most of his adult life helping people discover their potential. His envisioning workshops invited individuals and groups from diverse backgrounds to listen to the voice of their spirit and to search for their spiritual archetype.

Though the archetypes given here came to Warren in a flash, he studied them for many years through his seminars and classes, learning the types in depth even as he taught others how to connect with them.

His enspiriting work and his futures invention work changed peoples' lives by unifying all the aspects, roles, labels and aspirations they lived with. Even now I hear from workshop participants of twenty-five or thirty years ago. They tell me Warren's was one of the most brilliant workshops they ever experienced.

During the twenty-plus years I spent with him, Warren devoted his time perfecting the enspirited envisioning disciplines and practices. His own calling included helping people realize their purpose in life and create a new direction in their relationships and their work.

As you go through the book, you'll see that the end of each section has related questions for you to reflect upon as you read through the descriptions of each archetype. (In this instance, archetype means your spiritual essence, your inner wisdom, your spiritual voice.)

Whether one of these archetypes speaks to you or you discover a new invitation, Warren's methods teach you how to connect with your inner voice, to acknowledge and act upon what your deep spirit truly desires and is called to do in the world.

I encourage you to record your responses in writing, images, memories and futures as they come to you. By recording your journey as you search for your spiritual archetype, you can review and reflect on your discoveries until your spirit's call becomes clear to you.

At the time of his unexpected death, Warren felt strongly that his work needed to continue. It is my strong desire to fulfill his hopes that more people can experience the discovery of their spiritual archetype. His work is too important to lie idle.

In this revised edition, we have attempted to stay true to Warren's vision while making the book more accessible and readable.

As we move into the future, this guidebook has the potential to benefit the individual, society, the earth and the universe.

I hope you enjoy the book. Exploring the essential qualities and characteristics of each of the nine social archetypes can bring a central theme to your life. This provides a unique opportunity to learn who you really are, why you are here and how to put the future into your own hands.

Preface

As my reflection and writing began, I sensed that underneath my own earlier work on gifts and talents lay a huge reservoir of undisclosed and untapped spirit-energy that would give meaning and direction to those whose own gifts were unrecognized, unrealized, or misused. In short, the next step in my research and writing about the human spirit demanded probing into an arena of grand human possibility.

I asked myself about the gifts and talents of the persons with whom I and my colleagues had worked in envisioning the future. That work began with futures-invention in the early 70s when I was at Syracuse University. With the encouragement and support of Elise Boulding in the early 80s, I moved to the vocabulary and practices of imaging the future, and then to the enspiriting work, the enspirited envisioning, and the enspiriting disciplines and practices which I finally codified beginning in 1989 and which appeared in the 1994 publication, *Ways of Enspiriting—Transformative Practices for the Twenty-First Century.*

I brought together my ideas and experience about gifts and talents with the envisioning and deep imaging work of these participants. I began a mental review of this enormous array of compelling images which I had been fortunate enough to witness. They came flooding back like the sweep of a great, unending wave.

Indeed, sitting at my desk, I went into a kind of trance, an altered state of consciousness in response to my questions:

> *When these folks were envisioning the future, what were they doing? From where did their visions, their images, their intuitions, their mind-experiments come? What was their source? Yes, from their human spirit. But is that everything? Why this image rather than that, this vision rather than that, this sense, hunch, intuition rather than that, this call to compelling action rather than that?*

Gathered over 25 years, this rich futures-material covered almost all arenas of human endeavors, human concerns and problems, and human possibilities. Where did that stuff come from? In a flash, I woke and wrote down the nine spiritual archetypes, the nine calls of and from the human spirit.

Three-and-one-half years later, following serious reflection, analysis, and self-argument, they are exactly the same as first appeared:

- **The Entrepreneurial Spirit**
- **The Sustaining Spirit**
- **The Loving and Caring Spirit**
- **The Mending Spirit**
- **The Just Spirit**
- **The Organizational Spirit**
- **The Enlivening Spirit**
- **The Reflective Spirit**
- **The Poetic Spirit**

This book invites the self-exploration that may lead you to listen to the voice of your spirit and hear its call. These nine archetypes of the human spirit have come from the work of the envisioners among us: persons who stepped beyond the boundaries of their social biographies (roles, jobs, beliefs, attitudes, affiliations) to envision a future to which they were called by their own spirit.

The invitation is to explore these archetypes of the human spirit as avenues to the call of your own spirit. Your spirit invites you to listen, to hear, to translate into your own biography, and to enact that to which you are called.

This is the invitation: Ask yourself, What are you up to? What is your project on this planet? What does your own spirit have to say?

And listen. *Deep listen*, as I have called it. Throughout the book are questions, enspiriting practices, and exercises that have proven helpful to many people who have asked themselves those questions.

Warren Ziegler

DECEMBER 2001
Denver, Colorado

PART ONE

1

The Search

IN SEARCH OF OURSELVES

The Quest

Since the awakening of our grand humanity on this planet, when spirit was breathed into us so that we became conscious of ourselves, the human species has been searching for its reality and its meaning. What is that spirit which is lodged within us? Why is it? How does it do its work within us? What is its call? These questions have intrigued us since time began.

That quest has not only been intellectual or of historic interest. It is also very personal, touching each of us in unique ways. Ever since I can remember, my own spirit has been talking to me, though my hearing has been severely impaired by a culture that denies spirit's presence within us. In our de-spiritualized age, we have forgotten that our spirit calls us. We have learned not to listen to that call.[1]

Is the human spirit lodged in each of us? Yes. When you learn the practices and do the exercises this book offers, your spirit will respond. Its voice, its message, its call await your invitation. It makes your presence on this planet unique and deeply satisfying. "Ah hah," you will say softly to yourself or proclaim to the world, "Now I know why I am here!"

Are you ready to respond to the call of your spirit? In working with thousands of people over the past thirty years in enspiriting and envisioning the future, I have found that many were ready and some were not. Nevertheless, no one is closed out. When you and your spirit enter into dialogue, you will discover how joyful and exhilarating this is.

The basic premise is that we all have spirit. It works within us, whether or not we are aware of it. Your spirit has emerged into your life spontaneously, particularly in childhood. My first exercise in Chapter Six invites you to reacquaint yourself with that experience.

If your spirit has been too long absent in your life, how might you best bring it back? How might you hear its call to you? By listening, a special kind of enspirited listening I call deep listening. This is a way of listening through silence, listening as an empty vessel, to be filled with that which your spirit offers.

A Transformative Moment

Bringing spirit back into your life is the central invitation and theme of this book... but it is not the only one. *Enspiriting*, listening to the voice of your spirit, is not a journey to be undertaken alone. You may well start out that way. But, ultimately, it is not a solo trip. Intimate friends and family may be with you, perhaps thousands of others, perhaps more. There is a broad movement toward the transformation point that our species is rapidly approaching. In my view, we are already there. This transformation requires the presence of our spirit in the fullness of its purposes if we are to make it through the mounting crises confronting human civilization. Each of us has his own contribution to make. This transformation is not simply an objective condition we can only observe or comment upon. It is not just a paradigm shift that pundits have been announcing for decades. You and I are in it up to our chinny chin chins. We must respond to its invitation, which comes from our spirit, or we are lost.

Who invites? Who calls?

How might this invitation come to you? In what guise? In this book, you should find an invitation that suits you. In one or another of its chapters, you will hear your own particular call. That call will speak to your deepest aspirations, your fondest dreams. You will find that you can wait no longer.

Your search begins in Chapter Two with *The Abundance of Spirit—Seeking Your Gifts and Talents*. If you are dissatisfied, if you sense that within lies a great adventure to fashion a new world for yourself, then these chapters start you on the path of reinventing yourself. The source of that invention is your own spirit. Its abundance is the invitation to your true self.

But what is your true self? Is it a psychologist's fantasy or a personal utopia? Is it a negative self-image, not knowing what is to become of you? No. Those are surface signals only.

The search is for your spiritual archetype, that which is your essence, that which gives direction and meaning to everything you are and do. The search begins with uncovering your gifts and talents, which express a spiritual archetype. It names who and what you are.

I am not talking about jobs, roles, labels, professions, or occupations. Roles and labels prevent us from seeing within to the unique person, to the spirit, to the full, dynamic richness.

Is your spiritual archetype captured and framed in your job, your occupation, or your profession? Too often, it is not. In the shifting winds of economic and technological change, too many of us end up seeking a holding place that provides economic security and a quick answer to the social recognition question, "What do you do?"

Listen, now, to hear if your spirit calls you:

- I call you to risk, adventure, making the curve, voices the **Entrepreneurial Spirit**.
- I call you to sustain the world, to rediscover our partnerships with each other, with all living creatures, and with our very Earth, invites the **Sustaining Spirit**.
- I call you to nurture, to empathy, to compassion, welcomes the **Loving and Caring Spirit**.
- I call you to mend our fragmentations, to make us whole again, to teach us not to wound each other in body, mind, or spirit, offers the **Mending Spirit**.
- I call you to bring justice back into the world, in all varieties of human, political, social and economic relationships and practices, calls out the **Just Spirit**.
- I call you to reshape our purposes and to re-create the organizational space among us so as to release our spirit-

energy in the interest of each and all of us, crafts the **Organizational Spirit**.

- I call you to generate, release, facilitate, animate the human spirit within, your human spirit, my human spirit, everyone's human spirit, in every situation and in every setting, welcomes the **Enlivening Spirit**.

- I call you to think the unthinkable, to unpack complexity, to unravel the knot, to uncover the criticals and go to the fundamentals, says the **Reflective Spirit**.

- I call you to re-create reality, to describe the world in its underlying metaphors, in images of sight, sound, language, feeling, to lift the edges of the holographic curtain to show us how we might reconfigure our world, shapes the **Poetic Spirit**.

Your Call

Does one of these call to you? Does one of these spiritual archetypes enfold your beingness? If it does, and if you so acknowledge, it becomes your very presence on this planet.

Perhaps more than one calls to you. Your biography, your action, your intention, your self-image may respond to a rich mix of these archetypes. Finding that out will be extraordinarily exciting.

But what if none of them calls to you? Are you lost? Of course not, just the opposite. You might well find your own spirit drinking at some other fountain. If so, you have embarked on the grandest adventure of your lifetime, to uncover your own spiritual essence, to learn to listen to your own spirit's unique call. That is why I have written this book, to help others learn to listen to the voice of their spirit and respond creatively and lovingly to its invitation, whatever that may be!

At this moment in history, are we all called? In principal, Yes! But in practice, so many of us find it difficult to identify our spirit's invitation, much less affirm and respond to it. We try this and that in order to learn what is our project, our place, our beingness on this planet, in this lifetime. At worst, we seek fulfillment and forgetfulness through the addictions of acquiring power, affluence, material things, through the ideological or religious certainty of the true believer, and through alcohol, drugs, profligate sex, and running from one thrill to another, one job to another, one place to another. At best, we seek out the programs which offer empowerment, renewal, emancipation, self-help, or spiritual belief, in the hope that one of them will bring us to a nirvana in which we can lose ourselves and walk through life unconscious of our spirit.

The Abundance of Spirit

Here, in this enspiriting work, there is no "losing yourself." It is about finding yourself. You start by searching for your gifts and talents. Chapter Two, *The Abundance of Spirit*, is a fast track starting point. Its practices will move you quickly beyond labels and to a new space of discovery whose territory lies deep within and whose boundaries are unmapped. You will map them because this is your space, these are your gifts, your boundaries. How do you move from uncovering that inner space to enacting yourself in the world? This book will help you listen as your spirit calls, and it will help you live your response.

FROM THE EXPERIENCE OF THOUSANDS

Naming the Archetypes

What are these spiritual archetypes? Where do they come from? Are these all of them? Suppose you are called by one I do not name?

These are fair questions. My aim is not to close off your experiencing your own spirit. It is to open doors to the room where your spirit dwells, so that you may enter, explore, discover, enjoy, and enact, which means to come to your own true action in this world. Here again is the list of the spiritual archetypes offered in this book:

The Entrepreneurial Spirit

The Sustaining Spirit

The Loving and Caring Spirit

The Mending Spirit

The Just Spirit

The Organizational Spirit

The Enlivening Spirit

The Reflective Spirit

The Poetic Spirit

The Origins of the Nine Spiritual Archetypes

Our human spirit calls to us to be and to do what too many of us have neglected, dismissed, or hidden from. What is that call?

It is a multiple call, and each of the nine I have uncovered comes from listening deeply to thousands of people over the past 30 years. Who were these people? They have come from many different countries and cultures, different social classes, educational backgrounds, ethnic and historical roots, and religious identifications. Their work has been about envisioning the future. In that envisioning, they were asked to describe their concerns. Not surprisingly, these concerns covered the wide range of human problems which brought with them discomfort, conflict, unrest, unease, fears, even pain. They were invited to learn the discipline and use the practices of *deep imaging* to envision a future in which their concerns were well addressed. It is from that work that I have extracted the nine spiritual archetypes. These people focused their concerns and their deep images on the future of their schools and colleges, their cities and neighborhoods, their natural environment, their nation-states and how best to govern them, their religious communities, their healthcare, their prisons, their police, their corporations, labor unions, farms, professions, their civic associations and groups, their racism and their violence. Many did personal envisioning of their lives, their families, and their work. From their envisioning came, quite literally, thousands of images of the future, and of the compelling actions which those visions invited them to take.

Keep in mind, these participants were not "experts" on the future, those we have come to call "futurists" in the last 40 or 50 years. I asked them, "What kind of future do you want to bring about that is any different from the present?" "What are your intentions toward the future?"

Thus, the origin of the spiritual archetypes set forth in this book come from these envisioners, futures-inventors, and concerned citizens of all walks of life. And as the responses accumulated over the years from many workshops, seminars, envisioning projects, and one-with-one enspiritings, my own spirit was at work!

What lies under the vision?

My own spirit compelled me to ask: "What are these folks driving at?" "Where do these images—so varied in their focus, yet so detailed—come from?" Just their social history? Only their unique biographies? Mainly, their subcultures? The mass media? What they have learned in life and about life?

I was impelled by my own spirit to raise these questions because so much of these visionary materials announced new paths for them and sometimes for all of us. Their visions were not about making a lot of money, raising the bottom line, acquiring higher status, more power, greater influence, personal fame and fortune, nor about moving up the ladder of material success, practicing what Thorstein Veblen called "conspicuous consumption."

Mainly, their intentions toward the futures of themselves and their relevant worlds were about forging new paths, testing the waters of their consciousness of what was truly important to them. Their images of the future went against the grain, were counter-conventional, and sought alternatives to current realities.

Was something "wrong" with these envisioners? Had they been abused in their childhood? frustrated by their lack of success? Well, in a way, they were special people, for they dared to envision different futures. But they were really quite ordinary too. They were married, divorced, many raising families, some retired and some still in high school or college, paying off their mortgages, shopping for their food and sundries, often not pleased with the systems of healthcare and schools. They were fearful of nuclear war, or of an economic, political, social, or environmental catastrophe that would engulf all of us.

The Research

Perhaps more than any other "futurist" on the planet, I have listened to the heartfelt responses of envisioners and enspiritors to my invitation to go deep, to listen to their inner voice, their central beingness which is the voice of their spirit, to learn what is most important to them.

Their faces, their laughter and tears, their spirits are still with me as I write these chapters, though some I worked with as many as three decades ago. They were students, teachers, managers, doctors, nurses, consultants, farmers, artists, politicians, factory workers, government officials, ex-offenders, persons from all walks of life who wanted to invent their futures. As I worked with them, their spirit came to me. Give attention, Warren. This is what we are about.

So I learned to listen to their hopes, their intentions, their compelling images, as well as to their despairs, and their unrequited spirits that are the reverse side, the inner painting of the cultural canvas of the twenty-first century. In short, I began a reflection like the kind of deep questioning you yourself will use as you explore the source of your own intentions, aspirations, and dreams for yourself and your world. I sought to go underneath the enormous amount of their visionary data to its sources. I asked, "What drives them to envision these futures and to seek to actualize them in the here-and-now?" The nine spiritual archetypes described in these pages came to my awareness as I processed this amazing accumulation of visionary data from these participants. These envisioners, ordinary folks from all over the world, were responding to a call in them, a call to them, which came from their spirit.

The Concept of the Spiritual Archetype

What is a "spiritual archetype" as I use it in this book? How does this concept relate to the call of your spirit, to your spirit's voice, to that which lies at the core of your being? And why did these nine spiritual archetypes surface in my reflection? Why did they emerge into my conscious awareness, and not nine other spiritual archetypes?

At the outset, I think it's important to say that the spiritual archetype is a concept. It is an idea. It seeks to give an account of the underlying reality that your spirit is enfleshed in you, not by accident but by purpose. Your beingness, your presence on this planet is not random. It is not accidental. You are constitutive of a purpose that transcends your biology and transcends your particular culture and group. That purpose, your purpose, is known by the call of your spirit which I now invite you to listen for, to hear, and to enact in your life. In one way, that call is unique to you because your own spirit, the deepest and truest and most real part of yourself, is unique to you. My spirit is in me and your spirit is in you. The choice your spirit made to enflesh in you was and is not accidental. Please don't take my word for this. Please don't require "empirical" or "scientific" proof. Rather, query your own experience. Respond to my invitation to discover this for yourself, out of your own inner listening and out of your own deep learning about what your life experience says to you. Science and technology can do remarkable things for us. But they can't keep us from dying. They can't keep us from killing. They can't keep us from loving. They can't keep us from our choices. And they certainly can't keep us from listening to the call of our spirit.

I do not say that these are the only calls. I do not say that this is an exhaustive naming of spiritual archetypes. These are the ones I have uncovered, named, and offer to you. The nine spiritual archetypes described in this book are templates, or ideal-types, to lie beside your spirit's call and see if they fit. They should help you to identify, describe, and better understand exactly what your own spirit is telling you.

Why make this offer? Because so many good people I know, hear about and read about are not yet clear about why they are here. They are not clear about their purposes. They are not clear about how they might impact their world and give some direction to their own lives. So they try this or that, impelled by an inner source but not knowing what that is. They are frustrated, disappointed, unfulfilled. Perhaps their work is misplaced. Perhaps their lives are misspent. If you are one of these, read on. You have some joyous work to do.

But there is more. These archetypes, these essences of human spirit, are about transformation. Your spirit might call you to that. That call is to something new and vital, which portends a different way of living, of being and doing. It starts with you but might involve other people as well. That indeed would be beautiful.

But what if these nine spiritual archetypes do not speak to you? What if there is no fit between one or another of the archetypes and who you have been and are becoming? That's perfectly okay. Search for your own mix, your own uniqueness, the special quality of your own spirit's call.

DEFINING AND DESCRIBING THE ARCHETYPES

Unexplored Territory

It will be helpful to review in greater detail the focus and drive of each spiritual archetype before you begin your search and self-questioning. This is the landscape you are about to explore. For many of us, it is unexplored territory. But we know some things about this inner territory of the human spirit. For example, in the desert of our mostly de-spiritualized world, there are some oases. You can rest at one, reflect, relax, and drink at its always-replenishing fountain. Then if you will, you can move on. Some of you will reach the border, look back, say: "None of these archetypes represent my spirit's essence," and continue your search. Others will realize that all of their searches, dreams, and inner questions reside and are requited right here.

The spiritual archetypes described below are basic essences, ideal patterns for the human spirit's presence within and among us. They help us to understand who and what each of us is. They bring a clarity of persuasion, passion, project, and potential to those of us who sense, perhaps even from infancy, that we are called, but know not what is the call and who is calling.

The Entrepreneurial Spirit

One of the first spiritual archetypes I came to was the entrepreneurial spirit. It is explored in Chapter Three. This spiritual archetype goes far back in history, to the inventors of fire, language, cities, domesticated grain and animals, and to all of the other first-order inventions which put the human species on the path to its initial civilizations. But we have a long way to go. Our need for a vast number of next-order social inventions is now as desperate as at any time in human history. Who will make them?

Through the exercises in Chapter Three, you may discover that a sleeping giant lies deep within you, waiting to be called out to breathe the fresh air and roar its proclamations to the world. The entrepreneurial spirit, if it is yours, will take you to new places on your life's path, and it will encourage and support new activities if you heed its voice. This is childhood's insatiable curiosity resurrected in you to pull you to creativity and inventiveness. It will encourage you to do other than your peers.

The Sustaining Spirit

The chapters and practices in Chapter Four, *The Sustaining Spirit—Partnership Rediscovered,* are for those whose spirit calls them to create ways of partnering with the Earth and all of its living creatures, including human beings. Do you sense deep within that you are one of that group, who are called to uncover new ways of being and living with the Earth? Through these discovery exercises, you may hear your inner voice speaking clearly and compellingly about your partnering with the Earth.

The Loving and Caring Spirit

This spiritual archetype is about loving, caring, empathy, and nurturing. One would hope that these relational qualities were evenly distributed among humankind, among all parents, all teachers, and all counselors, and that they would pervade all of our human relationships in every form and content. Of course they don't.

Might your spirit tell you that herein lies your special strength and prowess, that the acts and competencies of engendering fulfilling relationships constitute an expression of your deepest self? The loving and caring spirit is the focus of the chapters and practices in Chapter Five. It is here that you may find your special call, if you will listen deeply when your spirit speaks.

The Mending Spirit

The call of the mending spirit is described in the chapters and practices of Chapter Six. Is that, perhaps, your underlying theme? It follows closely on that path of the loving and caring spirit. Yet here, spirit's purposes and methods are different, for we are talking about mending that which has been torn asunder. Mending is making whole that which has been separated into parts. It is about a reintegration in new ways that will stretch our imagination to its infinity. Healing, medical or natural, is one way to talk about the art of mending. But this spiritual call and competence goes far beyond the "doctor-patient" relationship, beyond healing the sick of body, heart, or mind.

Most people on our planet are split off from their centers. There is a pervasive separation that characterizes most of what we do. Job is split from work. Government is split from governance. Sex is split from erotic loving. Family is split from friendship. The institution of religion is split from God. Teaching is split from learning. And most important, the human biography is split from its spirit. All of these splits need mending. Who is called? Who are the menders? Chapter Six, *The Mending Spirit—Growing the Whole*, is designed to help you discern if this is the stream of the human spirit that flows through your life.

The Just Spirit

Chapter Seven, *The Just Spirit—In Search of Governance,* is offered to those of you who are ready to learn from your spirit's voice how we might live together without violating each other's spirit. That is the question of governance. Mostly, throughout human history, we have been unable to come up with a response to that question which favors us all. Now, in this transformative moment, we are in desperate need of springing loose these social inventors.

Note the phrase, without violating each other's spirit. This is the seminal ground in which to plant the seeds of human rights, a fairly recent social invention which seeks to grow in all countries and cultures but is more noted for its absence than its presence. There is more. The just spirit applies as powerfully to family life and to one-with-one relationships as within whole societies. How shall a family govern itself so that no one within its reach violates the spirit of another, whether it is child, wife, mother, husband, father, or the extended family? How shall schools govern themselves justly, so that we learn about each other and our world without violating each other's spirit? Justice and learning are inextricably interwoven. When those of you called by this spiritual archetype show us why and how, learning and its governance in education will never look the same.

The Organizational Spirit

The organizational spirit archetype speaks to those who are called to gather us together in our collective conduct in such a way that our human spirit flourishes.

In this day and age, "organization" has become the metaphor for social reality. It has long replaced the older social dimension of "community." In one major corporation with which I worked, managers sought to envision and actualize the spirit and practices of community into its organizational milieu, into the ways its members related to and worked with each other. But senior managers stonewalled the effort in their quest for rising profits. Consultants learned to substitute the notions of team-building, diversity, and learning to feel good about each other for the sacred idea of community.

It is still unclear, at least to me, if the organizational principle must pervade our lives so extremely. How might we best organize our businesses, our schools, our hospitals and health care delivery systems, our governments, our churches, and our families? These have become powerful questions, drawing upon so much of our intellectual resource. But we have not learned well enough how to create the space in every organization for each member's, employee's, participant's, or citizen's spirit to emerge.

Might this be your space? Is your path to invent the ways of our working and making and creating together? To break through the barriers of organizational omnipotence to the space where, together, we may be fully human? Such space lies far beyond roles, rules, making money, or being successful. This space reaches far back in human history to our early consciousness of ourselves as both creators and creatures of our basic organizational proclivities. It reaches far forward to a new era wherein we all will have learned how and why to release each person's spirit-energy in the interest of all, and everyone's spirit-energy in the interest of each. Probe the exercises in Chapter Eight, *The Organizational Spirit,* to see if this is your quest and adventure.

The Enlivening Spirit

Perhaps most dear to me because it is my call is the enlivening spirit, that inner voice which serves to bring to life spirit's expression in everyone else.

The enlivening spirit offers, invites, cajoles, soothes, provokes, and witnesses to each of us, one-by-one, that which the human spirit in each of us calls us to. It invites another person's spirit into its own inner well of spirit-energy, warms and loves it, empathizes with it, judges not, gives to the other full and complete attention, and provides the space for the other's spirit and biography to play together and to negotiate a new presence on the planet. Its main practices are deep listening and deep questioning, the first two disciplines of the spirit. Each of us is invited to become adept in these disciplines and attendant practices. But not too many of us are called with the strength of thousands to focus the enlivening enterprise on the singular person, one-by-one or in small groups of communities of learners. The enlivener offers herself to others because of her own vast reservoirs of spirit-energy.

As you respond to the invitation in the chapters and practices in Chapter Nine, *The Enlivening Spirit,* discern if that is your call. Or if the enlivening spirit joins with other spiritual archetypes which, all together, constitute your uniqueness.

The Reflective Spirit

Some of the envisioners with whom I have worked offer a provocative stance that comes from the spiritual archetype I have named the reflective spirit. Its most visible expression is the quality of thinking before speaking, sometimes even thinking out loud in the midst of the most precarious of situations. Here, thought truly precedes action. In this spirit's expression, there is no such thing as impatience. The practical becomes the ruminative. The pragmatic translates into considering all alternatives. No question, even the most shocking or foolish, is inadmissible. The action lies in the thought. Uncovering the criticals and going to the fundamentals is its métier, though all of us are invited to and practice these enspiriting crafts. Chapter Ten, *The Reflective Spirit,* provides the exercises of the inner space to ascertain how and why this might be your call.

The Poetic Spirit

Finally, there is the poetic spirit. It does not require you to write, or even to read, poetry, though some may. A little piece of this essence is in each of us because we all have imagination. Its full call is to those, special among us, who put anything and everything—human relationships, events, organized behaviors, history, the future, human dispositions and needs, problems, solutions, even our basic "human nature"—into a new language, into new ways of perceiving, sensing, and interacting. I call these depictions or metaphors, "stand-fors." In their being enacted through dance, music, literature, painting, sculptures, images, and storytelling, new ways of being and doing are uncovered that stretch our imagination to its borders and show us our human possibilities.

Overlap

I think we want to ask again, "Is there an overlap here? Do these archetypes of spiritual presence on the planet interweave, parallel, or offset each other? Might not each of us, in our biographies, our character, our works, our relationships, express several of these powerful forces of the human spirit at the same time?" Of course. Why single them out? One supports the other. They are sympathetic.

But I remind you that an archetype is more than a predisposition. In the ways of the human spirit, it describes an essence, a call, a stream of adventures as your spirit essays its journey on this planet through you and not someone else. When self-clarity is achieved, your biography, your persona, the space in the world you take for your own, may well be characterized by one of these archetypes, or a rich mix thereof.

Through the enspiriting practices this book offers, I think you will find the clear stream of your spirit running deep through the events and the choices you make in your life. Cultures, institutions, and biographies muddy those waters, so that too many of us end up dissatisfied and frustrated. Unclear, we may try this or that, but we are never as effective as we sense we have it in us to be. We are searching, true. But are we listening... deep listening.

I invite you to journey to the further shores to which your spirit takes you. On that new land, you may discover that which is special to you, your unique essence that you can offer to the world.

THE METHOD

How shall we proceed?

What has impressed me most over the years is that those who have deliberately sought to hear the voice of their spirit have *listened* for it. It was a special kind of listening which I came to call deep listening. I want to invite you to learn and to practice deep listening because it will give you access to your spirit when that is important for you to do. In searching for your spiritual archetype, deep listening is the main method. In Chapter One, I will guide you through the steps. Indeed, when I first learned, practiced, and offered this method, I called it *Deep Listening the Empty Vessel Way.*[2] Through deep listening, you will find the path to your renewal, your healing, your calling, and to your place in the world. I think we must all become deep listeners, now, not later, if we are to create a world without destitution, without hopelessness, and worthy of the promise that our human spirit offers to each and every one of us.

The Method of the Book

I have written this book to help open the door to the room within which your spirit dwells. That is my intention. As you read on, one of the chapters will lead you to your deepest self or will offer ways of uncovering it, of that I am sure. Why? Because in these rooms are encompassed our aspirations to become fully human, to be fully integrated with our spirit.

As the door opens, you will discover your compelling image and your compelling action. In these, your spirit speaks to you. You will shift from the mode of reading to the modes of listening and doing.

These are the practices of enspiriting by which we learn to listen to, for, and with our spirit.

What is this enspiriting? What is its language, its meaning, its application and relevance, its new place in our lives?

Enspiriting

As I have come to know it, enspiriting is a twofold action, a reciprocity in which there are two "actors." One actor, the one you know best, is you, the human person, characterized by your biography. The other actor is your spirit, your human spirit. Enspiriting is the dynamic interaction between the two.

On the one hand, enspiriting is the active voice of your spirit speaking out, often without words. Sometimes the spirit announces itself in feelings that won't go away, or in images that enter your mind as pictures or through one of your other senses. Sometimes the voice of your spirit comes to you in intuitions or flashes of insight.

Enspiriting is the act of listening to the voice of your spirit in its many manifestations. Unless you listen, your spirit's voice goes unheeded. So you want to learn to listen deeply to your body, your feelings, your images, your intuitions, and your altered states of consciousness. Are you ready to listen? Have you prepared yourself? Preparation, readiness, and competence are involved here.

Chapter One, *When Your Spirit Speaks—Practices in Deep Listening,* is about how your spirit has already spoken to you. It reminds you that enspiriting is our most human voice, that which spirit brings to us when it is enfleshed. It is the reason for our being here, living on a planet on an outer edge of our spiral galaxy, far from its center.

How do I learn to enspirit? Keeping a Journal

One of the tricks of the trade in enspiriting is to learn how to enter the space for spirit as a commonplace human activity, whenever it is wanted or needed. Using a journal helps open that space when you are ready to jot down your moments of insight as they come to you. Respond to the questions posed in this book, note and record the steps in your journey to the space for spirit.

From Exercise to Practice to Competence

Take your journal with you wherever you go. Enspiriting can and does happen very quickly when you are ready and prepared. Its modus operandi is deep listening. That mode you can learn to enter into as fast as you can take and exhale a few deep breaths, empty your tant'ien (see endnote no.6) and shift two degrees out of your mind's and your body's current perspective to the new one of your spirit's space.

You can use your journal to record in as you choose. As you engage with your spirit, you will enter a new space where your spirit feels comfortable enough to speak out because you are listening for it and can hear it. As your spirit learns that it is welcome, its space expands within you as well as outside, with other persons. That space becomes the ambience within which your transformation begins. You practice, then, at the different ways to listen for and to hear the voice of your spirit. These are the seven disciplines of the spirit. You learn, or rediscover, how and why to enspirit. You are on the path to discovering your true self. You are becoming spiritually competent.

The Enspiriting Matrix

The nine spiritual archetypes are "pure" in their naming, their description, their definition. They are ideal-types or templates through which you can search out the quality and purpose of your own spirit's presence in you. I have sought to convey their essences so that you can discover if, how, and why you respond to their clear invitations as your own calling, your compelling image, that which you **cannot not be** and **cannot not do**. Be elated at your "Ah-hah, so that is what my life is about!" Be overjoyed if you discover your own special mix, where one archetype explains your compelling action in one situation, another in a different setting.

Your spirit, even in its essential mode, speaks and acts through your personal history as well as through your particular role as a citizen in world history. The enspiriting practices often lead to a deep negotiation between your spirit and your biography. In that rich interplay, your biography may respond more fruitfully to a complex possibility your spirit offers, a mix of archetypes as in *mending* and *caring*, or *entrepreneuring* and *organizing*, or *sustaining* and *enjusting*.[3]

How do you discover if you are called to respond to more than one invitation? Intuition and a feeling for it, coming from your deep listening to and deep questioning of yourself, are effective ways. Another way involves a bit of recording.

As you respond to the invitations in each chapter, record and review your responses in your journal. You will begin to get a sense of where you are at this point in your life, to what extent you have responded to a particular call, to a particular theme.

This becomes a self-searching about the ways you have responded to the call and invitation of a particular archetype, or the extent to which you find that particular archetype speaks through your spirit to your biography, your intentions, and your actions.

For most of us, the calls are not a perfect fit. For many of us, there is little congruence between our call and our expression in this life. Many barriers and constraints block spirit's expression. Discerning that which your spirit invites may take a piece of a lifetime. Unlike Mozart, who perhaps knew and responded at age five, most of us take a lot longer. This is a small but an important point. The human spirit is not concerned with chronological, biological, or biographical time. Old, middle-aged, young are not its scale. When you are ready, you will respond to the invitation. Enacting spirit's call constitutes a joyful adventure yet to be taken, just starting, well begun, deeply into, or nearing completion.

IN SEARCH OF YOUR SPIRIT

Childhood Speaks

Spirit speaks in many ways, perhaps no more so than with youngsters. With youngsters it speaks through a spontaneous dance, through a laugh or a cry, and through wide-open eyes of wonder and curiosity when a butterfly settles on the knee, when the puppy nuzzles into the crook of an arm, and when fingers paint inner images on blank paper. Spirit speaks in the gentle cooperation of two youngsters building a sand castle, in an honest response without guile. Most often, it speaks in an inner listening, giving attention to internal sounds, feelings, pictures that come from a space both unique to that youngster, and yet part of the universal space in which all spirit resides.

When I speak of the search for our spirit, it is not about hidden agendas, tasks and goals, worries, or false stories we soon learn about how the world works. This chapter is an invitation to bring into your conscious awareness some stories of your spirit speaking out, and your listening to it. I invite you to search for these stories from your childhood years.

Do you remember your days of innocence? Can you reach and touch an inner memory, in recall or in flashback, when your spirit, unbidden, was simply "there" in all of its simple splendor? In these days of innocence, you were your spirit. That is what innocence means. Throughout humankind, that wholeness, that naturalness, that integration of spirit with body and mind is recognized and supported, cherished and celebrated until the youngster is required to grow up. Whatever the culture, wherever the country, before the growing up takes place, the child's spirit is completely present. That wholeness and integration are the marks of innocence.

Can your spirit's experience of another human spirit be recalled? Of course. The bonding of your spirit with another, the search for its welcome by others, lies within. Your spirit just awaits a jostle, a tickle, or a beckoning finger from your consciousness of yourself to remind you of these stories. Sometimes the stories are about another human being, sometimes about a forest, a tree, an animal, water, mud, leaves, or mountains. Once, I worked in a one-with-one enspiriting with a person whose spirit was nurtured by turtles, doves, mud, leaves, snails, and undergrowth, and whose spirit in turn called her to nurture our natural world. Perhaps she was an unrealized sustaining spirit. Her biography resisted. She is still learning to enter that space where her spirit and her inner biography can negotiate a new life for her and write a new script.

All living things welcome and bond as partners with our human species in that special space for spirit that is the universe, the "spiritual" counterpart of what Fritjof Capra calls "The Web of Life."[4] Youngsters have this space within them without being prompted. Some of us, distant from our childhood, need a bit of prompting. Here are a few of my stories that constitute a piece of my own search through my childhood and youthful years for spirit's presence in me.

Some Prompting Stories

I remember playing on the rooftop of my childhood school when I was six or seven years old. Twenty or thirty children were around and about, playing and making lots of noise during a recess from class. The roof was fenced in with those high mesh wire fences used mostly at street-level playgrounds, surrounding asphalt basketball courts. Ours was on the roof. And here was a young girl. Pamela was her name. We stepped aside to a corner of the roof, away from the shrieks and screams. She leaned back against the wall as I stood in front of her, our bodies not touching, neither awake nor aroused. We stood very close. My arms were raised, palms against the rough brick on either side of her head. And we made a kiss. I was overwhelmed by the surge of spirit energy. Her blue eyes opened in wonder as our spirits embraced. An offer? A speculation? A question? What would it be like if... ?

I also remember sitting by myself in a backyard sandpile, not yet three years old, fashioning a new world out of toys and sand. My back was to a two-story frame house that provided the security of home. The sun blazed down with its own offering of midmorning heat, and I heard, unmistakably, my spirit sharing with me, "This is your world to make, Warren. You are part of it. Don't let someone else fashion it for you."

I didn't hear those words, of course. Often, as Mary Watkins notes,[5] images of the past or future come to us as "meaning-feelings." The meaning carried in the memory of the feeling is absolutely clear, as clear as you will find your own memories of your spirit's speaking out in your early years, if you are ready for it.

That very early experience, as I remember it, is parallel to an experience in my young adulthood. I was home on leave from the U. S. Navy, 18 years old, talking with my mother about my future. We were seated in our living room, facing each other over a small coffee table. My mother's spirit always spoke to me through her eyes. As her eyes flashed and cut through the facade of my youthful biography, she spoke out of the depth of her own spirit's journey through her life. "Warren, you can do and be anything you want in this world. Just be clear about what you want to be and do."

And finally, in the in-between years when I was nine or ten, I recall one summer night. I was on a mountaintop in Vermont, lying on my back on a bedroll outside my tent. I looked up at the endless canopy of stars, not counting, not in wonder, not in fear, but with a great sense of belonging and longing, knowing that among those stars was my home to which I would return after my sojourn on earth.

These are a few of my stories. They are nothing extraordinary. They are the accouterments only of a restless spirit. What is extraordinary is my spirit. What is extraordinary is the human spirit's journey in each of us.

What about your journey, your spirit's presence in you?

Has your spirit spoken to you? Of course it has. This is not fiction or fantasy to which I appeal. It is grounded in the invitation your spirit makes to you to begin listening again, as you once did before you learned not to, and so, like most of us, drove your spirit into hiding deep in your core being, your tant'ien, where it awaits its calling out.[6] That calling out is an invitation. Your recall of your spirit's action in you is an invitation.

An Invitation

"Invitation" stands for an act absolutely central to enspiriting. Throughout this book, invitation is the mode of our action. Nothing to be forced. Nothing demanding that you do or be what you would not otherwise do or be. My invitation to you is to relive what it was like when your spirit spoke to you. But this is also a self-invitation. Eventually, your spirit will invite you to the discovery of your true self, for the first or the 100th time. That discovery lies at the heart of the inner work this book invites.

So... to the inner work. The mode is invitation. Relaxing, not forcing. Yielding, not overcoming.

The focus of the invitation is bringing back into conscious awareness what it was like when you felt spirit's presence in you. Describe that. Relive those moments. Practice putting yourself in that frame of body and mind.

You might choose to stop here, put down the book, and relive, by recalling, your spirit's voice. The time, the energy, and the space you create for this are yours. Keep your journal handy. That way, you can record salient features and events of your journey.

Some of you may be in frequent, even constant, communion with your spirit. But for some of us, a little help, a little support, and a little re-familiarization with the practices unlock the door to spirit's room. For some of us, that key has been thrown away, and so we must refashion another key. For those of you for whom this is more or less true, what follows in the next chapter is a "start-up" exercise which, when well undertaken, is a big, first step on the journey to the space of your spirit.

WHEN YOUR SPIRIT SPEAKS—
PRACTICES IN DEEP LISTENING

Some Ways of Deep Listening

This first exercise begins to create the space for spirit. It is an early step in that direction. By remembering what it was like when you felt spirit's presence in you, you may be able to recall some of the characteristics of that happening, making it easier to create that space again.

To create that space is to listen for it. Deep listening is the way. It is a discipline of the spirit, an enspiriting practice we use throughout our search.

There are many ways to deep listen. Some ways you do with other persons. Perhaps you have come to your own way. Perhaps you have deep listened to others. Have you deep listened to yourself? Have you entered into that inner state where all is silence, where all is empty, so that what is to be spoken is heard, what is to be recalled is remembered, what is to be offered is received? If not, here are some ways we have learned over the years for deep listening to your spirit.

One way is being silence. This is an inner silence in which there is no conversation with yourself. This is a feeling of silence that pervades your whole being: body, mind, and spirit. This is not a task to be undertaken. It is an entrance into an inner state of consciousness where the noise of your life, the noise of the universe, has departed. An emptiness pervades all.

A second way is giving attention. As the inner silence grows, you enter into a state of focus, of giving attention to the exclusion of all and everything. This is not a desperate concentration and it is not a task. It is a focus on what is to be spoken, remembered, and offered without expectation, without even knowing what that will be. It is a giving attention that is a readiness to listen.

A third way is to empty. Perhaps this is another way of saying Be Silence, Give Attention.

Here, move inside to your tant'ien. Empty all that makes you who you are, your inner biography and your social biography as well. Your hopes, dreams, wishes, problems, personal history, worries, and concerns are put to the side so that all that remains is the question, a great question which you pose to your spirit, a great question which your spirit poses to you.

What is this question?

Deep Questioning

Most of my work begins with a question. A deep question is one you are compelled to offer. It is not posed to start a debate or an argument. It is offered because your own spirit calls it out.

Here is my deep question, my offer to you. What is it like when your spirit speaks to you? I have learned that for many folks, the question is easier to address when it is put in the past tense, like this: What was it like when your spirit spoke to you?

Why the shift to the past tense, inviting a memory of a past experience? Because if you are unfamiliar with the language of enspiriting, or if you are suspicious of the invitations posed in this book, allowing yourself to search for and remember that it actually happened gives you confidence that enspiriting is not make-believe, is not a fairy tale, but is a very deep and living part of your inner realities. So much of our knowledge, beliefs, values, attitudes and faith (KBVAF) fight this understanding. We best begin by reminding ourselves that this actually happened. My spirit did speak to me... perhaps more than once! And this is what it was like!

Preparation

Each of us prepares ourselves differently. Some muse while they set the table for a meal or do the dishes after supper. Others organize the papers on their desk. Some of us arrange our bodies in our beds as we lie down to sleep and to dream. Some of us take a walk in the woods, do a meditation, or listen to music. There is always a personal preparation that opens the door to this experience. It is self-invitation which eases us into the enspiriting, which sets the stage for something unique and wonderful to happen when we have accepted it.

The basic preparation for most of the practices and exercises in this book is emptying. Emptying is a mode that fits all of the enspiriting, not this exercise alone. First comes a quieting down, an inner quieting, perhaps accompanied by some deep breathing, a half-dozen slow, deep breaths on which you concentrate, listening to the sound of your own exhaling. Or perhaps you prepare yourself by stretching your spine, standing straight, entering your body, and aligning your spine, vertebra by vertebra, as you push the top of your head towards the ceiling or the sky. I learned these from a yoga master, and they have stood me in good stead in enspiriting. They move me to a quiet inner space easily and quickly, unforced yet responsive to my need to generate the space for spirit.

These kinds of self-concentrations, including those of your own making, produce a special kind of focus I call "giving attention." Giving attention tends to exclude all else. As you exclude the most pressing of your concerns, you begin to empty an inner space. Worries, anxieties, and tasks begin to disappear so that you feel the empty space emerge within your body.

There is nothing to force here. Find and use your own ways of preparation which allow a silence in your body, an emptiness. Then you are ready to yield to your spirit.

Ask Your Spirit... and Yield

What was it like, my spirit, when you spoke to me?

Remind yourself that "speaking" means many things, not only "words." Your spirit may come to you as feelings that are loaded with meanings, as images that arrive in various guises like pictures, smells, tastes, body movements, or sounds. Your spirit may enter your conscious awareness as an intuition. Or, it may sneak in unannounced.

To yield to your spirit is to have no expectations. It is to empty, to be prepared for any and all manifestations of your spirit. It is to wait in silence. It is not forcing. It is offering. It is an invitation.

Now these become your questions:

- What was it like, my spirit, when you spoke to me? When I was a child? Before I learned not to listen?
- What did you say?
- How did you announce your presence?
- How did I feel it?
- What was this about?

As you recall, listen for your spirit's reminder so that the memory is a bit like the actual experience, so that you can live it and render the past present. In the past present moment, chronological time is obliterated and, once again, you are living the memory. This is your spirit speaking to you about a time in the past when it spoke.

To close this exercise, may I welcome you to the "order of enspiritors"? There are no medals, no special clothes, no smoke and mirrors, no gurus, and no high priests. This listening to your spirit will happen time and again. The memories will start flooding back. Now you can invite these memories as frequently as you choose, through these practices of yielding, emptying, giving attention, and invitation.

Sometimes your spirit will come to you unbidden, for it now knows that it is welcome. It too will learn what it is like to "come out of the closet," or the tant'ien, or wherever it has been hiding in your body. It too is practicing.

So the enspiriting begins. So the deep listening begins.

2

The Abundance of Spirit—
Seeking Your Gifts and Talents

THE FULL LIFE

Inner Sightings

Our spirit speaks about that which is important. But what is important to you? What is vital to you? Is it not your beingness in this world? Is it not the way your presence impacts on others as well as on yourself?

Opportunities arise in life to find that special ground on which you stand. I call these opportunities inner sightings. An external situation calls forth your spirit so that you, the human being, are caught up in its expression. Your spirit enters your biography, takes over, as it were, and embraces you with its special energy. You tend to lose your social biography, forget it for just a moment, as something else empowers your being. For that moment, you are fulfilled. You are lost, and thus found. You have glimpsed, or lived, the abundant life.

Each of the chapters in this book invites that inner sighting. The sightings take you on a path to the space where your spirit shows up. Sometimes your first sightings will be quick, at most a glimpse, a hint. But they will build as you become adept in the enspiriting. Then your spiritual archetype will make its case to your biography. You will listen deeply, without expectation or judgment, to discern what is there, to hear the call more clearly.

Where do you commence the search for the inner sightings? In what domain do your gifts and talents lie? Where do they play out? Suppose none of the spiritual archetypes fit you? Or fit well? Suppose that special arena of action, of work, of life itself to which your spirit calls is new, so new that we have no good words to describe it? In many scientific fields and technological applications of the modern era, new names, new words, new concepts had to be invented, or borrowed from Latin or Greek words and given new meanings.

Beginning the search for the call of your spirit, for its vital essence, can be difficult. So I invite you to start with uncovering your gifts and talents prior to naming your spiritual archetype. At the start, keep the enspiriting space open. Start your search and affirmation as if you were a plate empty of all nourishment except that which your spirit may offer. See where your inner sightings take you. In this first piece of self-inquiry, let your gifts and talents emerge without expectation or direction from you.

What is my work?

Presence and impact vary from one person to another. Much of it, however, is expressed in the world of work. There is no easy way to ignore this world of work as you seek to discover your true self. For most of us, what you are is what you do!

Work is such a central part of life. It always has been. For those of you who are unfamiliar with or unclear about its centrality, read Hannah Arendt's *The Human Condition*.[7] Work is the way we interact with our environment, impact upon it, fashion it, and make it something it would not otherwise be. It is a creative act, perhaps the most creative we humans are capable of.

Understand that this "work," at least for most of us, is other than "job," "employment," "occupation," "role," even "career." It is not about making money, though we all have to earn a living. Since the industrial revolution, many of us have become separated from the impacts and fruits of our work. So work becomes labor, a much narrower domain of effort. It is too often routinized, distant from its impacts on others and perhaps even more distant from our own inner sources, lacking the inspiration of our spirit.

The popular phrase, "Be all that you can be," carries the constant reminder that the parts and roles we often accept neither push us nor invite us to reach the heights to which we know we are capable. Too often our "work" leaves us empty and longing for something else, for something we might have been and done, for what we might still be and do "if only... "

If only what? If only you could uncover and recover your abundance: a right life for you that expresses the gifts that have been given to you and the talents with which you are endowed. This is the life of abundance. It is a life of fulfillment, a life in which what you have chosen to be and to do truly represents why you are here, why your spirit has chosen you for its human journey. When you live that way, your life is abundant—no matter what the world thinks about it and no matter what the world tells you to think about it. This book is about that uncovering and that recovering, through a special kind of self-research.

While earning a living is a necessary condition of economic survival, earning a living is not the same as living the life of abundance to which I believe the human spirit calls each and every one of us.

This book is not about how to earn a living. I leave that to all of the career development and job placement consultants. This book is for those of you who choose to bring abundance back into your life. It has been absent too long.

The Fallacy of Scarcity

So much of our social world is founded on the false premise of scarcity, that what we need or want is lacking or is in short supply. Nowhere is this more true than in the arena of gifts and talents. Think of all the people in your own life who are denied the space to express that which is within them by virtue of their social class, ethnicity, gender, skin color, religion, age, and all the other ways we label humans so that we need not acknowledge their uniqueness and need not welcome them into the human family. The gate of social opportunity is extraordinarily narrow. It opens for those who are talented in ways that fit a particular time and place. We humans have raised to a level of extraordinary power and effectiveness a set of criteria for "selecting in" and for "keeping out," what sociologists and educators call the "sorting out" process.

In the United States of America, the prevailing belief is that there is a scarcity of good jobs, good neighborhoods, unpolluted space, openings at prestigious colleges, kidneys available for transplants, and virtually everything else that human beings need or want.

Can we be free of this social canard of scarcity? Can we acknowledge to each other that this is a life of abundance if we would learn to express our multiple talents and gifts born into each and every one of us? Clearly, this is a matter for the human spirit, your own spirit, to take hold. We must go to our sources within and enter into a search and dialogue that the practices of enspiriting promote.

Plenitude or Scarcity in Your Own Life

I think now is the moment for you to confront directly what is missing in your life. How do you know its absence? Is there a vacuum in your soul? What are you looking for to fill that emptiness? More money? A new car? Selling your old house and buying a new one with a second or third or fourth bathroom? An increase in any kind of material comfort or possessions? If not these, then what? And if you're searching for abundance, the right life for you, why the search?

Captured as we are in a system of production, consumption, acquisition, and the law of the moving target (i.e., there is no such thing as "enough"), these questions are not easy. Is there something beyond consuming what we can get using easy-access credit cards? I believe there is a great deal more. Only you can answer that question for yourself.

If your sense of your work, of yourself, and of your life is not abundant, query your spirit. I lay out a course for that, but you have to navigate it. It is not always smooth sailing, but sure and steady steer you to a life of abundance. How is that possible? Is there a guarantee? Yes! Your spirit is abundant in that which you need to live a full life.

The Full Life, the Right Life, the Abundant Life

What is a full life? It is of course, many things. Is it children in health, a loving family, reliable work, and fitting in? Certainly, for some. For others, it is adventure, risk, variety, singularity. For still others, it is clarity of purpose and intention. For all, it probably includes food that is nourishing and shelter that is adequate.

Perhaps we might call it a "right" life, rather than a "full" life, in order to declare its abundance. I do not mean "right" in a narrow or moralistic sense but "right" in the way your spirit calls you. The "right" life is about little things, like teaching your children to play marbles, catch a fish, or bake a cherry pie. It is also about big things, like earth-nurturing. It may be about strange things, like partnering with whales, or trees, or elephants, rather than ravaging them. Or it may be about healing things, like helping neighbors to make peace, translating poetry from one language to another, deep listening with a person or a group so they can hear the voice of their spirit in their own times of turmoil and stress.

These examples just skim the surface of a "right" life of abundance. I think there are six billion examples! There is a great discovery in store for you. But my own sense is that abundance does not mean making a lot of money at the cost of another's livelihood, or acquiring power by diminishing another's, or being a victim rather than an actor in history. I think the human spirit calls us to a fullness and a rightness. Don't take my word for it. Listen to the voice of your spirit. It will tell you.

Some people might sense the possibility of an abundant life within them by knowing its absence. Those who have been denied an opportunity to express that which is within know full well its opposite: a life of denial. Sometimes this is self-denial and your spirit weeps for you. Sometimes this denial takes the form of barricades erected by others that you have to tear down or leap over. Despite the multitude of pressures to acquire, to own every conceivable consumable thrown our way by an omnipresent "civilization of false plenty," success in playing that game is the antithesis of abundance. This civilization of false plenty captures our soul. It smothers our spirit. I know and have worked with too many folks whose ways of life belie their unhappiness and hide their sense of not having done enough with their lives, perhaps not having done anything worthwhile.

Opening the Door to Your Spirit

What is the key, here, to open the door to a right life of abundance?

It is learning to open to your spirit. Your spirit is not out to deny you, as perhaps others have. Your spirit has chosen to make its human journey through you, not through someone else. It will nurture you as perhaps no one else has, if only you will love and care for it. That reciprocity of offering and receiving between your spirit and your biography is the key to opening the door to an abundant life.

Do you have a sense, a feeling, that within lies some capacity, some potential, waiting to be revealed and actualized? Do not deny your intuition. As you work your way through these next chapters and the practices they introduce, look for the marshaling points of your spiritual journey.

There are two kinds of marshalling. In one, you marshal your inner forces to search for your gifts and talents. In Chapter Two, *Seeking your Gifts and Talents—Practices in Self-research*, are some exercises in self-research: uncovering the criticals and going to the fundamentals. These practices are framed for those of you who sense, who know deep within, that who and what you have become do not represent your human possibilities.

THE DIVIDED BIOGRAPHY

The Inner Biography and the Outer Biography

So far, I have used the term biography as if it were a single thing, unitary and whole. In the modern world, it is not. It is divided. We humans have two biographies. One is the social biography. It is formed by the stories people tell you about yourself, about how to live, about what they expect of you, and about the way the world works: knowledge, beliefs, values, attitudes, and faiths (KBVAF)[8] which you have come to accept as your story. You also have an inner biography, which are your stories about yourself, stories that you rarely share, that constitute your hopes and dreams, and to which your own spirit makes an unending contribution.

The biggest wrench, the biggest wound, is not whether or not you fit within your family, subgroup, culture, or work situation. It is whether or not you fit within yourself! Let me tell you a marvelous story about that.

A Story of Healing and Regeneration

Some years ago, I conducted one of my many workshops on envisioning the future of education and learning. In a group that included about 40 teachers, school administrators, and concerned citizen-leaders, one of the participants was in her late 30s, the wife of a professor, mother of a young daughter, and the holder of the highest degree in a highly technical science. This woman had so much to offer the world. She also had a troubled marriage. Her husband could not tolerate competition. In the workshop, I quickly learned to appreciate her insight and her forthright spirit. I started off participants by inviting them to go deep to uncover what was most important to them as persons. The notion of personhood—being a person to the other, as distinguished from being a role-player—means that we are present to one another in the fullness of our spirit, sharing and celebrating each other's gifts and talents. So she learned not to hide her enormous capabilities as idea-creator, as listener, as question-asker, and as a person understanding what it means to go to the criticals and uncover the fundamentals.

When she arrived home at the end of the workshop, an event occurred which changed her life and, despite its initial pain, began the mending of her divided biography. After driving the 60 miles back to her home, she was greeted at the door by her professor-husband who said to her, "I am going to divorce you." He handed her a sheaf of papers that inaugurated that process and left the house.

That very evening, after seeing her daughter to bed, she sat by herself, caught up in the very human, emotional trauma of divorce. She communed with her spirit. Later, she told me, "I just sat there, emptied, and listened inside, as we had practiced in the workshop. After a while, my future came to me. For I recognized what was in me that no one could take away or any longer demean."

She was a methodical person. She got some paper and listed her skills, her education and training, her knowledge, and her experience, ranging from parenting and household management to volunteer and community work, and including her largely unused scientific background, all aspects of her social biography.

And then she went deep, to identify her gifts and talents, and to pull from her inner recesses what was truly important to her, her inner biography. She created her own journal. She realized from our earlier work together that neither her gifts nor her talents would see the light of day unless they were shaped into a compelling image. These made up her inner biography, stories that were unknown by an outside world in which she had been confined to the conventional roles of wiving and mothering in a college town which gave kudos to her professor-husband and defined her role as a loving helpmate. She certainly was that and was much more. She had accepted that role... until she was abruptly thrown out of it.

In the midst of the trauma of a marriage finally unraveled, six hours after the confrontation at the front door, this woman had the constitutional fortitude to move deeply into her inner biography. She uncovered her other selves, her fully human possibilities, possibilities unrealized and unaccepted in her previous life.

In short, that evening, she started on a new life for herself. She determined to carve a new social biography out of an inner biography. Her spirit had given her the courage, the energy to do that.

This person went on to become an eminent, highly paid executive scientist with a Fortune 500 company. More important, out of her inner biography fueled by her spirit energy, she rejuvenated a personal life expressive of some loving qualities that had always been within her. Not all in one day. Of course not.

Might you uncover your inner biography and learn to give it the light of day? Find your own reasons for entering into the spirit of rejuvenation and rediscovery.

Your Social Biography and Your Inner Biography

What are we to make of this tale?

Simply put, she moved to the border which separated her social biography from her inner biography and, energized and given courage by her spirit, crossed that frontier to uncover her genius, her uniqueness. Eventually, she returned to the familiar ground of social life with the determination to enact her gifts and talents.

Might you not also approach that border and cross the frontier to enact your inner life?

Your social biography is constituted by the stories people have told you about yourself that you have come to believe. Your inner biography is constituted by stories about yourself only you know and care about.

Why do I call these "stories"? What about the "facts" of the case? Isn't most of life a story? Don't we devote a good part of each day to telling each other stories... about what has happened to us during the day, the week, the year, the life... about how the world works... about why we should do this and not that... about how we feel... about what the chances are for just about everything? In our scientific era, we like to believe that there are objective facts about ourselves and our lives and that these facts tell all, or at least the most important.

But when we get underneath these facts, we come to the extraordinarily rich swamp of meaning and of interpretation. What do these stories mean? Why did she do this and not that? Some stories we share. If we share enough of them, we have a common culture. But some we don't share, like the adventures to which our spirit calls us and our deepest hopes and fears. These latter are part of the inner stories that give us the richness of individual variety and uniqueness that make life interesting.

Social biography stories come from many sources: from our parents and those with whom we grow up; from the larger family, from friends, schoolmates and teachers; and now, of course, the ubiquitous television which has so invaded our lives and carries the messages of mainstream culture. Many social biography stories are common to our subculture, our social class, and our locales. These all become the social matrix of the "you" everybody knows, your public life, your work life, even your family life. But where lies your genius, your uniqueness, that with which you are endowed by your spirit?[9] These latter become manifest in your inner biography.

For many of us, this divide is too wide to cross by ourselves. Help is wanted. Such help will arrive as you begin to listen to the voice of your spirit. Your human spirit, that piece of the universal lodged in you, is the foundation on which your inner biography has been built. It is the source of your genius, your uniqueness, and your gifts. Ultimately, it is the "why" of your being on this planet, born in this day and age, in this culture, of this family, under these circumstances, with these genetic dispositions. None of these is accidental. Your spirit has selected you, as mine has selected me.

This is not a random universe. As you open to your spirit, it welcomes you. It helps you to fashion your beingness, your action, your life in a consort with this inner biography. The two parts, the inner and the outer, will be joined. The imbalances, dissonances, frustrations, sense of inadequacy, even pain give way to a new wholeness that is your total, integrated biography expressing your gifts and talents.

Of Gifts and Talents

Are gifts and talents the same? No, though they may be importantly related. Common language tends to blur a distinction between the two. Here is the difference. Our gifts have been given to us so that we may give them away. I believe that the call of our spirit is that kind of gift. Talents, as I understand them, are that with which we are "by nature" endowed, and they are expressions of our genetic capacities. Sometimes, gifts and talents are the same. Sometimes, they overlap. Sometimes, they are quite different. And sometimes, you are so good at expressing your talents that you neglect or even forget your gifts.

In our common language, we come close to mixing up the two. For example, we say, "She is a gifted person," or "He has a gift for… ," meaning much the same as "She is a talented person."

The relationship of talent to gift is crucial. This understanding came to me 20 years ago, after I had put more than a decade of my life into the development of this enspiriting work. In 1978, I published my first Guidebook for Futures-Inventors. I showed it to a friend of mine who knew of and had participated in the early work.

"Now," he said, "You are ready to give it away. This is your gift to the rest of us." But he did not mean that I was particularly talented. He meant, and went on to say: "By publishing these exercises and practices, hundreds, perhaps thousands, will see them, read them, use them. You are now giving this away to humankind, a gift which many people will take up, try out, accept, and practice, and forget where they got it."

And this happened. My uncovering the practices of deep listening in 1982 from a story in the *Chuang Tzu* is also a good example. It is one of the disciplines of the spirit that pervades my work, underpins this book, and is central to hearing the call of your spirit. Deep listening is now known and practiced throughout the world, well or poorly, by many citizen-leaders as well as professionals in the fields of conflict work, envisioning, human resources training, mental health, community development, healing, sustainability, and various group and self-help processes. Many of these users don't have the faintest idea, or care about, where it came from and that's okay. Deep listening was a gift given to me when I was ready for it and ready to give it away. I myself had no talent for deep listening, as some do. I had to practice it to receive that gift for myself and offer it to other people. You may not be particularly talented in the expression or articulation of your gift, but nevertheless the gift is there, to be uncovered and offered, as best you can.

The call of your spirit to you is a gift. I invite you to discover your talents or to remind yourself of them in the context of your gifts. I prefer the word uncover, because your gifts, like your talents, are already there. What has to be invented is not the gift but how to give it away so that people will receive it, including yourself. That can be very difficult, especially if your gifts do not fit the norms. This I consider being the crux of social invention.

These remarkable offers of your spirit are for the world, or at least that part of it where you find your action. In later chapters, we focus on ways to invent the social space for your offer to be made in such a way that others can accept it. These are the social inventions of which we are in such desperate need: how to live and work and intermingle on this planet so that the decency, goodness, generosity, affection, and bonding in community that we all crave can come to pass.

Deep Questioning

Now I invite you once more to listen deeply; to prepare yourself for that which you are about to hear from your inner voice, perhaps some new insight into what you have to offer, perhaps some confirmation of what you have always known about your gifts and talents. The method, as I have said, is uncovering the criticals and going to the fundamentals. Going deep. Going to the "heart of the matter," as we say.

But how do you do this so that some inner truth emerges and you do not end up kidding yourself? How do you discern so that as your inner information emerges, it is not squelched by a social biography that tells you different stories about yourself? How do you quiet a social biography that says to you, "That is impossible," or "Who's kidding whom?" or "Nobody wants to listen to that stuff," or "You don't have the 'guts' to try something new," or "Come on, now. Be practical. You have to earn a living, after all." There are so many ways we "nay-say" ourselves.

Here is a moment for you to "yea-say" yourself.

For that to happen, we must all learn to cut through the subterfuges, the false stories about ourselves laid on us since childhood, the culture of scarcity, of "don't take any risks," of "that's the way things are." One way to do this is deep questioning. These are questions which only you can ask of yourself, questions which your spirit has been waiting for, hoping that finally you will come to it: What am I about? What am I up to? What do I have to offer to myself, to my family, friends, colleagues, loved ones? To the world?

In what follows, I have framed these questions into exercises to help you focus your spirit-energy on your inner biography, querying it as you seek out your gifts and talents. Here is a word of caution. Do not require that the phrase "gifts and talents" must stand for something remarkable. Fame, renown, and becoming a "star" are neither the focus nor the purpose of your search. The quest is not, in my view, for greatness, accolades, fame and fortune, world renown, and star status.

This search is for you, for your own genius, your own uniqueness, your own project. That may cover anything. What one person calls "ordinary" may be extraordinary to you. I have seen it happen hundreds of times: uncovering a quality or characteristic of your own action in the world, a way of being and doing which brings abundance into your life in your own special way.

Let's begin the search.

SEEKING YOUR GIFTS AND TALENTS— PRACTICES IN SELF-RESEARCH

Building Your Own Search Engine

Here are some questions to help you start. They may not be your questions. Try them out and discover what happens. As you learn to live these questions, to put them deep inside (and thus, begin the deep learning), they will elicit responses from your spirit and your inner biography.

These questions are intended to get you thinking about your possibilities; to help you to recognize the sources of your social biography; to help you to acknowledge the pull of your inner biography. These questions are designed for exploration. Don't be afraid of surprises. It's just there where you may discover your spirit reaching out to you, giving you the energy to continue. With these questions, you create a space where your spirit comes to the fore.

The search engine is an inner dialogue. Can you build toward that? Will you build toward that? Remember the enspiriting craft: emptying, yielding, deep listening. It all applies here. Let this inner dialogue happen. It is for you. Later, you may choose to share the gifts and talents, the self-acknowledgments and the adventures to which your spirit calls you with others who are also doing this work, perhaps with the world, too. I hope so!

There is no push and shove here, no failure and no success. There is the complex richness of your emerging "You," your true self, as your spirit, your inner biography, and your social biography weave a new fabric using old pieces with new threads and new colors.

The First Set of Questions

What is important about who you are as you understand and know yourself?

Another way of phrasing it is:

What is important to you? Perhaps even most important?

Still a third way is:

If you had your "druthers," what would you be and do?

And yet a fourth version is:

What do you long for?

I offer you these alternate phrasings of the questions because I don't know which of your keys fit which of your locks. You may come to your own question that will more easily unlock the door to your inner biography and to the space wherein your spirit will speak out.

Don't try to respond to these questions too quickly. Let them sink in. Different pieces of different responses may come to you at different moments of the day. Sometimes, responses will come to you in the living contexts and situations of family, work, and social life, when you will hear an inner question: "What am I doing this for?"

Alternatively, as you learn to empty and to deep listen, you might want to set aside some special time for a focused yielding to the questions and to the responses that begin to emerge. These are questions that invite you to go deep, to go to your sources as a human being, and rediscover and relearn who you are and what you're up to. So begins the deep learning.[10]

If you have decided to do this work of seeking your abundance, it may well permeate your consciousness of yourself throughout the ensuing days and weeks. You have opened the door for your spirit to enter, and believe me, it will—at moments and occasions of its own choosing! At work, at play, in thought-sessions with yourself, in dreams. By packing these questions into your tant'ien, into the inner space of your vital life-energy, they begin to take on a life of their own. These are very powerful questions. They will open up new vistas. Let yourself deep listen.

EXPECTATIONS

Whose expectations: theirs... or yours?

This chapter is about what you have learned to expect of yourself and what other persons expect of you. That reciprocity is the dynamic of your social biography. Sometimes, both sets of expectations are congruent. For example, one might think: People expect me to be meticulous in my work... and I am, for I expect that of myself. Or: My family expects me to make the money decisions... and I do. I expect that of myself. Or (God forbid): People think I'm a loser. That's how they act toward me. That's what they expect of me. They're right! I am a loser. So what else is new?

When you ask yourself, "What role do I play in another person's life?" in effect you are asking what does she or he expect of you and to what extent do you fill those expectations. Of course, not all expectations are met. That is the story of both personal and social change. A case in point is the rise of feminism, when women no longer respond with docility to what men expect of them at work, in family life, in politics, in sexuality. The civil rights movement radically challenged generations of the role expectations for black persons in American society.

Doing this self-research on what other people expect of you in any sphere of your life is an important key to unlocking the door to your own expectations of yourself and, more importantly, to your hopes, your dreams, and your aspirations which may lie dormant in your inner biography.

The Second Set of Questions:
Uncovering the Personal Culture of Your Social Biography

This second set of questions on the path to your abundance aims to help you differentiate your social biography from your inner biography. Here are four questions, any one of which may generate insight into your social biography.

1. What aspects of your life and work, including your behaviors, your feelings, and your actions do other people expect of you, and do you meet those expectations? List them—when they come to you—in your journal.

Do you see what's beginning to happen here? We take so much of our lives for granted. That's not unusual. How else can we so easily exchange pleasantries, go shopping, eat a meal, or rely on our hospitals and doctors, supervisors and employees to see us through emergencies or hard spots? More to the point, with family, friends, and colleagues: What about you do they take for granted? What do they expect of you and from you?

These expectations cover the range of human behavior, and thus are sometimes positively valued and sometimes negatively valued. For example, they may vary from bringing home a pay check to doing the family laundry; from offering affection, to freezing up when the going gets tough; from digging in and working hard to shoving work responsibilities onto someone else's shoulders.

With these questions, you begin to describe your own personal culture, what people expect of you to which you respond. Your personal culture is enacted in most of your daily living and like the larger group or social culture, we take it for granted. To uncover your gifts and talents, it's very helpful to bring into your conscious awareness these linchpins of your social biography so that later, when you come to your inner biography, you can find the freshness, the uniqueness, and sometimes the unexplored qualities and possibilities which you have harbored and protected from your social biography.

Begin, then, to lay out these fulfilled expectations. Not all at once. Perhaps the main ones. Make a list in your journal. After a day, a week, a month, that page will begin to fill up.

As you continue this self-research, other questions follow. These focus on the active side of your social biography, what you offer, rather than its passive side.

2. What impacts do you have on other people that they also would acknowledge?

Responses to this question help paint the picture of how you go through life and impact upon it as seen both through your own eyes and that of other persons. A person's social biography is a composite picture, one in which your views of yourself mesh with others' views of you. When there is a substantial disparity between the two, a good portion of the difference reveals how much your inner biography and your outer or social biography clash.

3. What skills do you offer and use that other people know about?

This is the "can-do" question. It goes beyond the potential to the actual that other people know about and accept. So-called job skills, home skills, and recreational skills make up a good part of your responses to this question. Perhaps a separate page for each in your journal is called for. It is important to remember that, in one way or another, these are public skills, known by others, which you use, enact, and express.

Often, gifts and talents are understood only in the vocabulary of skills. Of course, they are much more. This question, however, renders the social biography concrete and specific. The idea is to list at least some of your most important skills, whether at home, on the job, or in your social or public life, that are generally acknowledged, some perhaps even celebrated, by other people.

A final variation of these insights into your social biography may emerge from your responses to this question:

4. What do you know, understand, and believe that fits what other persons know, understand, and believe?

At first, this seems like an enormous question whose response will cover everything that makes up the totality of your human experience. It is, of course, a way for you to begin to specify the KBVAF (knowledge, beliefs, values, attitudes, and faiths) that make up so much of your social biography. This KBVAF constitutes the internalization of the family, group, and culture into which you have grown up and lived your life.

The idea here is not to make an exhaustive list. You might want to identify those values, beliefs, and attitudes which are central to the way you interact with other persons, close or distant: avoiding conflict; being a rah-rah booster of everything; being a super-patriot; being tolerant; being suspicious; trusting what persons say to you. This is to remind you that much of your external life, your social life of interaction with other persons is given over to acting in ways that most people have come to expect of you.

Take a Break

I have given you four questions in this chapter, and there are more to follow. I have suggested that you pack these questions into your tant'ien and leave them there so that wherever you go, you take them with you. As ideas, images, feelings, words, and intuitions pop into your conscious awareness, you can jot them down. When you are ready to do this work of unpacking and describing your social biography, it will happen quite quickly.

Making the offer of your gifts and sharpening your talents, on the other hand, may well take substantial energy. The next chapter begins the search of your inner biography. As you continue to explore and discover your spiritual archetype in the ensuing chapters, you will address the grand question: How can I forge the space for the actualization of my gifts and talents? In fact, many chapters in this book focus on the various ways your gifts and talents are actualized as an expression of your spiritual archetype. But be sure of one thing: your spirit wants action. One way or another, if you deep listen, you will find and respond to your call.

But first, you want to move from your social biography to your inner biography, for it is in the latter arena that the search is most fruitful. There might you find new insights, new responses, new drives, and new compelling images which lie at the heart of your self-vision, that will bring to fruition your right life of abundance.

This is not "overnight" work. There is lots of homework and lots of inner work. Give yourself the space for that.

SEARCHING YOUR INNER BIOGRAPHY

Shift of Focus

Now we shift from the outer focus, your social biography, to the inner focus, your inner biography, that aspect of yourself that we name as private. This is largely that aspect of yourself which you don't, or only rarely, share.

This is a shift toward that which lies deepest in your heart: your dreams, your hopes, and your aspirations. Often, these are unspoken, sometimes even to yourself. They may include vague phantasms that have drifted through your mind like bewitching wisps of clouds and ideas that you have never probed because you thought them too foolish or out of the ordinary. Perhaps you didn't understand them completely, so you put them aside instead. Your inner biography may offer up insights into your self and your situation that you have dismissed because they challenged your social biography, particularly your expectations of yourself that you have learned from other people. Yearnings and longings to be or do differently in some way, great or small, may be waiting to be recognized. They may have been frozen in the cold logic of, "Oh I could never do that," or "I don't know how," or perhaps, "People would think I'm crazy."

Self put-down, self-freezing, and self-doubt are the strategies by which your social biography—which, after all, is a living aspect of your total self—shuts down your inner biography, by which the common culture suffocates the innovative and extraordinary. For each of us, the strategy takes a different twist. I'm sure you know yours. Now is a good time to put it aside.

But how shall we make this probe to the marvelously rich inner world of your human possibilities? What questions will open up this inner space in a loving, nurturing way, absent of fear, without threat, and outside the social parameters of success and failure?

The chapters on the Entrepreneurial Spirit (Chapter Three) commence the foray into the practical, the possible, the feasible, and the believable, though even there the entrepreneurial spirit is born to break boundaries.

But not yet. Now is the moment to release your imagination and fly, perhaps as you've never flown before, into the space where your spirit breathes. This is a place to search out, to acknowledge, and to create the images at the deepest level that stand for your gifts and talents.

How?

Deep Imaging

The method I have used for years and seen work in so many people, the method for the inner search to uncover your gifts and talents is deep imaging, an enspiriting practice.

In all of the enspiriting practices to which I invite you, deep imaging is probably the most powerful way to bring into the open your spiritual archetype. In deep imaging, you begin to generate and let flow freely images of who and what you might be and do if you let yourself be and do that. Your spirit speaks out most fluently through deep images.

The images may come to you as memories, as when your spirit spoke to you in your childhood. But they may also come to you through self-vision, in which your spirit poses the adventures, the concerns, the possibilities, and the new realities of yourself to which your spirit calls.

Self-preparation is essential here, for deep images can never be forced out. Invitation, emptying, deep listening, yielding are your tools. These are always the start-up practices for this work. Then what? Pose the questions to yourself. Swallow them. Place them in your tant'ien... and wait. When your spirit is ready, it will speak out.

The Questions

"What have you to say, oh spirit of mine, about my possibilities?" "About my gifts?"

"About what I can do, be, and offer to the world?" "About what I can give to others?"

There are other ways to begin this dialogue with your spirit if the questions above are too forthright, too abrupt, and you're not yet prepared inwardly to ask them. The next question follows from the social biography work of previous chapters.

"What can I do that no one knows about?"

If it helps, transpose the question from "doingness" to "beingness."

"What can I be that no one has yet seen in me?"

You can further shift from the future of potential and possibility to the present of actualization.

"What am I now doing and being that no one else knows about?"

Now empty... wait... listen... in silence.

Might you not uncover some qualities of your inner presence as only you know them, which do not fit a job description or a role definition? Try that. You are not looking for jobs, careers, or roles. But this is no simple matter. Our consciousness of ourselves, of who and what we are, is invaded by our social life, our social biography, the KBVAF (the prevailing knowledge, beliefs, values, attitudes, and faiths). We have lost our inner biography in the search for a safe social life.

Given what's happening in our world, that safety is well on the way to becoming a fantasy. We need social inventiveness across the board, in every arena of our lives. And for that, we need to multiply exponentially the expression and actualization of our slumbering gifts and talents.

Perhaps you are satisfied with who and what you are. Then go no further. But if you have the sense that your inner voice, your human spirit is suffocating, then continue. The rewards are simply enormous. I would say that they are out of this world! And now, we are invited to bring those "rewards" back into the world—your world, my world, and ours.

Some Practices for Deep Imaging

Research shows that deep images come to us in many ways. Visualization—pictures in your mind—is a common way of imaging. But 10% of the population doesn't "picture" things. Sometimes for all of us, images may enter our conscious awareness as thoughts or as words, but without premeditation. Images also emerge as "senses," as you sense something hovering just outside your conscious awareness. Invite it in. Perhaps that image is born as a smell, a taste, a body feeling or movement. Perhaps you hear your image. Images come to us in all the ways we interact with the external world and with each other. Deep imaging casts a wide net into the ocean of our psyche through which our spirit speaks. Let this enspiriting practice bring into your conscious awareness whatever comes up in whatever form it takes.

Suppose nothing comes at first. That's okay. Have no expectations. Let your spirit speak to you when and as it chooses.

Some persons find it helpful to create a solitude in which they empty, focus, give attention, with no expectations, and wait. They create a special space for deep imaging, away from the noise of everyday living.

But too, the images may pop into your mind, into your conscious awareness, at odd moments, when you are least expecting them. Use your journal. Keep it handy. Stop what you're doing and jot down the images in words, pictures, symbols, whatever is easiest for you. Later, as these begin to accumulate, you can put them together, embellish them and ask of your spirit, "What are you telling me?"

Questions About the Questions

Perhaps we could dig a bit deeper. What is underneath these questions about your gifts and talents? What are the criticals here, the fundamentals?

Way underneath, in your heart of hearts, are you hoping that you harbor a talent, some special psycho-motor skill or natural ability that will carry you to an outstanding career, a stellar performance, a unique act of public expression?

For most of us, that is not too likely. But through deep imaging, we can begin to explore and to uncover some aspect of ourselves fundamentally different from the tempting and ego-driven need for star-status. To the contrary. You have a gift. We all do. It is from your spirit, some aspect of yourself in which your spirit offers to work its presence and promise in and through you. Empty your tant'ien of your social biography. It is your inner biography that poses these questions and you must give it the freedom and the confidence to do so. Just place the questions inside and wait.

Eventually, sooner or later, in bits and pieces or in a great roar of recognition, will come the images of yourself being and doing in new ways. What ways? That is for you to listen for and to discover, without initial judgment and with no expectations.

These images come to you in a concrete and specific dimension. You can see, hear, sense, and feel yourself in concrete imaginings with people, within contexts, and in situations. You can live these in your imagination, which is a way of trying out, testing, rehearsing.

Is this fantasy? Yes... and no. If the images return, if you can't get rid of them, if they keep speaking to you, if you have a sense that they draw you to their expression in action, then they may be the seeds of a new reality.

The "gifts" within are that which you have to offer. See what these are, or might be, with no final judgments, outcomes, or conclusions. Not yet. Let your spirit begin to build the stories. Don't let anyone, and particularly your social biography, censor them. Eschew judgments of probability and feasibility.

Don't be too hasty. Eventually, you will move from the images of your gifts to your compelling images—that which you **cannot**

not be and that which you **cannot not do.** These you will then seek to translate into action, into newly invented roles, new institutions, into enacting your call in the world. In the later chapters in this book, where you explore your spiritual archetype and seek to come in contact with it, you will discover and invent the occasion for creating your new realities.

That is why self-censoring is so damaging to the work. Do not cut off your gift; bury it in some dark dungeon, failing to nurture it to see how it might grow. We humans have developed such powerful ways to deny our creativity, just when we need it the most, as we continue to devastate our home—planet Earth—and destroy each other in the name of time-honored ideologies, prejudices, attitudes, beliefs, superstitious knowings, and faiths bred of damning exclusivity rather than welcoming inclusivity.

I'm sorry, folks. God has no entrance fee. However you name her, She is loving, welcoming, and nurturing, without guile or machinations, to all of us, whatever our social biographies, whatever our KBVAF, inviting us, as always, to listen to the voice of our spirit which She breathed into us, to push the boundaries, uncover our calling, why we are in this world and not some other.

If you live outside her domain and find the "God-language" unintelligible or threatening, no matter. Your human spirit still awaits your readiness to listen.

Let the images of what you might yet be and do, what you might yet offer to the world, to yourself, your loved ones, your work, and to your settings and situations enter into your conscious awareness. Here is the "grammar" of deep imaging.

- Let your images flow without forcing them. Listen as an empty vessel that your spirit will fill.
- Don't interpret your images.
- Don't censor your images. No judgments of good or bad, possible or impossible, practical or impractical are called for at this moment of creativity.
- Let them build in you. If initial images are vague and ephemeral, or if they arrive as a feeling, a word here or there, or a piece of an incomplete picture, then let these initial images be nurtured in you, growing, becoming more specific and concrete, warmed in the bosom of your loving welcome. Return to them. "What more, what else have you to say to me, oh spirit of mine?"
- And live them. Render them as alive inside as you can. Specificity and concreteness help. When you're ready, your spirit will tell you a story about yourself. About your gifts. That to which you were born, that which you have to give to others.

PART TWO

3

The Entrepreneurial Spirit

WHAT HAVE YOU TO LOSE?
WHAT HAVE YOU TO GAIN?

That Special Drive

Do you remember that old saying, "Born, not made," applied to some special prowess or skill, as in, "Leaders are born, not made?" Does it contain a modicum of ancient wisdom, a recognition by us ordinary folks that the extraordinary in life succeed through factors other than sheer training or education? Are entrepreneurs born with a special drive that only the genes can supply? Or is entrepreneurship a call from the human spirit, perhaps yours? If so, what are its characteristics?

One quality of the entrepreneurial spirit is risk-taking. Who are the risk-takers? These are persons who break the mold, try out new things, create their own lives and make the curve rather than following it. Like Billy Mitchell, a U.S. Army officer in World War

I, who advocated a strong air force, flying in the face of military officialdom? Like Pablo Picasso painting his two-faced women because that's how he saw them... or wanted us to see them when some of us had a difficult enough time looking a one-faced woman straight in the eye?

And Henry Ford decided to pay his auto workers an unheard of 1914 wages of $5.00 per day ("Then they can afford to buy my cars.") when the other auto magnates thought he had gone mad.

Second, these risk-takers have the courage of their convictions, which means that their vision, their idea has to be translated into action. That characteristic is central to the archetype of the entrepreneurial spirit. If you don't hold to the beliefs grounded in your spirit, who will? These days, we might assign that courage to a person who challenges the omnipotence of political or cultural structure.

A third characteristic of the entrepreneurial spirit is to make your own opportunities. The person called by this archetype does not sit around, waiting for the world to come to her doorstep. These persons seize the moment. They create their own emancipation from the mundane, the ordinary, the habitual.

Put them all together: Born, not made. Breaking the mold. Keeping ahead of the curve. The courage of one's convictions. Making your own opportunities.

These are what entrepreneurs of the spirit do and have. Are you one of them? In part, this is what enacting your gifts and talents mean. But as with the relationship between abundance and scarcity discussed in chapter two, the notion of entrepreneurship, and thus the availability of the idea for the enspiriting work, has been severely constrained by its economic overtones. In the history of humankind, the entrepreneurial spirit has never been confined to business ventures. Its scope covers all activities in which humans engage.

The Malfeasance of Economic Themes

Current thinking confines the idea and practice of entrepreneurship to business ventures. This greatly limits our appreciation of the broad sweep of risk-taking throughout life. It obscures the discussion about what lies within you, about your potential, your genius, your inner voice, much as the notion of scarcity has so denied the human capacity for creating abundance. Once again, the tremendous influence of economic themes over our lives, our institutions, our culture, the very ways we think and feel and talk about ourselves has greatly limited the emancipation of the human spirit.

In the old days, at the birthing of our highly capitalist civilization, we attached the notion of the entrepreneurial spirit to the great capitalists of the day, the Henry Fords, the Andrew Carnegies, the John D. Rockefellers. What fortunes they amassed as they changed the face of industrial society. Today, a culturally correct description of an entrepreneur points to starting up a new business, designing a new product or service, or finding a new market niche. Success and the mark of achievement are indicated by making lots of money.

This chapter is not about the economic or managerial themes that dominate our culture. Entrepreneurs are not only, or even mainly, business persons. Do not allow the business metaphors to claim your soul. In principle, the entrepreneurial spirit may reside in each and every one of us. That has to be discovered. In principle, it may activate in any arena of human endeavor. In practice, we want to learn to release that spirit, to give it space for expression.

Searching for Breakthroughs:
The Entrepreneurial Spirit at Work

Entrepreneurship is about enacting and bringing your dreams to life. That is its "subject-matter." It is about your wildest idea, about risk-taking, about getting a life for your own uniqueness, about being and doing what you are called to be and do. About that which you **cannot not do** and **cannot not be**. As you search for its qualities in you, how will you discern that the entrepreneurial archetype is the essence of your spirit's call?

You might commence your search with this question:

Do you recall your breakthroughs? That is what you are looking for. These may be little things that perhaps no one but you knows about. But for you, they are still breakthroughs.

That question begins your search. Remember those occasions when you went against the grain. Recall a time when you tried out something new, by yourself or just for yourself. When have you broken your own mold, found a bit of your own voice, despite what everyone imposed on you in the formation of your social biography? That's the entrepreneurial spirit in you coming to the fore.

I remember a marvelous spirit I met and worked with some years ago. We were part of a project to reform a major Protestant church denomination seeking to return that church to its roots in the local congregation rather than the bureaucracy.

This person was wheelchair-bound.

You should have heard the speaking out of this young man, his clarion calls to re-covenant in the congregation itself, as if the group of worshipers he was calling to were still in the catacombs, not members of a national church with its hierarchies and its bureaucracies. He asserted himself, gave voice to his spirit, and confronted the powers and principalities of his national church. He claimed all as his peers, accepting no one, churched or unchurched, physically able or physically disabled, as either his superiors or his inferiors. He broke the social boundaries of his "disability" in enacting his own convictions, invited, demanded, and pushed us all to interact with him as a fully human person... which he was. He broke the mold.

Does your spirit touch you thus? Does it seek to help you break through the social boundaries? Does it goad you to try new things, to ignore the cautions of your century, your culture, your world as it has been given to you? Does it urge you to err on the side of creativity rather than to succeed on the side of the habitual and the ordinary?

You have to ask it. How? By entering into the space where your spirit will speak to you, unencumbered by expectations of what you will hear. In other words, empty, and deep listen.

Why might your spirit touch you thus? Why give expression to your entrepreneurial spirit, if that is its course and direction? You will have to uncover your own reasons. Your spirit will listen to them, as you listen to it in your inner dialogue. But I would also like to make the argument that human civilization is rapidly reaching the point of no return, as our destructive and negating habits, institutions, and proclivities outweigh our creative, nurturing potential. We are in desperate need of great social inventions adventured by our human spirit which moves us to new heights, new risks, new modes of being and doing—the entrepreneurial spirit at work in us.

Is not each of us called? For some, the call is loud and clear. Sometimes, it is only loud. Clarity comes later, with experience, with inner work, and in dialogue with other enspiritors. In my earlier years, I tried out and left job after job, position after position with foundations, universities, businesses, governments, education, politics, and labor unions. In all of my jobs, I was reasonably successful, taking on a rising load of responsibilities and receiving upscale monetary rewards, status, and position in life. Why did I routinely leave? Because my spirit was restless, egging me on, driving me to listen to its call, its offer, its invitation. Finally, I heard the call clearly and responded to its invitation: to bring the human spirit back into the world through the disciplines and practices of envisioning and enspiriting.

For some of us, the call is heard neither clearly nor frequently. The social biography has encased and suppressed the inner biography. The spirit has never been given its chance. Are you now ready to hear the call of your spirit?

Your spirit is not all-powerful. Like most of us, it too wants invitation, nurturing, loving, and caring. For those of you whose social biography has been overwhelming, I hope that you will find one or another pry points so that you may open the door to your spirit and begin to create the inner space and, eventually, fashion the outer space for its expression.

That is why we began this search by opening the inner door first to our gifts and talents. These give us clues as we search for the call of our spirit. For some of us, the entrepreneurial potential is there, standing at the back screen door looking in on our life, waiting to be invited into the kitchen.

You have to extend your own invitation for it to enter. I can't do it for you.

How might you make that invitation? Remember, we are talking about:

- Breakthroughs
- Taking risks
- Acting your convictions
- Putting your creative energy into new ways of being and doing
- Enacting your gifts and talents; and
- Marshaling your inner resources to a point of action.

In the short exercise that follows in the next chapter, search out examples from your own life.

BREAKTHROUGHS IN YOUR OWN LIFE

As you begin your reflection, do not look for the big breakthrough. This exercise is not designed to make you look larger than life. Search out the little things. Give yourself some reflective space. Try breathing deeply a half-dozen times, listening to the sound of your own exhalation. It works wonders to open up a little space inside. Forget the pop-psychology and interpretation of why you did what you did. At this beginning, just describe what happened, what you did of an entrepreneurial character. Deep learning begins with the reflection and the search.

An Initial Question

Can you recall a breakthrough in your own life and experience?

You are looking for a certain kind of action, something you did that included an inner action. That in which you penetrated, addressed, or overcame a problem, a barrier, or even a confusion. That in which you took the first step toward something new—a skill, a relationship, an experience. The act might have been mental, physical, emotional, or a combination of these.

Once again, your breakthrough need not be big and earthshaking. Recall the small acts of courage, curiosity, and risk. Our lives are peppered with them, though the internalized social biography tries to cut them off, to stop them before they are enacted, or dismiss them after the fact rather than appreciate the little miracles the entrepreneurial spirit gives to us.

Cooking is one of my little personal examples, a "breakthrough" that only I know about. I contemplate making a new dish, one I've never tried before, reading the recipe and remembering that my mother never took a new recipe too seriously. And I think to myself: "I'm making a new dish for the family supper table tonight. My wife and son will eat it. Will they like it? What if it tastes bad? Have I the courage to try it?" All of these questions, momentous to me, asked in the safe, cozy space of the family kitchen.

When I was a youngster, I received a fabulous introduction to art and painting, both from family and school. Can you imagine this? Vito Tomayo, the great Mexican artist, taught me painting in the third grade, at the Dalton School in New York City. But I moved on in my life. Sixty years later, I bought a sketch book, took it with me to foreign countries rather than a camera, and began pen and ink sketchings of old churches, old barns, old government buildings, even trees and vines and growing things that move and twinkle and shake before your very eyes. For me, that was a breakthrough, looking at everything through new eyes. Never mind that my sketches are mostly unintelligible and illiterate. No matter. However small, I brought something new into my life and in a minuscule way, into the world.

Isn't that the key to the question? Isn't every breakthrough creating something new? Isn't that what risk is about: the new, the fragile, the just born, in need of nurturing? We have so narrowed the domain of entrepreneurship to the economic. But it is so much more. Look for it in your own life. Look for it as an expression of the entrepreneurial archetype that speaks in all of us, though for some of us, it is the very essence of our lives, the call of our spirit.

My invitation is for you to describe these actions, inner or outer. What? When? How? Perhaps even, Why? The why focus may even evoke your spirit. The self-dialogue might go like this:

Why did I do that?

Well, I had to. I just had to!

Yes, but why?

Well... I felt compelled.

You mean impulsive?

Maybe a bit. But much more. As if I were in control and at the same time out of control.

I just had to do it. I **could not not do** it.

Oh... a compulsion... like the psychologists talk about it?

Oh no, not that. My spirit invited me to my breakthroughs. "Why not?" it spoke. " What have you to lose that is not worth losing?"

Record these precious moments, these events. Jot down the memories as they come to you, whether from your childhood or from yesterday.

Of course, the breakthrough experience is not all. Doing or being something new always involves risk. Sooner or later, we must come to risk. What are you risking? What is at risk? Questions like these may go to the heart of the entrepreneurial spirit.

WHAT IS AT RISK?

Fortune 500 Risk-takers

Some years ago I did an enspirited envisioning workshop at a Fortune 500 corporation with 30 of their senior executives. During the first day, their images of the corporation's future were not very exciting. There was no sense emerging that its future would be much different from its past. The corporation might be bigger, have a larger market share and produce a rising bottom line for stockholders. But in their domain of combining high technology with service to millions of people, their visions of the future were taken from the last 300 years of a ubiquitous cultural belief that bigger and more is better! Is that a vision? Is it something new, a breakthrough, making the curve?

In my own frustration, I took a bit of a risk. Something wasn't working. There was no inventiveness coming through... and my work is about invention. "Stop the process," I said to myself. Everybody is too comfortable, including me. "What are we afraid of?" I asked. "Why are their visions so ordinary?" I asked, first to myself and then to these senior executives. "What's to lose? Will anyone care 500 years from now? What's at risk here? Who among you is at risk? What does 'risk' mean to you?"

Sitting in a circle, these 30 executives began half-an-hour of chalkboard work about the nature of their risk as they understood it. Here are their words and images about what risk meant to them.

One input sparked another in this sequence.

> Frustration   Not moving ahead   Fear Losing it   Afraid
> Power   Self-actualizing   Empowering   Commitment
> Blast off   No guarantee   Hope   The future   Courage
> The new   Trying out something new   A waste if you lose
> My heart picks up speed   Protecting your ass   No protection
> Learning from losing   Reorganizing   New clients
> Market niche   Breakthrough   Personally, on the line
> Being responsible   Not knowing   Caring but not knowing

As you can see, this group of executives imbued the notion of risk with their own experience of it, including lots of personal as well as organizational connotations. Feelings were involved. There weren't many cost-benefit type words, or much input-throughput-output analysis. Rather, the words were expressions of feelings and meanings that emerged from their social biographies and from their inner biographies.

Then, we returned to the work of envisioning the corporation's future with new elan and a new spirit. Their images were mind-boggling. They put together all kinds of components in new ways. Now, almost 20 years later, that corporation is acting out those futures within a new competitive, technological, and global environment. That organization is mostly ahead of the curve, indeed mostly making the curve itself.

The Next Question

The first question was, "Can you recall a breakthrough in your life or experience?"

The next question is, "For you, what is or was at risk?"

This question involves a deeper reflection. It invites you to consider the risks undertaken in one or more of the "breakthroughs" you identified in the previous chapter. Ask yourself, What was or is at risk? Can you describe that risk? Can you identify its qualities, the feelings associated with it, your weighing of the possible loss or threat? You see, if we couch the entrepreneurial act only in the terms of money, finances, capital, we can usually quantify the risk. But in the ways that the entrepreneurial spirit expresses itself throughout one's life, that quantification, the "measuring of risk" becomes more difficult and much more interesting.

Expectations are a central component here. When expectations are clear and grounded in habitual patterns and activities, we generally know what will happen as a result of our action. You can balance the inputs with the anticipated outputs, the intentions with the results, because your expectations are not contrary to what actually ensues. There are no surprises to unbalance the equation.

In true risk-taking, however, the adventure is just the opposite. You don't know! You enter an area of unexplored territory for which the map is at best fuzzy. Perhaps there is no map! You may have articulated your goals, described your action-setting, and identified the actors. But you don't know the results beforehand. If you did, there would be no risks!

If it's a new arena of effort, you have no expectations. You may have hopes, even a well-laid-out line of possible consequences. But there are no guarantees. Expectations are replaced by hopes, the past is replaced by an intended future, and the KBVAF is replaced by the compelling images that emanate from your own spirit. This is the critical quality of newness: there are no expectations.

So, there is risk. It may be small, but it is deliberately undertaken. As you dig more deeply into one of your breakthroughs, you say to yourself: "I intended to do this even though I did not know what would happen." In all of my own work in enspiriting in which I sought to open up participants' hearts and minds to the calls of the human spirit in each of them, my intentions were strong, my hopes were fervent, the voice of my own spirit impelled me to all my breakthroughs. But I did not know what would happen as a result!

The Illusion of Failure

What an oppressive monster is the notion of failure. Often, people will say that the risk is failure. We must come to grips with the idea and experience of failure. Once you have uncovered a gift and are prepared to give it away, the "trick" is to help others to receive it, to create those conditions wherein the recipient can receive it wholeheartedly and in the spirit in which it is given.

Often, that doesn't happen. The gift is not received! What is that? Not succeeding? Was that the risk? Was the attempt worth the failure? For example, I have known people whose gifts of their own spirit were offered to God. Some of the local congregations received those gifts wholeheartedly, with transforming results, at least for those members. But the "official," national church would neither receive nor facilitate those offers because its protocols were violated and its powers and principalities were threatened. Perhaps here lies the biggest risk: not that you will "fail," but that you will "succeed," and the world, the institution, or the person, won't be ready. And is that failure? And is that a risk?

We have developed a love affair with success and failure, particularly in America. Banal standards of measurement have permeated our culture based on prevailing economic themes and metaphors. (For example, a "failed" marriage. But marriages don't "fail." They are not businesses. Something much deeper happens.) A large portion of our social biography balances on the teeter-totter of success and failure. But while success and failure may be the watchwords of our outer life, what about our inner life, your inner life, your inner biography, that which probably only you know? That is the area to which these questions now lead. So on to your inner life, a passageway to your spirit.

THE ENTREPRENEURIAL ARCHETYPE AT WORK

Outer Risks and Inner Risks

Is yours an entrepreneurial spirit?

I don't mean occasionally. I mean, are you a risk-taker by the call of your spirit?

The difference between the outer and inner is just this. In our outer lives, as we participate in the human condition of being in the world, we humans are all at risk. Ultimately, nothing is guaranteed by high technology, modern medicine, wonder-working drugs, safety-net social programs, or any of our social institutions. In the end, these guarantee nothing. Twenty-five years ago, I lived in Dubrovnik, Yugoslavia for a month. I was facilitating an envisioning seminar on the future of education at the International Center for Post-Graduate Education. The participants came from many European countries, a group of highly educated professionals. Such a beautiful, ancient, sophisticated "city-state" was Dubrovnik. Its citizens included lawyers, doctors, architects, judges, engineers, professors, merchants, old ladies in babushkas sipping tea, factory workers buying their nightly half-liter of plum brandy on their way home. Televisions, telephones, computers and electronic networks filled the airwaves. On Dubrovnik's ancient, narrow cobblestone streets busses and autos vied with pedestrians for some space to move, and jet planes landed and took off at the airport. Dubrovnik and its citizens occupied the sophisticated spaces of the modern, the industrial, the refined, the polite, the high-technology society. Croats, Serbs, and Muslims sometimes lived and worked together. A modern culture of security and habit permeated the premises.

What was at risk? These folks lived out their lives, married, had babies, maintained their homes in the old Twelfth and Thirteenth Century three-story houses leaning up against each other for support, went to school, bought a new fridge, calculator, what-have-you. But what happened when the old Marshall died? Ancient enmities, ancient blood-lusts, vengeful memories of carnage burst forth once again, heated by leaders who wedded their power-lusts, their ideologies, and the political vacuum to their ethnicities in a way that fed their egos. They did not deep listen to themselves and to others in those very moments when our loving spirit might begin the mending, the loving and caring, the sustaining, the just governance, in new ways.

If we look now at the carnage that ensued, we ask, who are not at risk in the world we have created? Do you think that the millionaire, the Bishop, the TV star, the professional athlete, the political leader, the successful professional is void of risk in her life? They are as much at risk as everyone else on the planet. The "risk" is just plain living—and dying—in the world we inhabit and the cultures and institutions we have invented.

The entrepreneurial archetype calls you to an inner action, to an inner risk that is yours to claim if your spirit calls and you respond. Is it calling you to that inner space where your intention emerges to be and do differently, newly, freshly, creatively?

Is this you? Is this your core? Do you feel the blood rushing to your head, your lungs bursting, your heart beating rapidly, your musculature tensing in preparation? Of course, the rush of venturing an enterprise of the soul differs from one person to another. In the very moment of initiating a risk, you may well exhibit inordinate calm as clear purpose pervades your very beingness.

How do you find out? Continue the search if this archetype calls to you.

Clues to the Inner Risk

Some of your inner territory is already mapped. Have you not already recalled some of your breakthroughs? When you marked a new standard for yourself? When you made a venture, however small or large? When you judged the risks and went for it?

These are clues. The inner risk is this: that you will lose, or at least threaten, something that has become very dear to you in your social biography. It may be a belief. It may be a habit. It may be a personal relationship imbedded in your life. The call of the entrepreneurial puts the habitual and accepted relationship between your inner biography and your outer biography at risk. That's the nub of it! The dynamic between your inner and your outer biographies will shift. For a moment or a longer period until mending takes place, your biographies may fly apart. I can't tell you what is the substance of that risk, its content, its meaning to you. Only you know, and by now have investigated and recalled your hopes, your dreams, your aspirations, your gifts and talents. If you have come this far in your search, know now that expectations fly out the window. You are with your spirit, in deep dialogue. Listen.

A Third Set of Questions

Now we come to a third set of questions in this entrepreneurial sequence.

The first set of questions:

Do you recall your breakthroughs? Can you recall a breakthrough in your own life and experience?

The second set had one question:

What was or is at risk?

The third set of questions:

Are you an entrepreneurial spirit? Does your spirit speak to you of adventures, of trying out new things, of exploring your gifts and talents, of enacting them without fear either of success or failure?

How might you best respond to these questions? One way is to review your life by looking at it through the lens of the questions already posed. Perhaps new responses and additional images will come to you. Perhaps you can identify more clearly the nature of your inner risks.

What will your spirit say? This is a more direct way of posing this question. The question may well lead you into your future, for that is where your hopes, dreams, aspirations, and intentions are actualized. Your past certainly illuminates the future. But it does not control it, it does not determine it, and does not own it.

The future is a grand act of the imagination. It is the space within you where you live out your new stories. It is the space where you try out new things, where you explore your gifts and talents, where you can dream a little, where hope creates its own realities, and where you can live your inner biography free of the constraints, inhibitions, and limits that your KBVAF has imposed on you through your social biography.

Deep Imaging a Response

Imaging the future is cumulative. It builds upon what you have done so far, and carries you to the next step. Remember the imaging methods you have already tried, as you searched your gifts and talents.

- Preparation. A few moments to get you into the imaging space.
- Specificity and concreteness of the image.
- No censoring.
- Letting the images flow. Yielding to them.
- No psychological interpretation. Let them speak to you in their own language.
- Return to the images and see if they stand firm.

Now, bring this competence, which is truly a discipline of the spirit, to the foreground. Use it. How? With what focus?

What would it be like if you enacted that which has sparked your imagination? Lived it?

Felt it? Breathed it?

Let your imagination go. It is the bridge that joins your spirit to your inner biography, to your social biography and eventually to the world. When you ask yourself, "What would it be like if… ?" You are testing out your risk-taking quotient and your inner capacity to take a step forward, in advance of other folks. You are testing out the entrepreneurial spirit within.

As you live and rehearse these enactments, what do you feel? How does your body respond through its senses and feelings? Some slow us down. But some propel us forward with a faster heartbeat, a jaw firmly set, a gleam of determination in the eye and perhaps a trembling in the voice.

There are so many ways to ask these questions. Find yours.

To what are you called?

What new adventures or directions in the domains of everyday life compel you to take action?

Let your images roam the unexplored territory of your human possibilities. Record them all as they come from you.

Of course, your genius may surface in the arena of another spiritual archetype you have not yet explored. Still, if you are of the entrepreneurial archetype, you will feel that in your bones. Your images, your inner voice, will reveal that substance. Your very flesh may tremble in anticipation of your enacting the images your spirit announces to you.

There is nothing to be forced here and no games to play on yourself. Your deep imaging is cumulative. Perhaps you want to map the whole territory before your own path becomes clear. Perhaps you might visit the other callings, for they might make clear that, after all, you are the venturing type par excellence, that your ambition is to give, help, suggest, and challenge the others whose focus has also become clear but who lack that inner drive to chance the breakthroughs that their spirit calls them to. In that way, persons called by different spiritual archetypes can work together hand-in-hand to accomplish extraordinary things.

In the business world, we call that person the "venture capitalist."

Are you a venture capitalist of the human spirit? Are you willing and able to lend your spirit-energy to those of us who know what to do but dare not do it?

Do your own deep imaging. Then read on. Search on. And return to your entrepreneurial spirit if that is where your genius lies.

4

The Sustaining Spirit—
Partnership Rediscovered

PARTNERING

It's all about power.

In our history on the planet, we humans are the one species
that possesses a presumed ecological advantage: we have at least
some control and choice over our destiny. To exercise control and
choice requires that you have some power to do so. Competent or
incompetent, wise or stupid, without efficacy (the power to produce
a result), the human being's control and choice are illusory. Who
has the power to do what? What kinds of relationships are most
efficacious in our newly-emerged, complex, interdependent world?
The sustaining spirit offers an alternative to the historically popular
responses of Bossism and Stewardship. It is Partnering. Partnering
and sustaining are powerfully interwoven.

Bossism

It matters not what sophisticated name you give it or what forms it takes, in the end, bossism stands for a hierarchical relationship in which the one (person or group) holds sway over the other (person or group). However subtle or explicit the commands are, the former has the power to get the latter to be and do what they might not otherwise be and do. Control and choice reside with the boss. And until that relationship is changed, we know not what the latter would be and do.

That relationship, no matter what its political, moral, or social forms, has held a powerful attraction throughout human history. Some proclaim that God holds sway over the Earth and all its populations and manifestations. The industrial civilization made no bones about the human species using the Earth and often each other for whatever purposes suited the ruling industrial elites. Some religions hold that men hold sway over their wives and children, though a few cultures and religions have placed women in the prominent and superior roles, not only in family life but also in the economic and political sector.

I recognize that "bossism" is a vast simplification of power relationships as they have existed throughout human history. But there is a reason for this simplification. Despite its popularity in human affairs, I do not believe that the human spirit calls us to this. Bossism diminishes the call of our spirit and often renders our response to it impossible to enact. Spirit's call in all of the archetypes moves the relational quality of our species to absolutely new grounds in which the power motif disappears. Are there alternatives?

Stewardship

A kind of a "moral" stature was added to bossism when we came to the relational notion of stewardship. That notion, which is relatively modern in the history of our species, seeks to soften the rawness of the boss syndrome by stating that he or she (or the group) in the superior role or position knows what's best for whomever or whatever is in the subordinate position.

We use the concept of stewardship to account for the prevailing belief among some of us that we can "husband" our forests, our streams, our cattle, our wives, and our children. We also believe that we are given dominion over our Earth and all of its other creatures, organic and inorganic, by virtue of an obvious cognitive disparity: we humans "think" and "learn." As far as we know now, very few other species do this.

Stewardship simply means using that power wisely in someone or something else's best interests. But hold on for a minute. Perhaps our earth holds an enormous capacity to teach us all sorts of things, if we will but learn to deep listen.

Partnering

Is there still a third way of relationship, one that has also existed since time immemorial? Yes, there is. It is partnering. Partnering is the mode of action of the sustaining spirit's archetype.

Some of us are called to sustain a partnering relationship with another human, our society, or with the entire world in all of its organic and inorganic manifestations. The call is to make a relationship that is rechargeable, enduring, self-nurturing, and intrinsically creative; one in which that which is given is freely given, and that which is received is freely received.

Through great social turmoil and planetary degradation, we are slowly learning that beyond bossism and stewardship lies partnering: partnering one with another, men, women and children together, blacks with whites, humans with animals, birds with trees, poor people with social workers, the sick with the healers, victims and perpetrators (restorative justice).[11] Every instance of the sustaining archetype at work, in fact or in imagination, is about this underlying quality of partnering. If your spirit calls you to sustain the world, I invite you to discover, or reconfirm, its natural environment, your society or group, or yourself through the action of partnering. Perhaps the sustaining spirit is calling to you. Perhaps it is lodged deep within your vital source and just now, as you read this, it awakens.

Partnering Starts With Self-nurturing

The initial move in partnering is with yourself, not with another. I believe that the sustaining quality of self-nurturing is a part of all of our lives. No one is left out when they start with themselves. Even for persons who are despondent, self-doubting, perhaps in despair and without hope, this sustaining quality of self-nurturing is always there when they are ready to listen.

We begin with ourselves. To sustain yourself is the bedrock, and not only of this spiritual archetype. It is the foundation on which all spiritual archetypes stand to launch their call. With all of the archetypes of the spirit, we start with this profound recognition: that our very spirit invites a partnering relationship with our biography.

They learn to listen to each other. They nurture each other so that the relationship is rechargeable, enduring, self-nurturing, and intrinsically creative.

This partnering is enacted through a deep listening and a deep questioning between your inner and your social biography, between your spirit and who you are becoming. Its mode is the enspiriting dialogue.[12]

Indeed, the very first deep listening I invited you to in Chapter One is an introduction to that inner dialogue. By now, I hope you have become acquainted with it as you listened and queried about your gifts and talents, or focused on the possibility that your archetype is the entrepreneurial spirit.

The partnering quality of the sustaining spirit is not about team-building. It reaches beneath every group process I know of to call people to learn what it means to be a partner in life, with oneself, one's loved ones, one's fellow citizens, and emphatically with every aspect and feature of the natural world which will listen to us if we will listen to it.

Partnering With the Earth

What about the nonhuman voice of partnering? Can we humans render our planet sustainable? That is the steward's question. The partnering questions are: "Can the Earth, in all of its expressions and manifestations, sustain itself, including us humans? Will we let it? Will we get out of the way to let the earth do some of its own self-healing? And will we enter into partnership with it?"

Do you understand that our rivers weep when we pollute them? Deep listen.

Do you hear the wrenching cries of our virgin forests when we demolish them to assuage our lusts for farming space, mining extracts, cattle feeding, or wood boards for housing for our out-of-control population explosion? Deep Listen.

Do you hear the groans of our very Earth as she tries to carry a bursting human population far beyond her own limited resources, some not replenishable, as precious to her as your teeth, your fingers and hands, your ears and eyes are to you? Deep listen.

The response to all of these questions is the sustaining spirit's call to partnering with the earth. Partnering, then, is not only inner dialogue. It is also outer dialogue. The sustaining spirit carries its powerful call and invitation into the external world, not only to people but to the very earth itself, to its spirit, and to its myriad aspects and expressions. Learn to listen to these too. They all enter into dialogue with us humans because spirit, theirs and ours, acts in a multidimensional reality far beyond the solely cognitive, far beyond the realities we have chosen to construct.

I learned this first hand from envisioning with aboriginals in Canada who call themselves "First Nation Peoples." Working among the bands north of the Arctic Circle, I learned from the elders their stories of living in the bush for months at a time, in temperatures often below minus 50 degrees Celsius. Some of the elders still live in a state of reciprocity with their environment; not fighting it; not eroding it; but listening to it in all of its manifestations. This is not the same as "living off of it." It is living with it, with its animals, its birds, its fish, its flora, its climate and snow and black flies; living in a way that can only be understood as the expression of the sustaining spirit working its way into the very sinews of their histories, their biographies, and their cultures.

Since time immemorial, these arctic peoples have lived with the earth and themselves in an unavoidable partnering which sustained both, in every way... until we high-tech, high-analytic, high-forcing, high-consumption folks intervened, to the detriment of both sides. Now, there are not many left to teach us what their spirit and history might best contribute to a fully human future.

Do you think that this is Western-type romanticism? Do you think that I am weary of the noise, the crowds, the automotive exhausts, the waste and plunder, the "who wins and who loses" in the throw-away cultures in which human beings are the prime targets for disposal? Not at all. Returning to the past is never an option. Learning from it is. Nor are the aboriginals without negatives and deficits. But they have something to teach the rest of us about learning to deep listen to our earth as she speaks to us. Our ability to learn this is crucial to the future of the earth and our place in it.

Partnering in Our Own Lives

So we might all look for this partnering in our own lives. We might look for the examples, the indicators that tell us how much the sustaining spirit has called to us, and yet awaits a response.

Can you find the examples of this sustaining partnership in your own life?

The Inner and the Outer

In the early 1980's, Elise Boulding and I did an envisioning workshop whose participants were mainly young people, members of various environmental groups and associations in New England. Hundreds were involved for a couple of days of hard work. Their compelling images of the future looked mostly to the external side of policy, program, and institutional reform. A much smaller number of environmentalists understood that changing our social habits of profligacy, waste, and the trashing of our nest, habits lodged in our social biography, would require some substantial inner work that might be best invited rather than forced.

In enspiriting, the inner and the outer are inextricably interwoven. It's a whole new kettle of fish that requires us to revisit many of our most hallowed traditions and cultural beliefs:

- that all "truth" is objective
- that "evidence" is the only aspect of human experience to which we should give credence
- that there is a kingdom of God and there is a worldly kingdom, and they don't have much—or anything—to do with each other
- that scientific psychology and psychiatric intervention are the therapeutic antidote to spirit's absence in our lives
- that the sacred is a very small portion of human's experience of their world rather than pervading everything we are and do.

What this means is that self-nurturing and the nurturing of others go together. Discerning this interlock is a powerful clue to this archetype's presence in you. We all need self-nurturing. One way or another, your spirit is ready to partner with you. But are you ready to partner in the world beyond your inner biography?

Such is the call of the sustaining spirit.

QUALITIES OF THE SUSTAINING SPIRIT

Beyond Stewardship

But a question remains for each of us to answer. Are we stewards… or are we partners? Are we stewards over children, over aboriginals, over animals, forests, ore mines, the Earth in all of its myriad living things… or are we partners in sustaining them and in their sustaining us?

This is a very deep question. It invites us to consider the most basic of stories we tell ourselves, as a human species, about who we are and why we are here on this planet. One such story is the modern one that celebrates our scientific genius and its technological applications. We marvel at the way we can coat our frying pans with the same Teflon that coats our space vehicles. We take for granted the computerization of our communications culture and believe that some day all of humanity will surf the net. Yet we humans are still plagued, as in days of yore, with the same deficits, injustices, hatreds, blood lusts, and national interests that lead us to make wars on each other. So the stories we tell ourselves, the events and interpretations we come to expect, are not without their dark side.

Can our self stories change? They have before, in the history of humankind. Is it inevitable that we must be prejudiced against different skin colors, languages, ethnicities, social classes, histories, cultures and ways of living, one gender over the other? When we say that it is "natural," that it is "human nature" to prefer our ways to other ways, to what are we appealing? We are certainly not appealing to the spirit breathed into us, alive in us, waiting to be invited into the dialogue of how we might best live together on this planet.

What is the sustaining call's story?

Most of us are part sustainers, of one kind or another, in one situation or another in order just to keep things going and to maintain the minimum level of our beingness through thick or thin. We call that survival, which doesn't perhaps differentiate us from other species. It's an ecological principle.

But is sustaining the same as maintaining? Certainly, one of the ordinary qualities of sustaining is maintenance. If you don't maintain your car, it's going to go "kerplunk". If you don't move your cattle to a new pasture, they'll overgraze the old field. If you don't do the minimum amount of work required for your job, you may get fired.

The sustaining spirit calls us to a land far beyond maintenance and the status quo. It is a new land of creativity and transformation, wherein we have so changed our ways of living that a visitor from another star system would see a new culture, economy, and ways of living, the people unattached to previous ways. This is more than a gradual shift to the environmental perspective. A remarkably reflective spirit, the management genius and futurist, Peter Drucker, had for years called this a discontinuity, a "systems-break," where the birth of a new system is generated by and from a space inside us for which the usual statistical, logical, or behavioral accounts no longer suffice.

Discontinuities, systems-breaks, paradigm shifts can be described. Explaining them is another matter. Explanation seeks to bring them under control. But the inner side of discontinuity is enacted by the spiritual archetypes at work in us so strongly that we respond creatively to their call. We bring forth, in practical ways, what was until that moment inexplicable... and so create a new reality. If we listen deeply enough, we begin to hear a new story waiting to be told.

I believe we are called to listen to our spirit tell us a new story about ourselves. I believe some members of our species have been doing that since time immemorial. I think it's time now to raise the level of consciousness about our spirit so that it becomes manifest in each of us, and in the world. Not everyone is ready to do this, but more and more are ready. Are you one?

Nowhere, to my mind, is this "new spirituality," as people like to call it, more clearly in tune with our predicaments, challenges, and threats than in the case of the archetype I call the sustaining spirit.

What is it? What are its qualities? How do you discover them in yourself?

Qualities of the Sustaining Spirit

I have introduced the notion of partnering as the modus operandi of the sustaining spirit, and I have suggested that sustaining spirits so invited may well show the rest of us the multiple forms of partnering possible.

Listening to envisioners and enspiritors, I have uncovered at least four qualities of the sustaining spirit. The sustaining spirit is signified when two or more persons partner together in a common endeavor or activity:

- which they jointly or collectively intend
- with parity throughout the relationship, though in any given instance one may have more to offer to the other, and vice-versa, in a technical sense
- which requires continuous mutual and reciprocal learning and

- which is grounded in the practices of giving and receiving.

Are all of these qualities to be taken together? In the true sense of the archetype, yes. But in its expression in us, as with all the archetypes, we humans are less than "pure" because our spirit always interacts with our biography. There is a negotiation between the human spirit and its social biography in which the inner biography acts as mediator.

Between our species and its home on earth a new covenant is emerging, just as between your spirit and your biography a new covenant is to be fashioned.

In the sustaining call, there is a myriad of relationships. Marriage and family life might be a good candidate, though too often, the partnering relationship is incomplete. Sometimes the two do not sustain each other in occasions of stress. (And stress is the symptomatic quality of modern life for which deep listening is the healing response, not Valium, not Prozac, not alcohol, not buying and consuming more and more. Deep listen to your own spirit, deep listen to others. You will discover this. Don't take my word for it.)

What of teachers and students? Might their relationship exemplify the sustaining call? The best of them learn to enter into this sustaining mode of partnering, into their reciprocal and mutual learning.

We can all learn to partner with each other and with our earth and its creatures, organic and inorganic, so that each of us and all of us are sustained. Without that, I think we are lost.

Because the archetype of the sustaining spirit expresses itself in so many different ways, it may be instructive to recount a story of how I myself experienced some of these partnering qualities in unusual circumstances. The story may also remind you to look for your sustaining stories in unusual places: far from work, which is rarely sustaining; away from family, which sustains less and less; far from the mass media, including most TV, which is not designed to sustain at all.

A Learning Story From Nigeria

Some of my learning about partnering entered my experience during my Peace Corps days, in the mid 1960s, when I lived and worked in what was then the Eastern region of Nigeria. Of course, I knew that the idea of the Peace Corps was to create a partnering relationship between peoples of different nations, as the volunteers lived among and worked with their counterparts. No doubt, that is why I was attracted to it. But I did not realize how much my Western, or American, or high-technology, or white ethos would get in the way of the new partnering... until a little girl taught me.

As a Peace Corps Rep. ("Representative," an official name for a staff position), one of my responsibilities was to visit Peace Corps volunteers in the field, to see how they were doing and how the in-country Peace Corps administration could help, if at all. Volunteers in Nigeria lived among the local people, teaching, helping to develop Farmers' Cooperatives, constructing water-holding reservoirs, building bridges, and making other access improvements. Some volunteers, who were mostly young persons in their 20s, partnered well. Some did not. And while the latter group did provide skills and human energy to help "modernize" the traditional Nigerian society, that group found it difficult to participate fully in the partnering and reciprocal learning theme that was part of the Peace Corps' birthright. Some found it difficult, for instance, to imagine that the Nigerians had something to teach us.

Partnering as mutual sustaining is not easy. Unlike the prevalent nation-state practices of bossism and stewardship, the U.S. Peace Corps was a grand experiment in partnership amid the cataclysms of a world in constant social upheaval, cold war conflict, and wars of national liberation. In Nigeria, I learned the realities behind the brave words that call for parity in the relationship between the volunteers and the indigenous people.

The story is about my learning, taught to me by an eight-year-old girl in the jungle forest that encompasses both the southeastern part of Nigeria and the northwestern part of Cameroon. This jungle forest consisted of huge, ancient trees, a virgin forest of climbing vines, rich undergrowth, and a density of total vegetation that you would not believe unless you had been there.

I was visiting a volunteer as far distant from the Eastern regional capital, Enugu, as you could get, several hundred clicks (kilometers) away. At first, I traveled on laterite roads, driving a large, bright blue Chevy. In late afternoon, I parked the truck in a small village by a riverside and, after negotiating the price and putting bike and knapsack in a canoe, I was canoed down a river for perhaps two or three clicks. Then I disembarked onto a narrow path disappearing up the riverbank into the undergrowth and forest as the canoeist pointed the way with a few words of English and a huge smile.

By now, dusk rapidly approached. I biked the narrow, rooted, overgrown path, brushing shoulders with huge tree trunks, for another two or three clicks, hoping at each turn of the trail that I would find succor. I could hardly see ahead. My bike lamp was of little help, so twisty was the trail. At last, I biked into a little clearing with half a dozen huts. In one of the huts the dim light of a kerosene lamp shone, and on its small front porch stood a man, a villager, whose skin was as black as blue steel.

My heart rose to a louder and more hopeful thudding. It was so far into nightfall that I could scarcely make him out. I rode my bike to his porch step, stopped, and put a long toe on the ground for balance.

"Peace Corps?" I asked. What else was there to say?

"Ah… Peace Corps. Keith," he replied. He pointed. The path continued out of the clearing. It was not really visible, but I saw a hint of an opening into the jungle.

I gestured, my arms out, a bit hopefully, a bit forlornly.

"Where? Peace Corps, Yes, Keith. Where? How do I get there?"

He understood. He turned to the open door of his hut and said something in his own tongue. In a moment, a young girl dressed in a blue school jumper came out the door and hopped off the porch. Without a word, she motioned for me to follow… and was off.

Hastily, I dismounted my bike, left it at the side of the hut, and rushed after her as she disappeared into the jungle on that scarcely-visible path. I followed, tripping, half-jogging, trying to keep up. And she kept disappearing, flitting among the trees on that twisty path. It was now dark. A faint light from the stars and the moon crept through the forest canopy and somehow caught her blue jumper, so I could see her… just barely. Hoping my eyes would catch her and keep her from disappearing, I stumbled, then caught myself. She had disappeared. I yelled for her to slow down, probably just a loud "Hey," or "Yo." She came from around a tree, now suddenly five feet in front, smiled a brilliant smile so that the whites of her teeth illumined the path, and lifted my spirit. Then she turned and was off again, skipping around the bend. I tried to keep up.

And so it went for 15 or 20 minutes, just like that. My heart rate was up. My big knapsack bumped up and down on my back. I kept losing sight of her. And when I thought, *Now I am lost,* there she was, waiting for me, smiling with such a loving, sustaining warmth that only an innocent child without fear could give in the middle of *her* jungle. Then she was off again.

She was a partner when I most needed one. I was completely in her hands. A 37 year-old Peace Corps Rep. A know-it-all. A "Representative" of my powerful and affluent country, completely in her hands, as lost as I have ever been.

Then the jungle forest opened to a large clearing, fields, brilliant rising moon... and Keith, standing in front of his hut, waiting as if he knew I was coming. The young girl went up to him, said a few words in her language, motioned toward me, turned, jump-skipped past me, flashed her beautiful smile... and disappeared back into that jungle path.

I had a learning. She had sustained me. Out of our joint intention, we had agreed to have her lead me to Keith. Who knows if I would ever have found that volunteer that night. Unlikely without her help. There were a common intention and a reciprocal learning, for she learned to slow down a bit for me to catch up in her journey, and I learned a humility completely foreign to me before that.

She must now be a woman in her late 40s. I hope that she is alive, with children, perhaps grandchildren. Does she remember our little partnering? I can just see and hear her now, sitting with her friends or family over a cup of tea, beginning:

"I have a funny story to tell you about this big white man, totally lost, came to my village when I was a little girl... "

Do you get a sense of the partnering? Of the sustaining spirit? Can we organize ourselves internally and with each other so we can give sustenance to our own spirit, to each other, and to our earth? Can we organize our relationships, our work together, and the ways we go about our daily business so that we give sustenance to each other's spirit and receive it back tenfold? I think partnering is the way this is done, the method, if you will. In this sense, citizens are partners with one another, not just shrill or one-issue advocates. Government officials are partners with citizens and vice-versa, a far cry from bureaucracy. CEOs, ministers, school principals, "heads" of family are not rulers, governors, executives, senior managers, stewards, or gurus. They are partners.

I have seen the sustaining spirit issue its call in some of the many envisioners with whom I have worked. I have even come to know some of those whose every action expresses this partnering way of life.

Are you one of them?

The next chapter may help you so discover.

ARE YOU A SUSTAINING SPIRIT?
INTENTIONING

What does intentioning mean?

As you listen for the presence of the sustaining spirit in you, look for the occasions when you have joined your intentions to another's so that a partnering has been inaugurated and pursued. It is not the whole thing, but it is a beginning.

What exactly is this intentioning?[13] Intentioning is the act of coming to your intentions. It shifts unthoughtful behavior to mindful action. It substitutes intentions for habits. The sustaining spirit shifts the nature and quality of relationships from a non-intentional to an intentional character.

You may have to dig deep in your search. In all of my years of futures-invention and envisioning with communities, organizations, universities and schools, corporations, churches, and governments, the biggest hurdle I have had to overcome with so many good peoples from all walks of life is to hold out to them the idea, even the possibility, of an *intentional future,* one that they could help create and enact, as distinguished from somebody else's future to which they could only withdraw, prevent, or adapt.

Why was it so difficult? Because they had never been asked. They had never been invited to discern their intentions for the future, a future they thought desirable, worthwhile, even compelling!

I think many of us are coming to the realization that too much human behavior is unintentional. Perhaps that is why so many programs in "goal-setting," from the most personal to the most organizational, have blossomed in the last 50 years. These are a social recognition that habit and tradition are no longer enough.

What is this "behavior" that I call unintentional? It has its source in many of us who believe that we act out of a determining past rather than toward an open future that we can configure with our own possibilities. To be unintentional in your conduct means that you are not in charge of yourself. That belief results in a vacuum which other persons, organizations, and belief systems of all kinds are eager to fill.

We study human behavior as we study animal behavior. We analyze it. We compare it, explain it, seek its causes, quantify it, and report it. These are the social sciences, the "behavioral" sciences at work, in which we seek "causes" and statistical correlations rather than acknowledging that human action, intentional action is known by the choices made in its behalf.

More and more, our behaviors don't work as well as they used to… or don't work at all. The framework of our KBVAF (knowledge, beliefs, values, attitudes, and faith) disintegrates, leaving us directionless. "Family values" erode. Citizens carry concealed weapons legally. Children don't listen to their parents; parents don't listen to their children. Service at the counters, garages, banks become negligent at best, surly at worst. The security of the lifelong job disappears into thin air as one corporation buys out or merges with another. Old skills become next to worthless in the competitive environment of new technologies. Knowledge about our private lives becomes public property. Our social contract, that which binds us together as a society, disintegrates into an ideological swamp as true-believers and single-issue advocates argue over every aspect of morality and public policy, instead of deep listening with each other.

Motivating... or Intentioning?

Clearly, intentioning lies at the heart of the human expression of the sustaining qualities of this spiritual archetype. The act of coming to your intentions is constituted by your spirit's stating its call to your inner biography. It is an image of the future which compels you to actualize that call, not motivation from the past. Here is a major distinction between psychologizing and enspiriting. The former seeks to uncover your motives—why you do what you do and are what you are—as an expression of your history, your personal culture, and the dynamic relationship between your inner biography and your social biography. The latter, enspiriting, offers you an alternative perspective: that your spirit invites you to consider your human possibilities through deep imaging. Your spirit gives you images of the future that compel, that attract you with the powerful magnetic force of spirit-energy. You end up saying, feeling, thinking: I **cannot not do** this. I **cannot not be** this.

Intentioning Partnering... and Partnering Intentions

What is the practical implication here? How might you join the ideas of partnering and intentioning to begin to build your search engine? Is it like combining fire and water? Impossible—unless what you seek is steam. You look for the cases in your own life when your purposes joined with another person's purposes—perhaps more than one person, perhaps many.

Impossible to find? Not at all. Difficult? Yes. It is increasingly difficult because we have neglected the enspiriting discipline of intentioning in favor of the adaptive culture of "behaving." Political and cultural correctness tell us to adapt, to behave ourselves, not to invent.

Nowhere is this more crucial to our collective future and to your intentional participation in it than in framing a new social contract. Can we enter into a grand, intentioning relationship with our fellow citizens? Can we intend to live together, to sustain each other and the world in matters of justice and governance? Not as a cultural artifact, not as a social habit, but as a matter of civic partnering that we can sustain with our civility? (This is, by the way, the specific call and focus of the just spirit. See Chapter Seven.)

The Self-question of Intentioning

Look, now, for a common experience, activity, or endeavor in which the intention is shared with another. There is a reciprocity of spirit in which each contributes to the expression of the other. What is it like to experience that? Sometimes this partnering is unspoken. Many things we do with other persons are unintentional. We do them together out of habit. We fulfill each other's expectations without asking, perhaps without even knowing the reason. Then occasionally, with a lover, a colleague, a fellow-worker, someone in your family, or even a citizen who is a stranger, we are caught up short. The relationship doesn't work anymore.

Then we ask, "Why?" And we come back to the act of intentioning, which means coming to your intentions by listening to your spirit as it creates for you a compelling image of what it is like to do what it is calling you to do.

Here, then, are some questions. Enter through your memory of yesterday or of earlier years. Uncover the events, the situations, and the settings characterized by shared intentions. Empty. Ask. Wait. Listen.

- What was jointly intended? A goal, a strategy, a common endeavor, an action?
- What were the intentions that joined you to another who shared them?
- How did the sharing come about?
- How did the intentioning happen?

The Search Practices

This quest begins with that which you have uncovered in previous search exercises. By now, your journal may have become an increasingly rich reservoir of recorded experiences, events, self-feelings, and self-knowledge. Your social biography has been exposed to your reflective talents. Your inner biography has announced its presence when you opened that inner door on the way to your spirit. Perhaps the entrepreneurial call reminded you of the times, places, and circumstances when you took your risks and lived your adventures.

There is nothing to prove here. Finding no basic call in you to a joint intentioning is no loss. There is no failure here, no defeat. Each of us is learning to listen to the voice of our spirit. Deep questioning is an enspiriting discipline of discovery, not proof.

You may want to give some time to sifting through your relationships to discern which expresses this joint intentioning. A remarkable description of combining to share an intention through partnering is recounted in Sam Keen's personal story of his learning trapeze flying in his 62nd year, a story about risk, courage, spirit-energy, and technical know-how which culminated in a joint intentioning between his neophyte self and his trapeze-flying mentors.[14] His story reveals as few others I have read or heard what it is like to listen for, hear, and enact the call of your spirit.

When you place yourself in this reflective moment, when you can prepare yourself for your meditation, probe the joint intentioning quality of the relationship I call partnering. It may be a one-time thing, a longer time, or even a lifetime, in which the joint intention sustains both or all of you.

The new partnering is called forth by this archetype. I'm not talking about soup kitchens for the poor or indulging others who wallow in self-pity or self-righteousness, but about coming to shared intentions to be and do something different. How is this possible, absent of group pressure, bossism, or stewardship?

It is possible because the sustaining spirit knows how to act in a group setting. It knows how to transform uniqueness into shared purposes, into shared adventure, into a common experiencing of unique spirit. It knows how to transform different compelling images into common action without violating each person's spirit and its call.

Has that happened in your life?

Empty. Ask. Listen.

THE SUSTAINING SPIRIT—
SOME OTHER CLUES AND QUESTIONS

Do you find the sustaining archetype appealing? To your liking? Even part of your life? Is the call moving through your body, your feelings, your mind? Have you been able to identify the enactments of partnering in some of the ways you have been involved with other persons or perhaps even with the planet in one or another of its manifestations?

Clues are everywhere, but they have to be uncovered, for they hide in surprising places and indicate qualities of living that often lie beyond the norm.

Parity is one such clue.

Parity

Is there parity to be found within the sustaining relationship?

This question brings into conscious awareness the experience of parity, of equivalency, where partners recognize that each offers to the other something of worth which is crucial to the relationship. I am not talking about sameness. The sustaining spirit calls for equivalency but difference. What the Amazon jungle forest brings to the sustaining relationship with our species is quite different from what our species might learn to bring to the Amazon jungle.

Consider that the forest jungle, born into the infinitely complex ecology of our planet, offers the rest of the world a multiplicity of gifts: healing properties, for example, of its plants, flowers, herbs, and barks, many of which we humans of the Western scientific cultures have yet to discover. Do the aboriginals who have lived for ages on that rich, vegetative mass understand their part of the partnering?

Perhaps not in an intellectual way. Yet the deep structures of their social life and the fabric of their cultures represent an equivalency of "live and let live." Their spirit and biography have created a way of life in which that forest jungle and its human inhabitants—like the Gwich'in and the Inuit in the arctic north—sustain each other. We moderns, of the population explosion and more-is-better mythology, do not sustain either the jungle or the frozen tundra, and we do not let them sustain us. We decimate them. Parity, equivalency married to difference, takes many forms. We have much to learn here. The sustaining archetype invites us to learn parity through the persons whose spirit responds wholeheartedly to that call.

Parent and Child

Do you realize that parity sometimes emerges between parent and child? They have learned to listen deeply to each other in order to create an ambience in the home where spirit is not thwarted but is emancipated. This is not "bringing up." It uncovers the unique gifts and talents of the child in such a way that her social biography is expressive of her inner biography and, through it, her spirit.

The parent is also sustained, for the child nurtures back in that loving, surprising, and sometimes challenging way that calls the parent's KBVAF into question and breaks through the mold of generations, offering a new way of understanding how things might work better. Sometimes, in a mutually abusive, even violent, marriage relationship, it is the child who sustains the family.

The invariable response to the youngster's questions need not be: "But son, but daughter, this is how the world works." Together, from the very beginning, parent and child form a sustaining bond that may spread to other people and settings, as their orbits interact and they enter the modes of invention, of intentioning, of creating.

Do you find instances of this emancipation of spirit in your own life? You, emancipating others? Others, emancipating you?

The Ram's Horn

I use the child-parent relationship as an example because our culture does not generally see this relationship as partnering, as joint intentioning, or as parity. Every young person is a potential Joshua, blowing her spirit's ram horn so that our adult walls come tumbling down.

Every aboriginal is a potential Joshua blowing her spirit's ram horn so that the protective walls of stewardship come tumbling down.

Every river unleashed at the flood stage, every undergrowth brush fire rampaging into a forest fire, every mudslide on a built-up, defoliated mountainside where humans have built their homes remind us that we humans have sought to subdue, control, decimate that piece of the Earth rather than to enter into a profound relationship of partnering which sustains us all.

Marriage

Another place to look for the sustaining spirit's call is the marriage relationship. Marriages endure, or break apart, for many reasons. Sometimes they endure when the uniqueness of giving and receiving sustains, when together they intend and create a partnering relationship conducive to joint intentioning.

Partners sustain each other as each invites the other to the dance. One leads. Then the other. Parity. Reciprocity. Not sameness.

The River Invites

Canoeing down the Current River in the Ozarks as part of an eight-day Boy Scout expedition, my son, Zach, then 14, took the stern paddle. I had suggested he do this. I took the bow paddle and supplied power. He was the steersman, and I was the engine. We had to learn the harmony of parity out of a joint intention to do so. I had to learn not to give orders, not to yell at him "Watch Out!" not to be a boss, not to be a "Daddy," not to be a mentor. Zach is and was a better canoeist. He had to learn how to help me be a more skillful partner as he learned how to be the "steersman."

But what of the river on which we canoed? We steered, we paddled, and we drifted silently as the turtles sunbathed on half-submerged logs and as the blue herons soared overhead and winged splendidly down the river, in the direction of its flow, ahead of us, always ahead of us, saying in effect: You can paddle. You can steer. But this is the river's movement, this is the river's direction. Be with it, in partnership. Don't fight it.

Learning

Do you sense now that one quality of this archetype leads to another? They are intertwined and cannot get loose from each other as far as the sustaining spirit is concerned. As you move among these questions, do not be surprised if one anecdote, one memory, or one image breathes life into the next as you watch the sustaining spirit birthing in you, if it is the archetype that resonates for you.

Another question may be percolating in your consciousness. Is the partnering conditioned by a mutual and reciprocal learning?

The sustaining spirit does not offer certainty. Where there is certainty, learning is finished. We have so much to learn about how the new partnering works in practice. Thus, you also look for a relationship characterized by a learning dynamic, the learning stance, wherein each person intends to learn from the other. The learning intention is mutual and reciprocal. The learning of one depends upon the learning of the other.

This is not mentoring. Mentoring is a one-way street. Mentoring is not the call of the sustaining spirit. Mentoring is stewardship. Cast into the stream of your life to catch those occasions when you realized that to teach, you had to learn, and that the other, to teach you, had to learn with you.

Giving and Receiving

Partnering, parity, and learning call for the beneficent acts of giving and receiving. Earlier, I said that as we uncover our talents and seek to offer our gifts to others, the difficult part may be to invent the ways in which these others can receive our gifts. If we charge enough money for the "gift," the others know they are valuable, and so might seek to receive and learn from them. If we offer little or no money for the work, it is seen to have little or no value. It is easier to say "No thanks," and to shrug it off. That is the money culture. Yet Alan Tough, the great Canadian educator and futurist, discovered 40 years ago that adults (and children) learn from each other all the time, without fanfare, without money, without credentials, in a partnering relationship of teaching and learning which is both intentional and reciprocal.

Do you find that your gifts are received? Do you find that you are receiving others' gifts?

The sustaining spirit calls for that reciprocity. It is characteristic of the new partnering. It is the basis for a new kind of human ecology. Look, then, for that receiving. Look, then, for that giving. In any or all of the relationships in which you have entered, look for that reciprocity: with mountains and streams, birds and snails, wetlands and deserts, family, friends, and colleagues... whomever and wherever.

A Totaling Up

I have said that we are, all of us, sustainers a bit. Who among us are sustainers a lot?

As you reflect on the entries in your journal, see if the joint intentioning, the parity, the mutual learning, and the giving and receiving coalesce into one stream of your spirit at work in you. Discern if they coalesce into a whole.

You will know this as it has happened, or is happening, or might yet happen. You will know it as an integration that stretches beyond habit, maintenance, mutual admiration, and self-satisfaction to a sustaining relationship that is rechargeable, enduring, self-nurturing, and intrinsically creative... with yourself, your very spirit... with others whom you invite to this way of being and acting... with the Earth, which now invites you back.

How do you respond?

5

The Loving and Caring Spirit

WHAT IS THE CALL?

Spiritual Archetypes Revisited

Before you begin this part of your journey, I wish to review the very idea of the spiritual archetype. Is it more than idea? Now that you've come this far in your own search, might we dare to question the very premise of this book: that we all have a human spirit and it calls to us to be and do that which expresses its essence?

In this modern age, the space for spirit is murky. For most of us, the inner truth is obscured by the pseudo-certainties and partial truths of psychology and sociology, by the emotional attractiveness of ideology and true belief, and by the brain-clogging appeal of catchy slogans. The space within is also clouded by our unreadiness to hear our spirit's call. In search of meaning, we settle for explanation. And when that is provided, how easily the explanation of our conduct turns into an excuse for our conduct. Our culture has fashioned no clear glass through which we can find that inner light which illuminates who and what we are. Your first obligation is to yourself. The obligation is to discover your spiritual archetype, to cut through the swamp of false interpretations so you can hear your spirit.

In the field of logic, a distinction is made between the concepts of the necessary and the sufficient. Listening to and enacting your spirit's call is not sufficient for anything. No world problems, no private dilemmas, no interpersonal conflicts are thereby resolved. But listening to and enacting your spirit's call is necessary for everything. Even to growing radishes, as the great Zen master Ikkyu might have said five and one-half centuries ago. Without that we are as flotsam and jetsam, floating directionless on some vast ocean of basic indifference to the fate of the world, and ourselves as creatures in it. This is your ground on which to stand, to say, "Here I am and no other."

Thus, the call of your spirit is first to you. It is yours and it is unique. How you express that call in the world through your biography is also unique... and not easy. An infinite number of unique calls have been recorded in the annals of humankind, in legends and myths, in stories told around the fire, in novels, plays, and poetry, in song and dance, in music. What has emerged is the recognition of our humankind's spiritual archetypes.

You can say, "My spirit calls me to loving and caring." How do you know? Because, you can say, "I have listened." You can say, "My spirit calls me to the new partnering which is the sustaining spirit's particular mode of action in the world." Yes, but how do you know? "Because," you can say, "I have been listening."

From Anecdote to Insight

Does the loving and caring archetype play out in real life? Does yours? What if the practices of the loving and caring spirit are so widespread that we have to ask: "What has this to do with the human spirit?"

After all, we might argue, who doesn't have a loving and caring spirit? Don't we all, in some basic way? Don't mothering and fathering include lots of loving and caring? What about relationships with mate, family, lover, friend, a pet? Don't these also involve loving and caring? Aren't the giving and sharing of affection nigh on universal, however much its display varies from culture to culture, personality to personality, and situation to situation? Affection is very universal. But the giving and receiving of affection does not define the loving and caring spirit.

As we unpack the loving and caring archetype to discern its essential qualities and characteristics, I hope you will look through your own life to find your personal response to the questions posed above. Do an honest and forthright search, not only into your soul but also into all of the human relationships you have experienced, from the most private and intimate to the most public and social.

If there is a special spiritual call to loving and caring, how is that different from sustaining? Would nurturing and compassion be characteristic of both spiritual archetypes? Perhaps there is a gradation of one archetype into another, a substantial overlap.

Your discovery lies in listening for it. Those of the loving and caring spirit are scattered throughout the world, in every human guise. We might find them in any family or neighborhood, in any business or organization, in any school, church, or hospital, behind

a counter in a bakery, or behind the steering wheel of a bus. Have
you not known a loving and caring spirit, close to you or seen only
at a distance? Have you not been caught up in the warmth of a
stranger's spiritual embrace, as his eyes caught yours for a moment
and you just knew that he was offering a space for sheer lovingness to
replace the anger or fear or confusion which too often monopolizes
the human group?

What is sheer lovingness? Have you ever met a salesperson
whose concern for your purchase goes far beyond making a sale?
Did you sense that somehow, she was caring for you as a person,
even in those few moments of a commercial transaction? Has a
doctor, nurse, or alternative healer given you a sense that beyond
their credentials they truly care about your plight?

Death and dying sometimes reveal who is a loving and caring
spirit... and who is not. When it was clear that my mother's lung
cancer was soon to take her, she was moved to a room at the end of
the hospital corridor. Her doctor stopped visiting her. The nurses
left her alone, providing minimal care and, sometimes, no care at
all. Her sister, trained as a nurse years before, requited her needs
and gave her the loving care which perhaps eased her journey to the
land of spirit.

And when, 25 years later, that very same sister, my aunt, now in
her mid-80's, lay dying in another hospital as her body just stopped
working, I was a thousand miles away teaching a summer seminar
I could not leave. I called the hospital, connected with her floor,
talked to the shift head nurse, and asked: "Who will be with my aunt
when she dies?"

In the exchange that followed, it became clear that being present at the death of a patient was not within the bailiwick or concerns of the nurses or doctors on the floor. Computer stations, medical technology, record-keeping, and insurance forms for the living were the matrixes within which dying had no place except as something to record on a medical chart.

"Yes, but who is there to hold her hand as she goes? Who will be with her as she starts her journey?" I asked into the hall phone in the corridor of the university building. Perhaps she heard a plea. But silence. Then, as the pay phone cooled in my hand, a soft and warm voice responded.

"Hi. I'm Clarice. I'm a nurse's aide. I have been sitting with your aunt. She is now my patient."

I told her my concern. She reconfirmed that my aunt was about to pass. She heard the distress in my voice when I told her I could not be with my aunt in her dying.

"Will you be with her? God, somebody has to be with her."

She heard my plea, my desperation and my ordained sense of deep loss. It was in my voice. She understood, this nurse's aide in a Florida hospital a thousand miles away.

"I will be with her. I will sit with her. I will hold her hand."

She did not say the secret word. She did not have to. But the message was so clear over the electronic wires and plastic and satellites... *and my spirit will be with hers.*

The Tree House

Once, at a marvelous gathering of 30 or 40 envisioners in Vancouver, two in particular imaged a "tree house community," building their images into an alternative loving and caring community which found all the rest of us longing to be invited in, all of us silently weeping inside because our world, what the pragmatists like to call "the real world," was not loving and caring like the make-believe community of these two loving and caring souls. One worked in an art gallery. The other was an administrative officer of a foundation.

"Yes," one of the other participants said as we sat in a great dialogue circle doing critique of each other's futures, "But what happens there? What do people do?"

"We just are," the two responded. "We welcome all. We give each other love and care, first and foremost, so that it permeates everything else we do. Making things, building, fashioning, extracting, planting, harvesting, cooking. All of the doing things are undergirded by the spirit of this place, which is loving and caring."

They slowly cast their eyes around our medicine wheel circle of learning in which sat professionals in culture work, business people, school teachers, government officials, media experts, knowledge workers, a few from the hinterlands of farms, and said:

"You are all welcome."

QUALITIES OF THE LOVING AND CARING SPIRIT

At the Center is the Person

The loving and caring spirit, as I have come to know it in others, is like a warm, nourishing rain that follows the thunderclaps and flashes of lighting. It is a quiet snow that blankets the landscape and soothes the roughness of crags, stumps, broken branches, and sharp edges of metal carcasses. It places a hand lovingly on the hunched-over shoulder of one grieving a loss. It gives a smile to light up the cold room of anxious executives or turns a joke to relieve the boredom of the assembly line.

It is a hug that embraces spirit and mind as well as body, so that every aspect of you is invited into its grasp. It is the recognition— which we all so desperately need—that we are persons in this moment, in this place; that we have some unique and inevitable presence, so much more than the multiple roles and labels into which each of us is divided and certified.

Somehow, in the word, the gesture, the body-sense or the spirit-sense, the loving and caring spirit affirms to each of us that the troubles, the worries, the little defeats and partial victories that are the stuff of growing up and being a grown-up will pass. It is the loving and caring spirit who knows the full person in you, who seeks out the full person in you, who embraces your personhood on all occasions, and just when you need it most, who reminds you that this joy shall endure and this pain shall pass. It's in phrases offered often to children, not enough to adults (*There, there. It's okay. It's going to be all right.*) that tell of the presence of the loving and caring spirit.

The Gift of Personhood

The gift of the person who lives out this archetype is a great and unique gift. Our modern era is not an age of persons, full, complete, whole, integrated in body, mind, and spirit, living with and treating each other as such. In our ways of living, in our daily practices and habits, we hardly know what personhood means, what it is, how to be and act as a person even toward ourselves, much less toward others. We have let ourselves become objects, designed to respond to sales pitches, news media sensationalism, the demands of technology, human relations training, and certification by others as to our worth as human beings. We are caught up in an infinitely complex network of roles and labels, ideologies and loyalties, situational ethics and appropriate behaviors, so that when the real person is invited to stand up and be counted, there is no longer any ground on which to stand.

Do you remember Pastor Martin Niemoeller's words about this, spoken as his reflection on the German people's response to the conflagration that Hitler ignited?

"In Germany they came first for the Communists, and I didn't speak up because I wasn't a Communist. Then they came for the Jews, and I didn't speak up because I wasn't a Jew. Then they came for the trade unionists, and I didn't speak up because I wasn't a trade unionist. Then they came for the Catholics, and I didn't speak up because I was a Protestant. Then they came for me, and by that time, nobody was left to speak up. You and I must act. Together we can make a difference."

The loving and caring spirit enters onto this stage, and for a moment or for a lifetime, completes us. We are complete in her eyes. You will understand this, if you have met this person, if you are one.

How does she do this? By being a person herself.

She transforms our human interaction from separation to integration, so that we change from a partial appearance, to being fully present to each other. She reminds us and witnesses to us that personhood, being persons to each other, takes precedence over every other human act.

It is not surprising that this spiritual archetype finds her location most easily with the youngster. The child is more readily touched by this special presence than the adult, for whom the loving and caring practices of personhood sound like a foreign language.

Presence

Presence is a quality that expresses itself in all of the spiritual archetypes. It is the spirit's presence in the whole person that is so powerful. Like a hearty oak or a delicate tulip, the presence of the loving and caring spirit lies in its just being there, grounded in its own offer. How can any of us refuse? So many of us slip and slide through life barely aware of who and what we are, solely reacting to life's stimuli, even gorging on false plenty, and angry and frustrated if we don't get enough. Then the loving and caring spirit holds us close, each of us who comes within the orbit of her presence. "Be yourself," she says, "I welcome you and cherish you in the potential of your full personhood no matter what else."

Who and what we are is our spiritual archetype, in action and in relation. We will know ourselves by its singular presence in us and through us, fully integrated, so that we can be and do no other in the world.

The loving and caring spirit offers its special presence to the solitary you and to the you in the group, to the you in the crowded bus or airplane, to the you in the hospital waiting room.

Her presence invites out yours. That is her essence, so that at once some mutual recognition is posited. I am here. You also are here. In a flash of reciprocity comes recognition.

In short, the loving and caring spirit is a special presence or beingness that acknowledges and calls out yours. We are persons to each other, says the loving and caring spirit. I accept you fully. I acknowledge you fully, despite your foibles, aside from your labels, and apart from your roles, tasks, accomplishments, deficits. You are accepted for whom and what you are by the loving and caring spirit because whatever else you are, were, or may yet become, you are first and foremost a person to her. She offers complete and unalterable acceptance in situations and settings that, for the rest of us, defy credulity. That is why the "mother" is often thought of as its prototype. The true mother accepts her child and loves her child totally and unconditionally, everything else notwithstanding.

KNOW THYSELF

Variety and Multiplicity

Most interesting about this spiritual archetype is that it expresses itself everywhere, in all situations and settings. It is recognized in all cultures that I know of. Yet it shows itself differently and uniquely through the persons who carry this archetype within. We may know the loving and caring spirit by its being present to us. However we may react at the moment—not always graciously or in a welcoming way because the offer is nonnegotiable—there remains the enduring sense that we have met a loving and caring spirit.

Yet there is no behavioral receptacle to confine this spirit. It manifests itself in any and every human situation, from the most dehumanizing concentration camp to the most superficial glitter of our civilization of false plenty. We know when we are well met with the loving and caring person.

How would you know if the archetype is part of your essence, perhaps at its center?

Questions to Yourself

The questions that I now offer will be helpful. What if I were a loving and caring spirit? What would that be like? What would I expect of myself? What would others see in me?

Because of its essential quality of being present, you know if a loving and caring spirit lies at your center. No self-research, no guesswork, no "wouldn't it be nice if... " are needed. If it is there, you have heard this spirit's call in you for a long time, perhaps since your birthing day and its birthing day in you.

Here, nevertheless, are some questions I have found helpful in listening to the call of my own spirit in regard to this loving and caring archetype.

- How do you view your fellow human? What is your perspective on the human species?
- What has been your experience with your fellow human?
- What offers do you make by your being with your fellow human?
- Do you get beyond the anger, the fear, the competitiveness, the loneliness to see the potential of personhood in each of us?
- If you have been a target for abuse, put-down, sarcasm, being diminished by word or deed, or if you have accepted the least as goods are portioned out, has the offering of your spirit's warmth been a transforming presence that has overcome these negative intakes?
- Do you transform the other person's anger or fear into her self-recognition that the sources of those feelings lie within her own make-up, not someone else's?
- Are you that selfless person for whom the other's completion is paramount?
- Do you invariably see the potential in the act, the underlying presence in the superficial, the whole in the partial?
- What is most important to you? Is it the loving and caring of the other, always, invariably, in all situations and settings?

I have known three such persons in my life, friends and colleagues, really sisters who have reminded me, by their presence, of whom I am, was, and will be. They called me to my personhood by way of their own loving and caring, not as a task, not as a moral obligation, but by virtue of their caring that I be who I am, and loving me for that, for my own sake and not for the sake of anything else.

Would there were more.

Are you one?

6

The Mending Spirit—
Growing the Whole

MENDING OR HEALING?

What is the call?

Some years ago, a colleague who is a channeler gave me this message: "Warren," she said, "Your work is about healing. That is what the world needs now. That is the meaning and purpose of your enspiriting. Listening to the voice of your spirit is a way of healing. Healing must become the watchword of all that we do, and everyone on the planet is involved."

That caught my attention, you can bet on that. What a promising goal. What a hopeful message. And isn't it true? Aren't the wounds we inflict on each other, or on ourselves, running deep? Aren't we tearing ourselves apart by seemingly endless wars of identity, ideology, and dominance? Aren't identity politics escalating from verbal assault and defense to physical viclence? The underlying argument goes like this: only by advancing my identity at the expense of yours is mine made more secure. This takes us from group identification to ethnic cleansing.

But this great spiritual invitation caught me up short. For I am not a healer. And my work in enspiriting and envisioning has neither generated, identified, nor called forth many healers nor has it led to much healing. I have met some healers or, at least, some who purport to be that. But as I look at the calls of the spiritual archetypes that have emerged from the envisioning and enspiriting work of thousands, and which are recounted in this book, healing, by itself, is not one of them.

If we are all called, someday, to become healers on this planet, some of us must begin prior to that "someday." Doing what? Mending. Being what? A mender.

What is the spiritual archetype of mending to be and do? Is her call to heal the "causes" of wars, this absurd violence that has endured since time immemorial?

Of course, you don't heal "causes." Each of these conflicts is complex in its sources, be it historic, linguistic, ethnic, religious, ideological, or economic. The mending spirit is not quite in the business of healing any more than the loving and caring spirit is about the giving and receiving of affection, or the entrepreneurial spirit's call is only, or even mainly, to make a lot of money. In fact, the mending spirit's work begins before healing. This you are now invited to discover. Healing may take years or centuries; for the individual person, often a lifetime. Mending makes healing possible.

What, then, is the mending spirit up to? If not healing, then what?

Fragments

So many of us on the planet, now, are asking,

- How do I bring my life together? How do I unify myself so that I am at one with myself?
- So that I am clear about my identity?
- So that there is solidity, a fitting togetherness in all aspects of my persona?
- So that I present a unified front to the conflicts within and the competing demands without?
- So that I am no longer oppressed by money worries, by an overfull calendar, by family responsibilities, job requirements, deciding what to consume, and the unending bombardment of telephone, TV, and e-mail messages which have nothing to do with who I am?
- So that my inner biography and my social biography meet in some place comfortable to both?

You might want to plead: I have only so much to give. I have only so much to be.

Here is a famous Zen Koan whose innermost reflection turns that plea into a search. "All things return to the one. To what does the one return?"

What would unity, wholeness, oneness look like to you? Feel like? Be like?

Do you know your fragments? Are any of them these:

- Your creativity not expressed in your work?
- Your human purposes not enacted in ideologies that demand true belief and offer a false certainty in an uncertain world?
- The fullness of erotic loving diminished by the objectification

of your inherent sexuality, so that pornography, frigidity, or physical habit replace the joining of your spirit with another's in this loving and creative act?

- Learning constricted, prevented, or denied through lockstep schooling?
- Governance of self and governance with others so separated from government.

The litany is endless. What is your fragmentation? How do you put things back together again? Some people, in their frustration, advocate a return to the "good old days," as if the fragmentation were absent then. It was not absent. It was only different.

But is mending the same as healing? Do we choose another word, another metaphor, in the hope that what we don't really know how to be—healed—will somehow come to pass? Healing is not a doing. It is a being. You don't "get" it. You are it. Who offers a healing program? Do the New-Age practices and philosophies borrowed from Eastern cultures offer it to Westerners whose social biographies have for so long inhibited the celebration of the inner spirit, the speaking out of a higher consciousness, and the sense of being at one with the universe? A myriad of self-help programs offers a diet for the body or for the soul as a way of healing. How many of us can keep to a diet? So we jump from one popularization to another, hoping that the new one will heal us.

The mender does not promise healing.

Then what is her offer?

What the Mender Does

The mender puts the parts together. She sews them up, closely, fittingly, so that there is no escape. She binds in a way that won't let go. The mender weaves a new fabric from old threads, mixes new colors from old. The mender digs deep into the ground beneath the shifting soil, even if she has to burrow down into the core of molten magma from which all things grow, to uncover a foundation on which a new house might be erected, a house that will welcome all people, not only some of them, a house that encloses all of your pieces in its embrace, not just some.

Will healing then take place? Who knows? Mended persons might go about the business of healing. But the mending spirit does not make that call. In marriage, family, racial and ethnic division, hate groups, in the courts, the government, in the offices and factories, and in the media, the mender mends on the sewing machine of her spirit.

I will bind up the wounds, says the mending spirit, so that the edges can grow together again, so that each side gains sustenance from the other, is nurtured by the other as capillaries, muscle, bone, and skin join together to create a new reality. What is this new reality? An invention, says the mending spirit, which is beyond my powers, I will not foreclose your healing possibilities. I will not select your healing alternatives. I will neither proscribe nor prescribe your healing futures. I am a mender, not a healer.

Do you get a sense of how the mending spirit calls out a very special set of practices? It does not heal. In this day and age, with mainly a medical model to follow, we haven't even begun to explore the byways and boundaries of healing. But mending we know about, because its archetype calls.

145

A Mended Kingdom

What would a place of mending look like? Would it be a community devoted to the inner unity of all of its members? Might it be a "kingdom" that mends?

Twenty-six hundred years ago, a small vision of a mended place to live was composed by one of the world's great poets, Lao Tzu. Listen with your spirit to one of Lao Tzu's stories. Transport yourself to that time and place… and listen.

There is a kingdom that is small and sparsely populated.

There are numerous implements, but no one uses them.

The people love their lives and no one wants to move afar.

Boats and carriages are available, but no one rides them.

Fine weapons are in their possession, but no one uses them.

The people are back in the times when knotted cords were used to record things.

They enjoy fine delicacies and are handsome in their dress.

They are happy with their residences and are pleased with their traditions.

Although the next state is within sight, and the sounds of cocks crowing and dogs barking are heard,

The people live their whole lives without traveling to and fro.[15]

This is a vision of a society, a little "kingdom," whose inhabitants know what it is like to be mended rather than fragmented, to live a life of unity, to have bound together the inner and the outer. What is left out? Nothing. The mending spirit calls you to a unity that encompasses all, within and without.

The mending spirit sets the stage for something glorious, splendid, and necessarily inventive to be fashioned out of that which is first mended. The most amazing of its qualities is that the mending spirit sees the possibility of mending among the people, parts, institutions, beliefs which the rest of us would never think of putting together. How? Often, by cutting the edges.

Cutting the Edges

When the fragmenting has occurred, when the tearing apart has rent the unity, when the whole is split up, what we often get are rough edges. Pieces of a long-lost life hang about. Fragments of what-might-have-been float in and out of consciousness. Memories of old events, old wounds have never been exorcized.

The Serbs go back centuries to a lost battle that they cannot forget. Ancient enmities resurface as the scar tissue breaks up and fresh blood spurts forth. Tito, the Communist master of Yugoslavia, formed the tissue of the postwar Balkans—Serbs, Croats, Slovenians, Albanians, Moslems, Catholics, Eastern Orthodox—that hardened into a great scab. Underneath that scab, the threads of ancient memories and more recent brutalities, of what-might-have-been-if-only, rough edges, deep wounds that would never heal by themselves festered. When the scab was removed, the blood burst forth in renewed freshets of obscene and unbelievable violence on all sides.

What are we to do with these edges hanging about, these old threads of a cloth torn into many pieces centuries ago, and torn and torn again? The one called to mending by her spiritual archetype now takes out her scissors and cuts away those edges so that the new pieces can be joined evenly, without threads, tears, remnants, and rendings hanging out and about.

Can you picture this? The archetype calls upon its embodiers to cut clean edges, to trim the ragged pieces until they can be well joined. She sews the pieces together. She does not throw one side away to secure the other's continued existence. She makes out of the two a new piece that does not deny the old pieces but allows them to together create a new fabric. In short, the mender sews the edges together. She is a quilt-maker, who binds together different colors, designs, and patches which, nevertheless, keep you warm on a cold night.

How does she do this?

Cutting to the Bone

Snipping the edges to make them clean so they can be mended: what does this analogy mean? The mender gets underneath the conflict, the tear, the wound, the separate parts that will not be joined, and discerns the rough edges, the stuff that gets in the way of the mending. Most often, these are aspects of the knowledge, beliefs, values, attitudes, and faith that make up the social biography's content. These are learned from others, from parents, family, schoolmates, and our institutions. The mender invites going to the criticals and uncovering the fundamentals. I call this cutting to the bone, getting underneath, so that the common ground begins to be uncovered.

Here is an example. Once, I gave a year to a mending project in a southern community fragmented into two parts, black folks and white folks. The community consisted of a city, suburbs, and rural area of some one million souls. One hundred of them gathered to envision what it would be like to live in a community not fraught with racism. I invited them to deep listen with each other and to deep image concrete and specific possibilities of living and working together in new ways. They arrived at the residential site emboldened both by their pain and by their hope for a new vision. I first invited these participants to get underneath their KBVAF about racism to ask themselves: Where and how did I learn it? From whom? When? Why? I invited them to their deep learning.

The 100 dispersed to different corners of the building and did their inner reflection. Then they met in small groups, black and white together, and compared notes while deep listening to each other. They discovered together that they all had begun to learn their racist way of life from parents and close relatives around the age of ten, just before the adolescent onslaught when growing up is so confused and stressed. In Western cultures, we offer our children no rites of passage to mend bodily changes with their spirit. Growing up for many is a psychological mess and a spiritual desert. In a racist society, however, one truth cuts through that mess both for blacks and whites, though it does no mending between blacks and whites. It is this, spoken by parents, by older brothers and sisters, and supported by neighbors: "You two stop playing together. You are growing up. You are no longer a child."

And thus did each of the 100, black and white, remember. There was a common ground of personal experience that they uncovered and shared. They acknowledged this learning in public, in front of each other. When we 100 gathered again, a few hours later, there emerged a hushed recognition that something had happened. The deep learning undertaken and shared might be a solid foundation on which to build something new.

The mending had begun. Rough edges were clipped and sewn together by the enspirited envisioning after that critical discovery had been uncovered. People who had not known each other, not worked together, divided by the historic institutional embellishments which commenced with slavery generations earlier and were signified by skin color and social class, now confronted each other creatively, however painfully.

That creative group of 100, out of one million area residents, did not know that they were menders. The archetype of the mending spirit had yet to be celebrated in practice, institution-building, legend, and lore. Is it to be celebrated in you?

MENDING STORIES

Start With Yourself

Is mending primarily a social endeavor? Not at all. To the contrary, mending begins within each person and ends with each person. It is the inner work that provides the experience and the testing ground for the outer work of social mending. Does this mean that you are mentally ill? Not at all. You may be fragmented in the different ways I have talked about it, but mental illness and fragmentation are not the same.

Once, I did a three-day enspiriting session with a group of senior psychiatrists. · This was a lively, thoughtful, experienced group, each with her or his own specialty and training, most holding high positions in institutions devoted to mental health care. Most were also in private practice.

I introduced them to the enspiriting disciplines by inviting them to listen to the voice of their spirit. They all did. Of course, it turned out that, like the rest of us, none of them were whole. Who is, in this day and age? Indeed, what is a whole person like? Each of these psychiatrists had old visions and dreams, old wounds and inner conflicts that were part of their history, the dynamic between their inner and their outer biographies in a partial truce. None were completely mended.

In those few days together, they learned how to listen to their spirit. In the enspiritng work, there is no pushing or shoving except as your own spirit calls you. Invitation only. When you are ready and your spirit knows you are ready, it speaks. You listen. The dialogue begins.

As these psychiatrists experienced their spirit, mending began for some of them. They acknowledged that they were not yet completed. These were skillful and compassionate people who were ready for some spirit mending because their spirit, their inner, and their social biographies were not aligned into a unified flow where inner call, aspiration, and social reality become congruent.

One of them said to me, some weeks later, as she began to apply her enspiriting practices to her psychiatric practices: "I don't have to sit there, always thinking, always analyzing, trying to make a diagnosis about what is my next step in the psychiatric consultation, as my patient talks. Rather, I have to listen to her spirit, for that is where mending begins. But to do that, I have first to listen to my own spirit. To learn what in me needs mending before I can help others to mend themselves."

To my own mending

Now shift the scene to my own mending which, in fact, happened a month or two after the experience I have just recounted. This is a story of mending in my own life that brought into close fit a piece of my history that, when it surfaced, mended a tear of 56 years.

In part, this is about my father who died when I was thirteen, just turning fourteen. He died at Montefiore Hospital in New York City, the very hospital where he had acquired renown as a great mender, as a senior physician, department head, and surgeon. A brilliant doctor, he died of cancer at the age 48, in 1941. And this story ends in 1997—56 years later!

I was at his bedside for five minutes one hour before he passed. For five minutes. Sitting in a chair by his bed, holding his feverish, trembling hand. I remember no conversation. I suspect he could not speak. Everyone gathered about his bed. His wife (my mother), my brother, and the doctors knew he was about to die. Everyone knew except me. I knew nothing of death. They sought to protect me from the knowledge and experience of that universal experience. They succeeded. When I arrived home an hour later, I was told that my father had just died.

For years, until I was perhaps 40, I looked for my father in men older than I, men who mentored me through college and my early work life. It was not a heavy thing, but it was there. There was something unresolved in my father's death, about that event. But I did not know what that was, and I never sought it out.

Put aside, now, over 50 years of a life. Mine, perhaps like yours, has been filled with the social accouterments by which we seek out its sense and meaning... or seek to hide from them. This is not wholly accidental, this life, though so much of our culture emphasizes randomness. Shift the scene one more time 56 years later to a workshop in Sweden, with 30 great folks who gathered for a week-long intensive in enspirited envisioning. This happened the morning of the first day. We were all sitting in a great circle, looking at one another, in quiet conversation and anticipation. What would we do together? What was this about? What about this fellow from the USA, one of several facilitators, the rest of who were Swedish.

We began, as is often my practice, by inviting the participants to remember what it was like when they heard their spirit, when it spoke to them. It's a great way to begin the enspiriting because for so many of us, the invitation draws us without threat into the space for spirit. Each of us goes just as far as we can the first time around.

I accepted my own invitation. We separated the circle into groups of three and gave ourselves five or ten minutes for bringing back the memories. Of course, what we bring back are more than memories. They are images of our spirit's speaking come to life. For the human spirit is not only memory, it is of the deepest presence, so deep, so real, so transformative, so palpable that we avoid it… until we are ready to listen.

After 56 years, I was ready.

The room quieted to that overpowering stillness, as we emptied, as we listened to our own exhalations, as we prepared to yield to these memories of our spirit's speaking, each in her or his own way.

Those five minutes in that hospital room where my father lay dying came back to me with a pristine clarity that brought with it the smell of the hospital room, the position of each family member in that room, the warmth and uncontrollable trembling and jerking of my father's hand clasping mine, his head held up a bit by the bunched pillows… and this, which I had completely obliterated for so many years. His hazel eyes locked directly into mine, locking mine into his. His face was so thin, not shaven that day, pale, his breathing already labored. And his spirit showing so clearly through his eyes, saying just this: How sad I am that I will not be with you in your growing-up years. How great a sadness that gives me.

None of this in words. We had not spoken words in that five minutes. But now, all of these years later, it came through like the cellos in the symphony orchestra. Cellos are easy to miss amidst the sounds of the high violins and the resonating trumpets, unless you listen for the cellos. I had not, then. Now, I was ready. He spoke to me now with such great sadness that the tears began to pour down my cheeks, not only for my loss. Also, for his.

Then it came to me while in that Swedish gathering of envisioners. He had given me his spirit. Just like that. As he was preparing to depart his earthly home, he gave me his spirit. Right into me. Its energy, its love, its hope, its great mending capacity, for that was his own spirit's calling, to be a mender, which he was pre-eminently.

I will help you find your spirit. I will help you live your spirit. Like a great force of energy, from his inner to my inner. Like a stream of sheer energy, through his eyes into mine. I will be with you in spirit for the rest of your life!

How had I missed that? Now, 56 years later, I missed it no more. All of that came to me to tell me that my father had been with me, in spirit, all of those years when my inner life and my outer life were seeking some accommodation, and my spirit was seeking its space in me to speak out. He had been with me all this time. And I had not known it.

When my turn came, in my group of three, to tell my story, this very story, my two partners deep listened. I wept as I spoke. There was some mending here. Some gap was filled, need requited, promise realized. Some part of my life, my work in envisioning and enspiriting that began 30 years ago, now had been joined with my father's spirit. I had come to realize that I was not and never had been alone in this work. In all the years of my search for my spirit, and in all of my work with others to do the same, to listen to their spirit's call, my father's spirit-energy had been with me. It still is.

Is history mending?

If mending is the fitting together and the binding of the parts kept too long apart, what of their history? The separation may be a very old story, one celebrated in stories grandparents whisper into their grandchildren's ears about the olden times. Among some peoples, old wars, and old wounds, have never truly been mended.

Mending takes place deep inside. That's where mending begins. Each person's spirit enters into the dynamic of inner and social biography and culture, the dynamic of the present with the future, as well as the past. True mending brings the parts into close proximity, finally binding them together so that they can't let go of each other.

Isn't that the mending which seeks its presence in South Africa among the blacks, whites, coloreds, and different tribal groups? Is Nelson Mandela called by his spiritual archetype to mend? If so, how long will the healing take after his mending? No one knows. Decades? Centuries? He had made a surgical cut by inviting the perpetrators of obscene violence to come forward in public, in front of all, to admit, to seek, and to receive forgiveness. Ragged edges of old wounds can be cleanly sliced off, followed by a seeking to invent new ways to bind together what had been kept apart for so long.

In the United States, Martin Luther King, the mender, brought together blacks and whites in new configurations of vision, of compelling images, and of civic action. Have we healed? Have we, as a nation, grown a whole that binds us together in loving community? Scarcely. But he showed us a mending way. His spirit called out to us to mend our ways. Blacks and whites, mainly young persons, sitting together at the all-white restaurant counters, was a mending. Underneath the civic action, the civil disobedience, was a mending, no less than a surgeon's scalpel makes a clean cut through a ragged wound. We are still mending. There has not been too much healing yet, so far as I can see. Sometimes, it starts with re-living the old renderings, entering our history, future and past.

And Rosa Parks? What a surgical cut she made when she sat in the front of the bus, slicing clean through the raised edges and seeping wounds of racial segregation. When Donald Trump is long forgotten, Rosa Park's spirit will live on.

With an individual, the mending also brings the personal history back in, even if that personal history has been forgotten, neglected, slandered, or denied. One woman with whom I worked in the enspiriting ways had been fighting with her personal history for more than 30 years. She had experienced severe parental abuse. She had not brought those events into juxtaposition with her present life, that of a highly successful professional with grown-up children. Her inner life, despite professional counseling, had kept her distraught, torn apart in her relationships and unable to express her great loving and caring spirit because she had not mended.

How do I mend? She asked.

You have to bring the parts together, I responded. Embrace the abuse. As the T'ai Chi master embraces his pain. Live the experience, as a now, rendering the past present just as you might render the future present when you have learned to live your images of the future.

Is there a lesson here? Yes. We must embrace our history, good and bad, joyful and painful, of ourselves as individuals, of our group, of our nation, and now too, of the world. It must be brought into the present, next to the rest of our persona, our biographies, our society, so that we can mend. It must be lived again, in its fullness, giving us what Aristotle called a catharsis, a way of coming out the other side, mended. Not yet healed but the wounds are cleansed, bound, sewn together, one edge overlapping the other.

That is what the mending spirit seeks. It is her call. The archetype can be expressed in many different ways and settings. Spirit transcends chronological history by telling stories that obliterate time because so often the parts that stand in want of mending have existed in different time periods in one's own life or in the history of the world.

ARE YOU A MENDING SPIRIT?

How will you know?

Certainty comes from listening to your spirit's call. Fulfillment comes from expressing it.

What will you listen for? Have you a sense from reading these pages that, perhaps just awakening, the archetype of the mending spirit calls to you? Now, perhaps, is a creative time, to deep listen, to prepare yourself, to empty, to listen to the sound of your own breathing, to yield, and to invite. Then, review your life to discern if you have ever walked the mending path. Have you? Perhaps now is the moment to imagine what it would be like were you to embark on that journey, hand-in-hand with your spirit.

Your journal should be a helpful resource. In it you have recorded some of your life's events, your history in search of your spiritual archetype. Your responses and reflections on the questions in previous chapters may take on new understandings as you wander through these questions posed by the mending archetype.

Discerning

In the ecology of mending, discerning is one of the mending spirit's competencies. The mender images the mending intuitively, in a flash of insight, seeing how things might come together. Indeed, she images that fruition long before any binding action has been inaugurated, sometimes in the very midst of the tearing and wounding as the parts assault each other.

This is an instantaneous recognition, a strong inner feeling that here, in this situation, is a fittedness of two or more disparate parts. The mender sees what the rest of us have missed, that the parts, somehow, fit together. That underneath the separation or the conflict lies a unifying force contained within the parts themselves. She may not yet know what that is, but her spirit tells her that it is there, and impels her to uncover it.

Such discerning is often instantaneous. Other times, it may be the outcome of a protracted deep listening. An emptying of the tant'ien, a quieting inside to a stillness so transparent that everything on the outside comes in, is filtered through the listening lens that hears everything and thus can get underneath the roiled waters to the underlying current of unity.

If your spirit calls you to mend, you will know it. You will have been part of a conflict, you will have observed two persons or groups striding their own paths, and known that they could be walking together down the same path.

Ask yourself this question: Have I felt this? Have I seen this? Have I sensed this underlying fittedness?

Note: I have not asked you yet if you did something as a result of the discerning. I am not yet posing a question about your action. This is a question about the discerning competence in the ecology of mending. Did you sense, feel, intuit that mending was there to be done, a possibility?

Mending what? Mending whom? It may be two people, perhaps in intimate relationship, torn apart by elements in them that brook no compromise, no further search for a common link. It may be your own inner mending. It may be more than two persons, perhaps within a group or between groups. Search your life history to seek out and recall these stories.

A Childhood Clue

A clue to this discerning competence might be located in your childhood. Do you remember puzzles, the toys and games that required complicated putting together so that the pieces fit? Do you remember assembling the kitchen, the garden, or the electronic gadgets you purchased at the store or over TV? Written instructions were provided, for those who read and followed them. But others might just look at the mess of parts on the counter top or lying on the ground, and put them together. Were you one of the latter? Mending is not only with and for human beings. Its spirit calls in every circumstance and situation. In the ecology of mending, discerning the fittedness and underlying unity is its first step.

Joining Together

In the ecology of mending, this is the assembling competence, actually bringing the parts together. If it is a human conflict, the competence is to bring the two sides together. But it is more than that, because often the parts to be joined are not only of the human species. Animals may be torn from their natural habitat. Resources are plundered, leaving gaping wounds that need mending. Fabricated parts that don't fit stand in need of re-engineering.

Here, patience is called for. What if the parts can't be fit together in a day? Or a year? Perhaps a lifetime? The mending spirit does not give up.

Years ago, during the cold war, some menders thought to bring together the Russian Premier and the American President, perhaps along with their children and grandchildren. They envisioned a week or so at a seaside resort, a few days of playing with the kids, cooking some meals together, taking a hike or a swim, meditating together, telling family stories as well as thrilling the gathered families with epic tales of their countries' histories. Never enacted, the proposal entailed the spirit of mending. Wild-eyed? The menders among you will shake your heads and say, "Not at all."

Sometimes, the mending is inner. The mender turns to her colleague, her friend, perhaps a stranger, and says: "Deep listen on the inside. I will deep listen too. Enliven your history, embrace it, do not run from it: abuse, pain, missed opportunity, a run of bad luck, whatever. Bring it together. Get underneath it."

In her own way, and unique to the situation, the mending spirit brings the parts together, juxtaposes them so they cannot run from each other, can no longer seek to destroy each other. For now she has sewn them together, so that to demean, diminish, or destroy the one side is to destroy the other. There are no longer two parts. Just one.

The questions:

- Have you done this mending?
- Did you feel compelled to bring the sides together?
- Who and what have you mended?
- Can you recount the details?
- What were the occasions?

What is important here is not success in mending but a strong urge to mend. Describe that. Describe the events, the circumstances, the feeling and sensing inside yourself. Describe the tear, the wound, the fear, the conflict that was just too much for you to stand aside. You entered the fray. But as a mender.

Scissoring

Sometimes the parts don't fit. The edges are too ragged. The wounds are torn. Perhaps history has formed scabs over the separate parts. In the ecology of mending, the scab must be removed.

The mender does this. She removes the rough edges, the tattered memories, the infected tissue. She cuts and slices. How? By her deep listening, by her silence as the others speak, complain, curse, berate, and insult, whether themselves or others. What is this about? She asks. She gets underneath, cutting to the bone. She gets underneath the semblances, the justifications, the excuses, and the self-supporting explanations.

Have you done this? Ask yourself:

When and how have I sat in silence in the midst of conflict, of old wounds bleeding again, of desperate times when all is tearing apart, and offered my self, my very spirit, as listener and mender?

If this archetype grabs at you, do ask yourself these questions in order to ground the specifics of your concrete experiencing of mending. Who? What? When? How? In your journal, recount these occasions. The mending spirit makes its call inside. Listen for that in yourself. Is it there?

Inventing the Future Through *Envisioning*

Finally, in the ecology of mending, an invention is called for. As I said before, the medical model of healing, of returning to health, doesn't work. Something new has to be invented, born out of the old but beyond the old. This is what futurists describe as "a new state of affairs."

A colleague brought together some working class Catholic and Protestant women in Belfast to envision peace,[16] to mend by invention, to image their responses to the question, "What would a peaceful world for us look like?" These women envisioned a future state of affairs in very concrete and specific terms, identifying factors and coming to images that included the absence of violence, as well as images of employment, community, healthcare, sharing, and cultural acceptance. In a way, it was their version of Lao Tzu's kingdom. They envisioned alternatives that went far, far beyond what the political leaders were trying to piece together.

That story is paralleled in the USA by the early days of the Clinton administration's attempt to "mend" the healthcare industry. But the healthcare industry was and is unmendable until the people are asked to join the dialogue (a piece of mending in itself), are invited to share their own deep images about what a healing and healthy society would look like in concrete and specific ways so that their incisive concerns are well addressed, and alternative futures are born. Instead of asking and inviting citizens to participate, the conventional power process brought together the interest groups, the affinity groups, the professional and commercial groups, each with their own agendas, their own histories, and their own axes-to-grind. So no mending took place. Where were the people, the citizens? Among them, are there no menders? In my envisioning experience with thousands of citizens, members, and employees, some of them are menders.

The person who is called by her spirit to be a mender knows how to invite out onto the mending stage the human imagination. She knows how to call out the vision of being mended that each and every person possesses. The mender creates an environment absent of fear of the unknown, of the future, of uncertainty, of change, even of transformation. She does this by virtue of her own spirit, for she has witnessed her own inner mending.

Have you done this? As you look at your own life, work, gifts and talents, skills, do you find occasions when you have invited out the imagination among other persons rather than telling them what to do, be, think, or imagine?

- How did you do that?
- What were the occasions, the situations?
- What were the results?
- Was something new born that day? A policy, a program, an idea, an organizational breakthrough that could only be enacted through the mending of the parts, the sides, the antagonists?
- These are the questions of vision-building from the ground of the mending.
- Have you stood there and invited others to stand with you?

Sum-up

The ecology of mending has its own structure of action to which this spiritual archetype calls.

- **Discerning.** Seeing into the situation, seeing how things might be brought together before they have been.
- **Scissoring/Cutting to the bone.** Removing the rough edges, the tattered memories, the infected tissue by cutting away, slicing through, sometimes having to get underneath to ask, "What this is all about?"

- **Joining together.** Assembling the disparate, even conflicted parts. Sewing them together. Binding them so that they can no longer tear apart.
- **Inventing the future.** Inviting out the deep images, the visions, the new and alternative ways of living, being, and doing together that gives substance to the mending. By asking the folks who are mending together: What would it look like to be mended?

This is quite a lot. Suppose you don't find all or even very much of this ecology of the mending action in your own house? Perhaps your spirit calls, but you are wanting in one or another of the competencies. Where might you best fit in? Is it all or nothing?

No. To the contrary. As you listen inside, search your life, review your gift and talents, you may find that one or another aspect of mending has been expressed, but not other parts. Perhaps there is some inner mending to look forward to. Perhaps one aspect calls you more than another.

In the expression of your spirit's call, in bringing it into the world, don't look for perfection. Rather, listen for the call, for the invitation, for the grand adventure. As you respond, as you have already responded, the enactment of your spiritual archetype does not demand all or nothing. Your spirit is not here to send you on a guilt trip, to provoke anxiety, or to hold you to an exclusive and unalterable set of tasks. Not in this world where so many of us find it difficult just to listen to the voice of our spirit. We begin, as best we can, as our spirit enters into dialogue with our social biography. Responding to the voice of your spirit is a great and loving thing to do. It is an act of inner mending that we all need. Take it step by step.

7

The Just Spirit—
In Search of Governance

WHO IS JUST? WHO IS NOT?

Who is the just one?

Most people on our fair globe will respond to the question, "Are you just?" with the response, "Yes." After a moment, some persons might add, "Of course, not all the time. But most of the time."

On the face of it, the just spirits in our midst are everywhere. Persons seek justice in many ways. Consider:

- The one who speaks out for the underdog
- The one who somberly discerns how many cows his daughter's hand is worth in marriage... a fair bride price
- The one who seeks retribution
- The one who proclaims that everyone can sit at God's table, not just those who are baptized or circumcised or whatever
- The one who seeks to make up the deficit imposed on others by reason of birth

- The one who rights wrongs
- The one who seeks his fair share
- The one who seeks fair shares for all
- The one who rewards on the basis of contribution and worth rather than favoritism
- The one who defends the wrongly accused
- The one who details how many sacrificial offerings will guarantee a god's intervention on your behalf
- The opposing sides in a civil conflict, saying that justice is on their side
- The one who stands up to arbitrary authority
- The one who disobeys the popular law on the basis of conscience
- The one who obeys the unpopular law on the basis of conscience
- The one who listens to both sides before making a judgment or coming to a decision
- The one who looks beyond the group label to the individual person
- The one who is outraged at unfair treatment, of himself or herself
- The one who is outraged at the inequitable treatment of others even when he is satisfied with his
- The one who revolts against the misuse of power and seeks a system of accountability\
- The one who complains or even takes back the purchase if he finds himself overcharged
- The one who quits his job, or joins a union, if he is underpaid.

This list could be endless. Scarcely a human interaction or a social institution does not form a context in which the cry of injustice will not be heard. Does that mean that something we call justice is built into our very bones? Justice in my case, justice in your case, justice for all even though we regularly disagree about the meaning, content, and application of justice.

Is this a universal proclivity of human beings? Is the just spirit everywhere? If so, how can this spiritual archetype call out to some but not to others? Perhaps it is just a matter of degree. Perhaps this spirit's archetype lies at the far end of a continuum that we are all on in one place or another, seeking justice to some degree.

If it is true that we all seek some version of justice, is it because situations of injustice prevail across the land? The discerning question becomes: Which situation upsets you?

Just consider the array of hurtful, unfair consequences and impacts of much socially legitimated human behavior.

- The factory worker shouted down in the union hall when he would speak up in opposition to the majority, or to the union leaders; or
- The longtime employee fired from her job in a merger of corporations while the now-superfluous senior executive floats to the ground of retirement on a golden parachute; or
- American citizens of Japanese ancestry interned in a detention camp during the Second World War; or
- The American corporate CEO receiving 450 times the average wage of the workers his business employs; or
- The youngster from a school in a working class neighborhood told by his third-grade teacher that he has no chance to make it into college, so to settle on lesser aspirations; or

- The hundreds of millions of human beings on the planet who are malnourished, ill-clad, insufficiently housed, ill-governed, with the light of hope forever dimming in their eyes; or.
- The starving infants, bellies swelled with kwashiorkor; or
- The female, the black, the old, the physically disabled, or the ones marginalized for any reason passed by when opportunity, promotion, more responsibility, leadership, and higher pay are made available to those favored by the "right" gender, age, skin-color, ethnicity, religion, or physical health; or
- A parent's favoritism for one child over another, so that the latter sits quietly watching while the sibling gets the choicest morsel of meat, the more expensive toy, the best education, or the most affection; or
- Forty million American citizens, mostly children, single mothers, and working poor, going without healthcare insurance; or
- A country's leaders egging on their compatriots to go about cleansing the population through brutalizing and killing those who look different, speak another tongue, or keep to a different culture; or
- The person who does not believe in her own possibilities, her own spirit's call, her own hidden gifts and talents because she was brought up to believe that none of these things were her portion.

Take your pick. We all have experienced bits and pieces of the unjust curriculum of life's chances. The just spirit takes all of that as her life work.

What a mess!

True, there are cultural differences. What you can and cannot do. Which behavior is rewarded and which behavior is punished varies from one group to another, often significantly. True, the social controls of self-guilt, shame, embarrassment, anxiety, task orientation, compensation, incarceration, and physical punishment are not uniform in their criteria and standards. Even a foundation stone as basic as the declaration and observance of human rights has yet to be laid in all countries as a theme unifying the human species. The great United States of America, "bastion of human rights," has not yet signed that declaration.

Here is the point: We may not know what justice is. We humans may vigorously disagree about what it means, and how, when, and to whom it gets applied. But in a given situation, we know when we seek it, and we know when it is absent.

Rare is the person who has not experienced some kind of injustice in her life. Is this not just the way things are in this world, forever past and forever future?

Beneath these differences of version, lying deep in the bedrock of human experience and feeding the roots of justice are two fundamentals: One is about feelings. The other is about governance.

It is in their interplay, at the roots of feeling and governance, that we shall locate the just spirit's invitation. Perhaps its call is to you.

FROM FEELING TO... ?

Knowing by Feeling

Speaking the words of injustice often commences with complaints about life and its handouts, or about this or that which rub us the wrong way. For most of us, the knowing of injustice is not a thoughtful knowing. It is a feeling matter. We may come to understanding justice by thinking about it. But we know injustice by feeling it. It is as if members of the human species had a gene dedicated to identifying when we are treated unfairly. For most of us, justice is fairness and injustice is being treated unfairly.

We of the human species have built into our basic make-up feelings about these issues. There is no question that it is grounded in our neurobiology and honed to a universal impulse by hundreds of millions of years of animal, primate, and human behavior. Of course, we have taken the justice-injustice impulse far beyond its territorial, defensive, and herd instinct antecedents. As we grow up, we begin to learn the games, make and test the rules of a moral code: a family moral code, a local moral code, a group moral code, and a social moral code expressed in a culture and embedded in our social biography.

However much investigated by neurobiologists, psychologists, social anthropologists, political philosophers, and theologians, our feelings always responds to acts of injustice. A moral code is learned, established, rooted, and expressed in our feelings.

But knowing injustice by feeling it does not yet define this archetype.

Sociopaths and psychopaths are devoid of these feelings. For the rest of us, the emotions triggered by injustice are universal. Together with language, thought, and moral judgment, these feelings mark us as members of the human species who forever seek to get beneath and beyond the territorial and aggressive/defensive impulses that are rooted in our evolutionary past.

Does the just spirit know how to do that? In principle, it does. In practice, the just spirit has to make her gift to the rest of us in such a way that we can receive it.

However much it begins in our feelings, this universal quest for justice takes us to the very ground on which our humanness stands. It lies at the center of our family life, our neighborhoods, our organizations and communities, our societies and countries, the United Nations and regional alliances... into every nook and cranny of human beings when they are together.

The just spirit digs in the soil in which the aspirations of humankind are rooted. An infinitely rich garden of weeds and flowers grow from that soil. The just spirit helps us to discern the difference between weeds and flowers. Its tool is a set of questions to the rest of us, questions that apply throughout our social experience. These questions take us beyond feelings to that which lies in the human spirit for all of us. The just spirit invites us, indeed insists, that we respond to these questions.

What Justice is About: the Questions

- How are we best to live together on this planet?
- Is this not why we are here, to discover this, to make the bold experiment, to try this and that until something works for all of us... and for our planet too?

These are the special questions which the spiritual archetype of justice calls to those of us in whom it is enfleshed. The just spirit invites us to move beyond the boundaries of our feelings, articulated in moral codes, to some new place. It teaches us that only through the empathic mode of deep listening can we feel and understand the justice issues on the other side of the conflict. It reminds us that of all the expansive and invigorating qualities of the human psyche, the most creative is the human imagination. Hence, deep imaging what justice would look and be like in the specific situation is its most proactive competence and offer.

The Ghost in the Machine

What kind of questions are these? They are not static questions. Thus, they do not invite worship. Perhaps most of us are satisfied with living with our complaints, believing we can do nothing about them. But if you have explored your own gifts and talents, if you have become adept at listening to the voice of your spirit, if you are one who acknowledges your call, then complaints no longer suffice.

Whatever your spiritual archetype, are you coming to understand at the deepest levels of your consciousness that we humans create our realities? Our system of life is not static and never has been. Change, slow or rapid, is our identity, no matter how strongly we struggle to halt that passage. From the lifetime changes built into our own bodies to the rapid changes of modern technology to those characteristics of our planet, geological in nature, which can take hundreds of millions of years, change is perpetual and inevitable.

We are not passive recipients of our bodies, our technologies, or of the planet's total ecology. We act. We judge. Even so-called "objective observation," in which we seek to be uninvolved, influences that which is observed, a reality that lies at the heart of modern science's quantum theory. We humans are not neutral in anything we are and do. We produce effects, consequences, results, and outcomes, some intended, some unintended with which we now have to deal. All of this life experience, captured in the concrete events of our lives, feeds back into our very selves and into our world, so creating new grounds from which we launch ourselves into new acts, new judgments, new experiences.

Enter our human spirit, the ghost in the machine, that which shifts us from mechanism to choice, from neurobiology to consciousness about our neurobiology, from reaction to responsibility, from past determinants to future options.

About what? How we are to live together on this planet.

Thus, the acts of governance.

JUSTICE AS BALANCE

The Two Sides of Governance

How are we to govern ourselves? This questions splits in two because if you cannot govern yourself, how are you to participate justly in the governance of others?

On the inner side, I ask: How far along are you in opening up the space for your spirit to speak out, to create a new harmony among your spirit, your inner biography, and your social biography? If they are all out of a kilter, then this question focuses on your own self-governance, on your inner governance. The tools to use are the enspiriting disciplines of deep listening, deep questioning, deep learning, deep imaging, intentioning, discerning, and inner dialogue.

The other focus is on outer governance in which we are all participants in principle though rarely enough in practice. The one who is the just spirit invites, cajoles, supports, and admonishes us all. Join in, the just spirit says. It is your world. Learn how to govern yourselves. If you do not, someone else will do it for you.

When I speak of outer governance, do I mean government? Not at all. Governments are a response to the question of governance: How are we to govern ourselves? Governments are institutions which we invent, and which we can render obsolete. Just governments derive their legitimacy from the consent of the governed. And that consent can be withdrawn! Just government, not simply any kind of government, is forever to be sought.

Tom Paine knew this, as did John Stuart Mill, Mahatma Gandhi, the authors of the Federalist Papers, Goethe, Martin Luther King, Isaiah and Jesus and Moses, Erasmus, the Buddha and Lao Tzu,

Sun Yat-Sen, and many others. I think this is God's question to us, living on a small planet toward the outer edge of one of our galaxy's spirals. How are we best to live together? Animals know their answer by virtue of their instincts and their place in the ecology of the planet. We humans don't have an answer yet because our place in the planet's ecology is ambiguous at best. We have to learn it.

Now return to the many examples given earlier in this chapter (*Who is Just? Who is Not?*). They engage our feelings. But underneath each example, each incident, each episode, and each behavior lies the question of governance. That is the call from the just spirit to the rest of us: from complaints to vision; from reactive behavior to intentioning action; from a worshiped, celebrated, locked-in past to an open future; from feelings of injustice to the issue of our sociability... how are we best to live together?

Like the mending spirit, the just spirit understands that the human spirit is sociable. Spirit is more than private, though your piece of it lies uniquely in you. But you do not own your spirit, as a piece of property to be disposed however you like. It is more than inner; it is also outer. It is called to interact with the spirit of others, not only about the special matters and calls that each archetype evokes, but also about the universal matter of how we can best live together on this planet.

Disharmony Within

Everybody knows about his or her balancing act. It's called keeping all the balls in the air. You attempt to respond to a myriad of pressures: the social pressures that demand conforming behaviors; being on time, often, someone else's time; maintaining or achieving a life style that is beyond your income or inclination, if you had your druthers; competing with your colleagues for your next promotion; trying to put food on the table for the kids and pay for their health insurance at a working wage that keeps you in poverty. These kinds of outer pressures often hide conflicts that tear at your inner balance and throw everything out of kilter.

In my enspiriting work, I have listened to many people who are dissatisfied with their lives, who at the core of their consciousness of themselves are unhappy, unfulfilled, frustrated. Yet most of them are well off. They have a high standard of living, as the world understands that. They have a good quality of life, if we accept the indicators of cars, indoor plumbing, meat on the table, vacations, and home computers. But for many, the inner quality of life is absent.

As we have talked, shared, and deep listened, some of these persons have begun to weep. They have thought they had lost, or could not find, their souls. The outward accouterments of the modern society, of the civilization of false plenty, vanished, for the inner search and confrontation had begun. Old stories of their spirit's speaking to them, stories forgotten, withheld, or denied, came back. Pain was there as the spirit was listened to, often for the first time in years.

I think that paralleling the engine of society, which runs erratically so often these days for so many, our internal combustion also sputters, coughs, sometimes grinds to a halt or picks up in a surge of emotional speed that splurges with adrenalin and leaves us breathless as we drop off the other side... empty.

Disharmony Without

Too many of us are as a spinning top that has lost its spin and topples over. We slip and slide on city sidewalks, afraid our feet will go one way and our bodies another. One woman told me, during a training session for facilitators, that she had come to her work in her city's school system, satisfied with her good job performance and thoroughly positive evaluations, to have her supervisor walk over to her desk and tell her, "You have one hour to clean out your desk. You're being downsized." In the last couple of decades, that kind of experience has become increasingly prevalent.

In every society that I know, human prejudice colors all social behavior and permeates all institutions. I can conceive of no relationships more unharmonious than those based on prejudice, whatever their criteria: ethnicity, skin color, language, levels of educational attainment, social class, region or locality of birth, gender, age, etc.

Too often governments, as distinguished from governance, use their legitimated force of laws, police, courts, weapons, and control of the media to maintain that disharmony and to accept, sometimes promote, the prejudices particular to the society they inhabit. Often the other side, the marginalized group, seeks redress, their version of justice. Both sides engage in violence that is physical, social, and psychological. The victims of prejudice meet the terrorism of the state with their own terrorism.

The wars and conflicts of the Protestant Reformation pitted Catholics against Protestants. And while the former burned the latter at the stake, when they could, the latter tore out the tongues of the Anabaptists. The Hindus and the Moslems tore at each other and killed each other's children when India was partitioned. Pol-Pot sought to rid Cambodia of the millions of recalcitrants in his killing fields. The German state, so advanced in science, technology, music, poetry, and all of the arts of *hoch kultur*, offered Jews, Gypsies, trade unionists, and the physically disabled a final solution to their presence on the planet by gassing to death millions of them. Scarcely 50 or 60 years ago, the "advanced" American Democracy, the "great experiment for humankind" regularly saw blacks lynched by whites to keep the former in their place. Just recently, in the decade of the 1990's, Eastern Orthodox Serbs "cleansed" their territory of Moslems with just a bit more elan than Catholic Croats cleansed their territory of Serbs.

And so it goes. What else is new in human history? Disharmony to one sounds a beautiful chord to another. Injustice for one is justice for another. What is this "balancing" nonsense, this harmony we seek? What is fairness as all-inclusive ethic and practice? Who can do anything about it? Where do we begin?

Ask the mending spirit. She has begun. Now ask the just spirit. She enters where mending leaves off.

Ask yourself.

JUSTICE AS GOVERNANCE

Knowing Spirit's Presence

The interaction of the inner and the outer proclaims the presence of the just spirit.

The questions for the group, the outer context, are:

- How are we best to live together on this planet?
- Can we learn to do that?

In all the ways those questions arise, it comes down to a matter of governance. Can we govern ourselves so that the human spirit flourishes? So that what each of us brings to this planet and to our very own lives is encouraged to flourish as it meshes with our biographies. So that we are not a population wasted by negligence, prejudice, deprivation, and denial.

The questions for the individual, the inner questions are:

- How can I best live with my very own spirit?
- Can I live, will I live, with what it calls me to be and do through the channel of my biography?

These too are questions of governance. How do I best govern myself? Exhibit restraint in the face of gluttony, empathy in the face of anger, and hope in the face of despair? How do I give purpose, direction, and fulfillment to my life within the dynamic interplays of my inner biography, my outer or social biography, and my spirit?

The purpose of the just spirit is the joining of these questions: how are we to govern ourselves on this.planet, both inside and out?

Seeking justice through governance, of self and with others, is not each one for himself, creating the wealth of some nations by ravishing our planet and impoverishing a good portion of its human population. Just governance is a way of balancing disparate parts, interests, proclivities, emotions, and purposes. It allows each to achieve its purpose to whatever extent possible without diminishing that same level of possibility in the other.

I call that "equity of the spirit." Key to its enactment is to discover how each of us and all of us, together, are to discern our purposes. Deep learning is called for, for without that discipline and its practices, our purposes are adrift on a spiritless voyage. They clash. They sink. They consume themselves, as desperate ambition fills the vacuum in our souls. Our spirit cannot give direction to the search for our purposes, for its voice is not heard and its call is abandoned.

The Tension

Imbalance is far more prevalent than balance. When we come to an ungovernable situation, we recognize it by this quality of imbalance.

Imbalance is a destructive tension. Balance is a creative tension. The tension may be within, between competing emotions of love and hate, anger and fear, pride and shame. The tension may lie within your total being, as you seek to balance the inspirations of your inner biography with the claims of your social biography.

The outer tensions are as variegated as the inner. The tensions are like these: a Japanese thirst for cheaper wood to build houses and a sustaining policy against clear-cutting mountainsides in Washington or Oregon; the aboriginal peoples of East New Guinea, seeking to maintain ancestral tradition and life style, and the modernization of all Euro-Asian cultures, a modernization which rests so much on the exploitation of natural resources; a powerful impulse to meet the emotional cravings of sexual need and variety, and loyalty to and love for your mate and family.

The just spirit seeks to redress these imbalances throughout the world and throughout the persons in the world. You can see that the human settings and situations to which her call might apply are infinite.

The Balancing Act

The prime balancing act of the just spirit is exactly between the inner and the outer. Right now, among all of the calls to competence and action which the spiritual archetypes invite, I think we do this balancing act least well: being fair to ourselves and being fair to others; responding creatively to the inner demands and participating creatively in the social experience. The just spirit, the one called to this, leads the way.

It is your readiness to act at the interface of these two polarities that alerts you to the presence of the just spirit's call to you. It is your recognition of this dynamic conflict in other persons that compels you to address its antecedents and consequences as matters of justice and governance. In the United States, for example, decades of exploitation of First Nations peoples (Native Americans) by the government (through the Bureau of Indian Affairs) must be redressed if a balance is to be restored. With all of its deficits and problems, the policy of affirmative action in the USA sought to redress an imbalance that had built the affluence of some of its citizens at the expense of others. Among the world's peoples, caught in the inordinate disparity between affluence and impoverishment, balance must be invented.

We don't know how to do that very effectively. Okay. Let the just spirit speak out. That is the clue that your spirit is calling you to act justly. As the embodiment of the just spirit, you listen, question, image alternatives, and invite the deep learning whose focus is both the inner and the outer.

Of course, we all try a bit of the balancing act just to live in this world. Does the just spirit do it a bit more, a bit better? Is this a matter of the old "continuum" again?

The just spirit has learned to climb the spiral from imbalance to balance, from inner to outer, from falling apart to governance, recognizing that this spiral has no termination. The just spirit climbs the spiral's next leg, on which what was outer has become inner, onto the next level of aggregation. She understands that justice is not a noun, a thing, a bounded concept. It is a verb, an action, a quest, forever grounded in the feeling by which we know injustice. The just spirit cannot get off that spiral. It never lets go. She holds to her witness among us by asking herself these questions in public:

- What justice do I seek, and for whom?
- What are my gifts and talents? What does my spirit invite me to be and to do?
- How do I further my inner claims and possibilities without denying that same surge of spirit-energy in you?

These are the self-balancing questions that lead up the spiral. And the just spirit will not let you leap off your spiral. Along with the mending spirit (binding up, joining) and the sustaining spirit (creating the new partnering), the just spirit seeks to help humankind invent the ways to walk firmly on the spiral, by seeking a new balance, new ways to govern ourselves.

The Self-discerning Questions

How might you discern if this archetype constitutes the call of your own spirit? The following four sets of questions to yourself and to your life experience seat you on this spiral, until you want to get off. I hope you will give yourself the space, both inside and out, for the reflection they invite. As you take a look at your life once again and listen to discern if your spirit has cried out to you about justice and governance, nothing much may occur. This particular section of reflection and recording may stay empty. If so, move on to the organizational spirit in Chapter Eight. But the pages in your journal may overflow with instances and evidences of your spirit's call.

The First Set of Discerning Questions

Here, your focus is on the outrage that comes with empathic feelings.

- In situations of denial, deprivation, prejudice, put-down, inequity, favoritism, situations that may be personal, relational, organizational, or cultural, is their ox being gored your ox too?
- Do you stand in their place, live their lives, feel their feelings?
- Is their outrage, their plea, their dismay, their despair... yours too?

In the hard-winning, free-for-all competition that signifies so much of the present world culture, a put-down phrase often used to condemn those who feel the outrage and deprivation of others is "bleeding-heart." The one called to be just by her spirit's archetype celebrates that description. When you bleed, so do I, says the just spirit without shame of embarrassment.

It does not stop there, the search for balance. But it certainly can start there.

The Second Set of Discerning Questions

- Do you have an innate sense of balance, of proportion, so that when you observe an imbalance, you feel compelled to right it, to harmonize it, to the exclusion of neither side, be it among persons, groups, even at the level of nations?
- Can you describe what that "sense" is? How and when it emerged in you? At an early age, or more recently? About what, about whom?

The Third Set of Discerning Questions

- What have you done so as to right this imbalance?
- How have you encouraged others to engage in creative acts of governance that address instances of misgovernance?

Finding specific events and actions in response to these questions is a clue to the just spirit working in you. It may reveal a curriculum for justice that, by your witness and participation, becomes a self-teacher and a teacher of others.

The Fourth Set of Discerning Questions

As you have moved from your inner life to your outer action, how has your commitment to the just calling responded in the face of ridicule, opposition, even threats?

The one called to be just acts her sense of justice. She cannot help herself. The call is too strong.

Do you begin to see the spiral of justice at work in these sets of questions? The questions are framed to help you search for the indicators and clues that you have responded to this inner call. But because your feelings have aroused a response to a vast multiplicity and diversity of injustice's occurrences, search out the uniqueness in your own life. There is no magic formula here.

If you are called by this spiritual archetype's presence in you, you will know it!

8

The Organizational Spirit

ARE WE NOT ALL ORGANIZATIONS?

Ubiquity

We are all organizations. We humans would not know what to be or do without organizations. We ourselves are organized, each one of us, a complex system of parts, working together to achieve its purpose, being human. From molecules building into systems of chemical and physical interaction from which the human organism emerges in all of its glory... we are organized. We have 20 to 30 billion cells in the brain alone, with trillions of transactions among them. And then the marvelous organizations called fingers and toes with their own motion and movement. Feedback and interaction, form and purpose: all of this organized within the singular human organism.

There is organization without as well. We have organized ourselves into a myriad of organizations to achieve a myriad of purposes. Sometimes we do so mindfully. But too often we enter into collective entities mindlessly, without the sanction of what our human spirit calls us to when we organize. So we participate in all sorts of organizations at the behest of some appeal, an inner appeal from neglected hurt or abuse, an outer appeal from a leader or idea which takes us beyond ourselves to something larger than individual life.

The Organization of Social Reality

Mostly, we live our lives in organizations that, in some mysterious way, recapitulate form and processes within the individual body. For most of human life on this planet, organization stands for social reality. Organization is the way we have invented to collect ourselves into intricate formations of complex human energy to achieve purpose: yours, mine, the world's.

I don't mean only the mammoth organizations like business corporations, governments, universities, multi-nationals, churches, trade unions, school systems, and hospitals. The organizational metaphor stands for regulated, patterned formations of human interactions, both large and small. A family is an organization in which the family behavior of its members is regulated and patterned by expectations and roles. When expectations change and traditional roles break down in the family, you know what happens: dysfunction, abuse, violence, pain and sorrow, and millions looking for something to replace that vital organization of human conduct. Sometimes we look inside. Sometimes we look outside. For too many of us, we have not yet found a replacement.

As the human population multiplies and open space for human variety disappears, more and more we take the meaning of our lives from the symbols, images, and appeals of the organizations to which we belong. These are all sorts of organizations: the university or school system, the profession, the ethnic group, the regional group. Sometimes the binding appeal comes from the church, the sect, the denomination, or the cult, or from the business corporation, shop, or workplace. For some persons, the symbols and images of the KKK or other hate groups appeal. Most of us maintain a deep-seated loyalty to our nations and to the national government. Like-minded persons satisfy some of their organizational need in cultural or affinity groups. These millions of organizations on earth are all different in some ways, and all the same in others.

To be sure, some of us are loners: artists, hermits, recluses, "independent cusses," what-have-you. Maybe thank God for them. They are a smallish minority in any society. Perhaps they are all enspiritors, those who listen to the voice of their spirit.

Can the human spirit enter here?

In the envisioning work of the past 30 years, I have worked with persons who seek to bring spirit into the organizational milieu. They intend to weave human spirit into the very fabric of the organization so that it speaks in the ways we interact with each other, mindfully. This call is not just to oil the squeaky wheel, which is what many consultants in organizational development seek to do. Their call is to transform the very nature of our organizational interaction so that, first and foremost, the human spirit will out!

Why do that?

The spiritual archetype I have named the organizational spirit calls to us to invent a new kind of interaction within the organization so that the human spirit of its participants will flourish. I believe these "organizational innovators" were called by their spirit. Not to make the organization become more effective, but to create the organizational space within which the human spirit of its members might be emancipated.

Are you one too?

The Call

Make no mistake on this. The call is not to organize the human spirit. Just the opposite. The call is to create the space within our collective conduct to promote the flourishing of our human spirit in that which we do together because, to paraphrase Abraham Lincoln, we can't do it as well by ourselves. It is to express the human spirit in such a way that it contributes to the organizational purpose in a creative mode, with zest, with love for the others' contribution, with high excitement for a purpose mutually derived. The organizational clime becomes personal. We are no longer integers, role-players, suppressed spirits.

But the impersonal organization is everywhere, one to which we may "belong" but which does not belong to us. Indeed, who does? The CEO, the top managers? Scarcely. If they did, they would not need their golden parachutes. The shareholders? They are all at the mercy of worldwide economic systems which no one controls, which let ten percent of the world's population consume 90 % of the world's "wealth." The workers, the laborers, the technicians? Be they 3000 feet down digging for diamonds in South African mines or 1000 feet up, in the high rise, sitting at a computer or a telephone, they do not own the organization either.

An Uphill Struggle

Persons who respond to the call of this spiritual archetype face an uphill struggle. The ubiquity of the organizational reality in our world today is matched by the absence of the human spirit in it. Some persons with whom I have done an enspirited envisioning of the future of their organization, after that deep experience, leave it. Their organization was not conducive to that which was reborn in them when they invented a space for their spirit to make a difference.

Efficiency, a byword of the organizational culture, may have to go out the window. Letting spirit out into the open is a messy business, particularly at the start, until we learn its disciplines and practices.

Take deep listening, for example. It is a way of sharing where the one is silence while the other speaks. She maintains her silence, becomes empty, so that the other eventually hears herself.

Lots of practice is needed, at least for those of us for whom deep listening begins a strange affair with our spirit. The space for it has to be created. Meanwhile, the computers are clicking away, the production machines are whining, the vote is about to be taken in the board room, the assembly line is moving inexorably to its destination, the phone banks are buzzing, and the HMO-controlled doctor has 15 minutes for you, if you are lucky!

Finally, frontiers: are there any left?

So many Americans move about, from job to job, marriage to marriage, city to city, seeking something that stays unfulfilled. In the old days, we could move to the frontiers to find some empty space for the expression of that which is unique to each of us. Of course, there were outer reasons too. We were poor. We were slaves, indentured servants, unemployed or terribly paid, and jammed into places that afforded no flowering of the human person. We had our private reasons too: relationships gone sour; seeking the gold or the good bottom land; all kinds of unhappiness with the present and hopes for the future. In the modern era, three frontiers remain open to us: the exploration of outer space, the exploration of inner space, and the exploration of the space between. The exploration of outer space speaks so powerfully to the human spirit just because we don't know what will happen out there, so we must make our own impact, create our own space cultures along with the new technologies and science. It is a great adventure.

The exploration of inner space is an equally great adventure. Might we not also open that up for our spirit to speak out, just because we don't know what will happen in us and among us, as we invite our human spirit to make its impact? Can we become intranauts as well as astronauts?

More than anything else, the organizational spirit wants to configure the space between. That is her special way of understanding the nature of human organization... as the space between. She intends to shape that space between and among us so that through our collective action, we learn how to liberate the human spirit in each of us and in all of us. That invites a very special kind of space that celebrates the creativity of the human spirit within us, and particularly in the organizational setting. That is the agenda of her call. In the social realities of the organization, the organizational spirit seeks to explode the organizational boundaries while at the same time imploding its structures so that the human spirit can breathe.

NEW WINE IN NEW WINESKINS

Show me!

Much of the work of those who respond forcibly to the organizational spirit focuses on creating new purposes. They seek not to tweak the system, but to transform it. How? By coming to new purposes derived from the call of their spirit. Keep in mind that organizational life was created to support human purposes. Often, these purposes reside at a much deeper level of cultural consciousness than the organization's ostensible goals and missions. Much talk and writing by organizational gurus about "organizational culture" miss the point, which is about unexamined purposes, human purposes. The activity of strategic planning has translated purposes into goals and missions. But they are not the same thing, which Aristotle knew and we have forgotten. Goals and missions are instrumental. That means that they carry their own meanings, their own imperatives, their own actions as strategies in search of some larger purpose: our spirit's call. This purpose is worthy of us in the fullness of our humanity; we are worthy in the fullness of our virtue: our competencies, our strengths, our gifts and our talents.

Sometimes, the organizational spirit starts with: Show me. Why? Who said so? Where does that come from? What is that all about?

Organizational loyalists might say: "Come on. Let's get on with it. Enough of questions. There's work to be done, profits to be made, services to be provided, goods to be produced, and information to be disseminated. A little reform here, a little shift of emphasis there, okay, just so long as you don't upset things too much."

The person who embodies the organizational spirit simply will not accept the habits and practices of the organization. She will not be stopped by the walls of hierarchy, officialdom, habit, protocol, threats of dismissal, or the way-things-are. She will seek to get beneath and beyond them to purposes that are of the human spirit. What are they? That is what this book is about. They are purposes that I call invitations from your spirit, to get about the business of being fully human, not to deny your spirit but to listen to it.

The probe, the deep question, the unease, and the sense of imbalance characterize the awakening call of the spiritual archetypes to the human psyche. With the organizational spirit, that awakening tension focuses on breaching the fortress walls, breaking them down so that new space can be created for something collective to happen, so we may be together in ways that fit our promise and our potential. It is the space between and among, a space that is now occupied by the spiritless organization.

What are our promise and our potential?

Part of my search has involved listening deeply, getting underneath the questions and images of fellow envisioners. I learned about the archetype of the organizational spirit from them.

Education and the schools, the modern corporation, the military apparatus, and the church: they encompass so much of contemporary society's institutional life, and so little of the possibilities to which our human spirit calls us.

Might you, have you come to the same kinds of questions? Now is a chance for you to explore your own fit within organizational life. If it is the case that organizational life does not emancipate the human spirit, what else could it mean but that the modern organization follows purposes that are counter-enspiriting? Yes. Deliberately so.

Is it possible that emancipating the human spirit, giving it the space for its action within us as biographical people is the most dangerous thing that could happen? Yes... but dangerous to whom and for whom?

All of the great literature, the great myths, legends, and stories of the heros and heroines are about this danger: actors in history answering the call of their spirit.

In the modern world, that call is often about dismantling the social fabric and habits of organizational life and replacing it with something else. What?

In the 30 years of listening to envisioners come to their compelling images of the future—that which they **cannot not be** and **cannot not do**—I have been exalted at the number who sought out a vision that literally takes us beyond the conventional boundaries of organizational life, in the very domains I have iterated above.

Let's take a look at their vision, as a lesson to us all about the alternatives posed to ancient organizational purposes, cultures, and meanings. As you read on, perhaps you will find yourself an eager member of the coming transformation; perhaps a leader, perhaps one who is now ready to respond vigorously to the call of her spirit to recapture organization for fully human purposes.

BEYOND SCHOOLS AND COLLEGES

Learning in a Circle

I found and listened to a basic challenge, a basic vision, a basic transformative quest offered by hundreds of envisioners caught in the labyrinth of their countries' education systems. From successful teachers, from successful administrators, and from students (young and not-so-young) wanting and choosing to call themselves learners, emerges a central, unifying vision.

Of course, that gives it away. For their emphasis was invariably on learning, not schooling, not reform, not certifications, but on learning that which human beings do by virtue of their being human. For some envisioners who followed their vision to its source in their spirit, it became deep learning, which I later discovered is the pivotal discipline of enspiriting.

What were their purposeful questions?

What should we human beings be learning? How best should we learn it? In what configurations of sharing, of questing, of supporting each other as learners can we most effectively learn? When, why, and how might teachers become learners and learners become teachers? Are they the same activity, or is this a question about role-reversal? Might these historic roles of student and teacher be subsumed by a more generous activity of reciprocal learning in which each helps the other to learn what is truly important to them?

Are you surprised that so many youngsters rebel as their imagination is throttled, thwarted, and given no space to play? It is amazing how effectively the organization can suppress the grand acts of the imagination that join the human spirit to the "real" world. In education, I'm not talking only about the dropouts who are the focus of so much establishment concern. The dropouts walk to another ground, a ground that is exactly where their spirit should be engaged and invited by those enspiritors who have the courage and the competence to do so.

What of the majority, the "drop-ins" and "stay-ins?" The organizational culture of schooling has become fine-tuned enough to capture their spirits and bludgeon their souls.

When I began this part of the envisioning work in 1970, I learned that the physical configuration of this ubiquitous human learning, its collective configuration, is the circle. Margaret Mead would have loved this, for it was from her that I learned a futures mission of the human spirit, which is to reconfigure the future. The images always included people, young and old, sitting together in circles in open buildings with no walls, on forest floors, sand, grass, even circles on concrete floors. No beginning and no end. No top and no bottom. I came to call this the medicine wheel circle of learning.[17]

What is the point? Among these Western, modern envisioners feeling the call of their spirit, the organizational rules and formulae for the circle are still in infancy. But their response to the call within was to say, in effect: Our learning comes first. That is our human purpose. What will the educational organization be like that follows that purpose?

BEYOND PEACE KEEPING TO PEACE MAKING

Imaging a World Without Weapons

In 1980, the great enspiritor Elise Boulding and I inaugurated a program we named *Imaging a World Without Weapons*. Lots of participants were members of peace churches and peace groups with an historic affinity to nonviolence, but not all. Some were ordinary citizens without that affiliation, attracted to envisioning alternatives to nuclear war because a fear of a nuclear holocaust still loomed large as a consequence of the American-Soviet confrontation.

Given the history of humankind, violence, wars, terror rampant throughout, how can anyone say that the human spirit is involved, calling us, in many different ways, to envision and enact alternatives?

In a marvelous essay written by Elise in 1990 during the Gulf War, [18] she had this to say:

"Why should the past help us to face the future? I have come to realize that there was a reason why I was ready to work with Warren Ziegler in adapting his futures-invention workshops to a format of imaging a world without weapons at the time we did it in 1980. It was because, as a peace activist in the 1960s, my travels had enabled me to go through an intense experience of reliving the Hiroshima bombing, in Hiroshima itself; and of reliving the holocaust, in Auschwitz. I had come to feel that there were no depths to which the human spirit could not sink and I knew despair. At the same time I came to know wonderful people in Japan and Poland who were envisioning, working for, building a new world on the ashes of the old. The human spirit seemed to be unstoppable. My despair had to take second place to my discovery of the human spirit that could survive despair and rebuild the world."

Among the many who participated in these workshops were some who asked: Can we turn around our military apparatus to make peace rather than war? (For if there is no peace, there is nothing to keep. It has to be made first.)

This is an old question. Translated into a contemporary relevance, it means: Might soldiers, generals, technicians, the highly-trained military personnel who give most of their time and energy to training now invent and learn the arts and crafts of peacemaking—i.e., mending, deep listening—thus using their primary organizational strategy and culture to formulate and achieve a new purpose?

That vision, peace making, will have to come from the organizational spirits within that apparatus, not from their so-called civilian masters who have been universally unable to challenge, redirect, or "govern" these enormous and elaborate self-serving organizational systems of "defense," be they located in totalitarian or democratic societies. In his farewell address, Dwight Eisenhower, who had been a great organizational leader and commander in the Second World War reminded us of the omnipresent strength of that encapsulated system he called the "military-industrial" complex. The same goes with the "education" complex.

New purposes, new understandings, new ways of being and doing will come only from within, from those who understand their organizational life so thoroughly that they know how to get beyond it, to transform it, to come to new purpose like freeing up human learning and making peace. They may come from the same source.

Do you see and hear the call, the invitation from the organizational spirit that focuses its aspiration on the military organization? The modern military apparatus is steeped in training. Civilians may not know this. The modern military organization, certainly in the United States, most probably in other nations, is the best training organization in the world: standards, criteria, learning styles and instructional strategies, evaluation mechanisms, curriculum development, and relevance to continuously-emerging technologies. It is skill-based and hands-on experience-grounded. Military training makes our schools and colleges look like neophytes in the business of honing skills to match instrumental purposes.

Of all the imponderables and impossibilities in the world that we humans have created, a senior one is peacemaking. Learning why and how to do that is, I believe, the central, not-yet-uncovered purpose of the modern military apparatus. It is the deepest, the largest, the best part of its own hologram, lying untouched through most of the ages. Its relevant organizational spirits have not allowed the alternative images and realities of itself into the explicate order, the "real" world.

The courageous work of organizations like Peace Brigades International and Doctors Without Borders, which get into the nitty-gritty of human conflict and desperate need, show us what is possible.

I suspect, as did some of these envisioners, that the disciplines of enspiriting will be very helpful to set sturdy foundations on which to build the new practices, new concepts, and new organizational culture that free up the human spirit of its members and its "clients."

Wild? Wooly? Far out?

The Air Force Academy

In the early 1980s, I was invited for a one-hour session on a Sunday morning to introduce *Imaging a World Without Weapons* at the Air Force Academy chapel in Colorado Springs immediately following Sunday morning services. The chapel, a circular amphitheater, was resplendent with cadets in their dress blues, and the training and support officers and NCOs, many with their families.

With few preliminaries, but with lots of trepidation in my heart, I invited the assembly of well over a hundred to imagine what it would be like in a world without weapons... and what they, the "troops," would then do.

There was silence and disbelieving. One or two clarifying questions were asked. In this huge amphitheater, folks sat side-by-side and looked at each other across the empty space. What is this fellow up to?

I repeated the invitation. I offered a few supporting words about how to do deep imaging. Then I stopped. Well, they were "trainable." Whatever else you might say about military academies, learning is at the heart of their culture.

They took ten minutes for their private, individual imaging, focusing on what it would be like in a world without weapons. They accepted the invitation; at least some did. Did they do the imaging because they knew how to take "marching orders"? Perhaps, for their operational culture imbued them with hierarchy, authority, and discipline. Perhaps, because the proceedings took place in a house of worship. But also, perhaps, because my invitation was also theirs, a self-invitation from their spirit, encouraged by mine. For some, at least.

Then I invited them, sitting side-by-side, to begin listening to each other without judgment. Clarifying questions were certainly permitted, but neither argument nor criticism. Mainly, I invited them to listen in silence, and then to advance the imaging with their partner. Deep listening.

So they began. Low humming filled the huge room. I gave them time to create their own space for this work; for those that could; for those that would. Then we shifted gears, reassembling, as it were, into the circle of reflection. I spoke up.

"What is it like to image a world without weapons?"

I invited them to share their ideas, their concerns, their images to the whole group. There was silence again. Folks shifted on the benches. I just waited, then offered the invitation again.

"We'll have to feed them."

This, loud for all to hear across the empty space, came from a grizzled sergeant, his dress uniform beribboned in multicolored reminders of his long service to his country.

"Say more?" I invited after another moment's silence.

"The starving people all over the world. Who will feed them? We'll have to." He paused for a minute. "And we can do that."

"Yes," spoke out a cadet from across the room. "But what about the borders? How do we protect our borders? With no weapons."

There was silence again, as the collective attention of the group, now focused, chewed on this imponderable impossibility.

"Perhaps no borders," spoke up a third.

"Maybe we can learn to do away with borders." This from a cadet who, a decade later, may well have flown a Stealth bomber to keep Kuwait's borders, or oil, sacrosanct.

"Then what will we do?" asked a fifth.

"Fly kites!" came a response. There was relieving laughter. This was getting too serious.

"We'll learn to man the borders in a different way."

This exchange continued for a little while longer. Then the energy dissipated. This was too much for most of them within that ambience; too heavy, too impossible, too frightening. I was unable to create enough space for spirit in that setting.

So we ended with my offering to those who had made their offering in their public, with and in front of their relevant others, that perhaps this kind of envisioning is just what the military, and all of us, from the then President on up to the citizens of the country might try to learn and to do.

It just takes one to say: Show me. It just takes a few, and there are always a few, to offer alternatives within an organizational context, history, and culture. "Why are we doing what we are doing?" asks the person who is called, pushed, enticed, invited by his spiritual archetype.

CIRCLES WITHIN CIRCLES

The Circle Again... Sitting

Picture ten middle mangers and supervisors, women and men, employees of a very large transnational corporation, sitting on the floor in the middle of a very large room. They are in a circle, looking at each other, gesturing in pantomime while the rest of us, 50 other managers drawn from a wide geographic area the corporation serve, watch as the scene unfolds. Shortly, it becomes clear that this is about some substantive work problem whose dynamic engages their attention and know-how but whose solution is beyond their grasp.

But what of their reach? During the next few minutes, they make clear their frustration. They turn to those of us sitting outside their circle, and gesture toward us with inviting and welcoming arm movements, to show us that they want our energy and know-how gathered into their circle too. But we just sit there. After another few moments, one after another, the "insiders" stand from their sitting or crouching positions, walk the fifteen safe feet between their circle and ours, take us, one-by-one, by the hand, pull us to our feet, and lead us into the inside circle. Within a few minutes, we are all gathered, again sitting on the floor in a close circle now made larger, regarding each other in different ways. Some look quizzically, some suspiciously, some distantly so as not to be drawn in too deeply. But the inner circle folks, living out the scenario, smile at us continuously, warmly, invitingly, making us feel welcome by their beckoning hands, until we cannot help ourselves, and our bodies respond as our intellects, our feelings, our presence within this gathering begin to speak out what our spirit knows even though much of the rest of our selves are still groping.

Standing up, a technical supervisor responsible for at least 50 of the corporation's employees says: "You have read our scenario. You know that we, this team, call ourselves the 'problem-solvers.' But do you now understand?" This is not playacting. He gestures to include all of us. "In fact you come from our 14-state region, from many different divisions, departments, and responsibilities, divided into hierarchies, enclaves, and specializations so demarcated with the boundaries of little subcultures that we have forgotten how to communicate with each other across these boundaries. We have forgotten how to solve problems together." He pauses. "Now you have been invited into our problem-solving circle. Problem-solving has become our way of life. Our compensation, our system of sanctions and rewards is based on that, and nothing else. We have so automated our systems that what is left are problems. No hierarchy. No bosses. No intra-corporate competition. No winning or losing. Problem-solving."

He smiles, this young middle manager, and then looks directly at the one vice-president in the entire group, a 50-year-old vice-president at the fourth rung, still three more to go to get to the top of the ladder, which he never will because he's far too creative… and anyway, there's only room at the top for one.

"This is the shape of the future. What does it feel like?"

RE-COVENANTING IN THE DIALOGUE CIRCLE

Returning to the (Your) Source

500+ members of a national church with 20 million adherents gather to rediscover their covenant with each other and with their God at the local level through an envisioning dialogue in which they share their pain and what troubles their spirit. They then commence their re-covenanting through a dialogue about joy, love, peace, sustainability, and justice.

This re-covenanting is repeated, in larger and smaller groups, for several years as the congregationally-focused project continues openly to infiltrate the national church. The national church, with pretty much an all-white membership, does not quite realize what is happening at first. Its bishops, it theological consultants, its outstanding preachers and some of its national staff get on board, seeking to sway this powerful resurgence of human spirit to the service of organizational purposes and personal advancement.

The re-covenanting members, now some thousands made up of local congregation lay leaders and pastors, one bishop, and many of the marginalized, are in the process of disembodying the regions, the synods, the horizontal and vertical demarcations of churchly authority, power, money, legitimations. They ask a deep question about who has been welcomed into the church and who has not, like native Americans, Latinos, blacks, homosexuals, the physically disabled, those marginalized in the national society of which this national church is representative.

Are they not grist for Christ's mill? Were you an Old Testament Jew like me, called to justice, you would think so. But Jesus has become organized, starting around 150 A.D. First, he's killed. Then his great spirit is organized. So the churches, not His, but ours, reign supreme.

Nevertheless, invited, stimulated, provoked by the organizational spirits among them, these folks embody their deep learning, once more, after nearly two thousand years, of how and why to cleave together, a covenanting beyond all the reasons human beings have stipulated to keep apart.

This is an intellectual group of church members and their pastors. So the deep listening, deep questioning, and deep imaging of the future of their religious ministry and community about peace, justice, and sustainability evoke fresh, sometimes strange, sometimes unfamiliar states of being present to each other. Feelings get involved, first along with intellect, then prior to it. After all, the human spirit speaks through feelings before it speaks through ideas and rationality and sharp retorts. The enspiriting dialogue rests on presence, intimacy, and vulnerability created in the space for spirit, not on intellectual dispute about theology, biblical "truth," righteousness, win-win or win-lose.

In their dialogue circles, the people of these scores of congregations rediscover each other. They believe that they have been taught how to know their God. They have not been taught how to know each other. Now, as they learn to become present to each other in new ways that cut through the organizational boundaries of their church, God's presence becomes palpable. They rediscover their courage, their human spirit, and return to its source. They find themselves because they have invited their own spirit to become present, to intercede, to announce itself in such a way that they can confront the barriers and step over the barricades that are not, and never were, of Christ's making.

The Princes and Principalities

My, how a mammoth church organization steeped in its rituals, its practices, its ideology, and its purposes, can protect itself. Is it reasonable to ask, if the human spirit will not, cannot, come out in the church, the synagogue, the mosque, the temple, where can it?

Why do the princes and principalities so often win? Because they are so skillful in tapping into inner biography through social biography. Because they have learned, over the centuries, to manipulate and celebrate the KBVAF so as to protect and maintain the organizational power structure. Earlier I asked: Can the human spirit enter here? And I reminded us that persons who respond to the call of this spiritual archetype face an uphill struggle.

Simply put, the mountain within this national church was too steep, too high, too sharp an angle of ascent to climb. The movement of the dialogue circle in the local congregation was skillfully shunted aside, its national staff supporters fired or transferred to other more conventional tasks. The regrounding of worship in the recovenanting of the local congregation remains on a siding, off from the main track. Church goers, peeking through their windows as their train speeds by on the fast track of national hegemony, can see the ghosts of these modern-day pilgrims who sought to cleave together in justice, peace, and sustainability.

What is the point of this story? What are its deep questions?

Do you work from within the organization to emancipate the spirit of its members? Or do you step outside that organizational hierarchy to initiate your own transformation, inviting others to join with you? And if you do the latter, how far can you go in that transformation without emulating the very organizational creature whose culture, whose mission, whose behaviors you have denied and sought to go beyond?

WHAT IS BIRTHING?

A Reason for Living

In futures-invention workshops, enspiriting dialogue circles, and enspirited envisioning projects, something is being birthed. It is not a reform. It is not a tinkering, using group dynamics, diversity training, organizational development, or strategic planning. It is transformative, of which we see glimpses here and there. The organizational spirit invites civic discourse about organizational life: its purposes, its strategies, its reasons. Employees, managers, and board members are citizens of their organizations, each contributing her vision, her competence and her spirit as equals in their transformative moment. Our eyes have been opened by those among us who respond to the call of this organizational archetype.

Exactly what is it that is birthing?

This is an extraordinarily exciting question. Clearly, what is birthing is post-organizational. It goes far beyond the attempt of the large-scale organizations like national churches, governments, or business corporations to "bring spirit back in," to "regain our soul." But it has something to do with the human spirit. That much is clear.

The spiritual resurgence of recent decades started on the fringes of mainstream society. But in no time at all, it got caught up with business and profit, with success and strategy, and with the claim of consultants and gurus that the spiritual domain was part and parcel of the Western civilization of false plenty now pervading so much of the world. Is this surprising, considering the persuasive power of a marketing culture which uses the tools of electronic information transfer? Now, as of this writing, all the talk is about e-commerce on the Internet, rather than about how might we create the space for civic discourse and civic action among the citizens of our planet.

And the New Age, the Age of Aquarius has not saved us from ourselves. Eastern rites, Eastern cosmologies, Eastern practices have vied with a resurgence of Christian fundamentalism to replenish the spiritual coffers of millions of folks for whom crass materialism is proving an insufficient reason for living. Our ways of living and working, shaped and controlled by the unyielding cultures of our subgroup and organizations, do not speak to our fully human possibility of an integration with our spirit.

Do you know, have you yet realized in your deepest self, in concert with your own spirit, that we humans want a reason for living, a reason for being? That is why I invite you to search out your own human spirit and listen to its call. For therein lies your reason. Some of you have always known this. Some of you by now have uncovered your reason. Some are still searching.

Barking

Have you ever barked at your boss? Or wanted to? Or just quit because your organization was not organized for barking?

Have you ever quit what you were doing? Ceased what you were being? Grasped for some openness in your life where you could float a bit?

This is the underground story of organizational life, about those who don't fit it, and are either fired or leave of their own accord. The story is mostly hidden, nothing like the publicity and wringing of hands we give to the school dropout problem. They too are quitting the organization.

As for me: when I left the Agency for International Development (A.I.D.) from a relatively senior position, for Syracuse University, no one really wanted to talk about why. They may have thought, Oh, he is just bettering himself. Truth is, I couldn't any longer stand the squelching of human creativity within government, no more than I could stand the bloody killing and self-deceit by American leaders, military and civilian, during those Vietnam years. But it was more than the Vietnam war, which had twisted all the better A.I.D. aims and motivations into supporting that depraved and self-lying "cause."

But then, after six years or so, I left Syracuse University for much the same reason. In neither organization could my own spirit flourish. I could no longer live with the protocols, the practices, the criteria for rewarding and sanctioning, the massaging of the egos of the "biggies," the unwillingness to speak truth about mistakes, deficits, and misguided aims, all in the name of achieving the historic "purposes" of the university. Yet by the norms of effectiveness and success, I did pretty well. My stories of leaving were reserved for immediate family and close friends, and sometimes, not even them.

Truth to tell, I was just beginning to realize, to feel the travail of my spirit. I was just beginning to do my own deep learning. I'm still doing it.

Learning to listen to your spirit is by no means an easy craft. And it is no panacea. Kidding yourself is a well-known trap. Moving from social biography through inner biography to your spirit, and then "back out" again is an exercise in the enspiriting disciplines of intentioning and discerning in which most of us are less than competent practitioners. In enspiriting dialogue, we love and nurture and hold on with fellow enspiritors and prepare for the next try.

Organizational gurus like to talk about organizational transformation, organizational creativity, and organizational learning. But I believe that they, and the rest of us, make a grave mistake here. It is human beings who transform, human beings who create, and human beings who learn. And they do it in response to the call of their spirit.

It is the case that we worship the organizational culture of efficiency and effectiveness, particularly when it comes to producing goods, generating and managing information, moving youngsters through school in the same lockstep that the education system learned from the industrial manufacturing systems of the 19th and 20th centuries: factory production, linear, hierarchical, and standardized.

Who would want to standardize human learning, particularly that which is responsive to one's spirit and to curiosity? Or do some of us want to standardize the product so that it fits into our organizational culture of look-a-likes? And if we weren't look-a-likes, how would we produce, market, consume, and render obsolete anything... to be replaced by the next fad, the next style, the next product, and the next piece of information?

So... to the questions, our self-questions.

These are, perhaps, the most difficult self-questions in the panoply this book offers, for they not only query you, they query the very bones and flesh of our organizational life, imbedded so powerfully into our social biography that the search, even for clues that the organizational spirit is amongst us, perhaps even in you, seems stupid, inadmissible, and so impractical.

Why waste the time and energy?

As always, you can move on to the enlivening spirit, the reflective spirit, or the poetic spirit. These spiritual archetypes have their own exciting, powerful invitations that, at least at the surface, are not about the ways we organize ourselves to the detriment of the human spirit's flowering.

But try out these questions. See if any of them fit. Remember that the query is first for your self and for your own spirit. The journal of your journey is yours, not anyone else's, until you choose to share with your fellow enspiritors.

The Generic Question

This is an overarching question that speaks to the deep images within us. At first, it is a kind of intellectual or reflective question. Unlike those which follow, it is grounded less in feelings, in the body, than in your mind. But you might keep it around, as a sort of guiding light for the other questions. If the organizational archetype calls to you, you might begin the deep imaging which will pull your responses from the source of your own spirit as it lifts the cover of the hologram to give us a glimpse into the implicit order of things.

The question is: What formations of complex human energy achieve purposes that emancipate the human spirit and give it full play in the arenas of transformation, creativity, and learning?

This question might initiate a long dialogue with your spirit and with others. At first, it may seem imponderable, foolish, and irrelevant to the organizational world we humans have invented.

Yet it is exactly out of a deep question like this, a source question, that new worlds are discovered and fashioned. Ask a competent scientist. Discovery comes before proof. Deep questions which assume nothing, or very little, begin the discovery. Do not assert, accept, and proclaim that this question is wrong, and a waste of good human energy because it is directed toward the omnipresent domain of human organization.

I remind you that we of the human species are not herds. We can be individually mindful about our collective conduct. We can make choices. We can query our spirit for guidance in these matters if we choose to.

All of the spiritual archetypes recounted in this book are called by this kind of question in their own domains. Here are several more. Some go to the roots of organizational culture. Some invite increasingly specific, concrete, and experiential responses. I hope they help open up the space for your spirit, so that you can assess your response to the call of the organizational spirit.

Questions About Inventiveness

The second set of questions goes like this:

- Do you recognize that we humans invent our organizations, even their essential forms, meanings, and purposes?
- Do you recognize that the organizational culture and its expression in millions of quite specific and concrete organizations are the product of human invention?

My argument goes like this:

Organizations are not invented by God. They are not invented by sociologists. They are not even created by history (though being locked into history can be a strong barrier to human inventiveness). Organizations are human creations, inventions, as I call them. But why ask these questions? Because of a corollary set of questions that goes to the roots of inventiveness.

- Do you recognize that if we can invent, we can dispose?
- Have you considered that we can render our organizational inventions obsolete and invent new ones?
- Have you ever done that?

Ethnic cleansing, religious extermination, starvation, and the dissolution of independence movements are ways we humans have learned to dispose of, or render obsolete fairly large numbers of human beings. Wouldn't you think that if we can do this to each other, we could render our organizations obsolete when that makes sense? But what sense? And whose sense? We must reinvigorate a civic discourse about our human purposes in their collective or common manifestations, a civic discourse wherein our human spirit is a partner in the deliberation.

We human beings can invent just about any technology we want, perhaps not in a day, but maybe in a year, a decade, a century, a millennium.

Someday we will invent new ways of rendering a bedroom in a home antiseptic, and possess micro-surgery tools and ways of hooking up the body to a central, computerized brain such that we no longer need hospitals. Ambulatory surgery is a recent step in that direction. Hospitals rendered obsolete? Thank God!

And the school? What a mis-transferred repetition and application of an industrial-age factory system. May we not render that hoary institution obsolete? It is less about learning than about custodial care. But don't the kids have to learn together as well as learn to live together? And adults too? Of course. Organizational spirits: Invent a new way that neither denies nor dulls the learner's spirit, which encourages mutual exploration inward into the recesses and sources of our human spirit, as well as outward to explore that organizational space among us, where we can live, work, love, learn, produce, and sustain in ways which do not hurt so often, so much, or so many.

In your journal, will you consider these questions? Have you ever thought of them, in your own language, in your own experience, in your own settings? If you have, no matter how strange are those thoughts, jot down some of your responses. Tell a little story or two, a few lines, just to remind you of how your imagination might create organizational conditions and organizational experiences in response to your spirit's quest.

Once again, it does not matter if these questions move across your path like a light wind that kicks up no dust. Take up some of the other questions below, or move on or move back to another spiritual archetype, even to the chapters on your gifts and talents. Over the past 30 years, some envisioners have been called by their spiritual archetype to enact their call in the organizational context, and have responded to these questions through their deep imaging and their compelling actions. They are powerful enspiritors. Might you be one?

Questions About Unsmothering Spirit

This third set of questions are good "testing out" questions. They go to the heart of the organizational archetype.

- Have you ever seen, heard, felt, lived the smothering of a person's spirit in the name of an organization's purpose? Was it your spirit? Was it someone else's?

- Will you describe what happened?
- Can you retell what you did about it... including nothing?

If these questions do not ring in your heart, dismiss them and move on. This is not a classroom quiz. But if they do, please give yourself space to make an exploration. Be specific and concrete. Tell the story to yourself in your journal, or to other enspiritors. Your own spirit emerges in the details!

This sounds like a justice question, one for the just spirit, but it is different. For the just spirit might recount the smothering of spirit in every conceivable situation and what she did about it. For the organizational spirit, this wine is in a very old wineskin.

And thus to the next set of questions, which might make this distinction clearer.

Questions About Organizational Purposes

The fourth set of questions is:

- What purposes are conducive to the expression, or the actualization of the human spirit?
- Will you now name (deep image, describe) the qualities and characteristics of an organization that places the human spirit's emancipation at the top of its mission statement?

This might be a small list. It may be a non-list. But you might invent or uncover a list longer than you surmise. This question might initiate a breakthrough in the invention of the enspirited organization.

The next set of questions need a little advance notice and another way of summarizing the dilemma that confronts the organizational spirit.

Crisis in the Organizational Culture

The organizational culture is in a state of crisis. It leaves little or no space open to the human spirit, that which calls us to live extraordinary lives and do extraordinary things. But at this time, we find ourselves at a new starting point, striking out on new paths, inventing new ways of working together in such collective enterprises as schools, churches, governments, prisons, and above all, the ubiquitous business organization which has served as a model for all else.

This organizational culture relies on the ordinary. It severely limits the inherent creativity of its members in the name of smoothness, efficiency, and single purpose goals like the bottom line, getting elected, or cornering the market.

A large part of this crisis can be found in the culture of organizational governance, which tends to be hierarchical, putting a few people in charge of other people, hundreds or even thousands, in that pyramid shape which narrows control to a point at the top. For mechanical administration, that sounds reasonable, though as Karl Marx pointed out, the state must wither away and there will emerge an administration of things but not of persons.

But no administration of the human spirit is possible; not by a board of directors, a chief executive officer, a doctor, a school superintendent, an oligarchy, an elite, an archbishop or Imam, a husband, a general, a dictator or a leadership group. There can be no monopoly over the human spirit. How do I know? Ask your spirit!

Are there too many of us? Is that the problem? We have a soaring population that increasingly deprives a portion of us of minimal health and good nutrition standards and perhaps all of us of a sustaining planet, our home! Is the response that we have to organize ourselves just to keep out of each other's way, like green lights and red lights on the streets? Stop. Now go. Now stop. Now go. So much for the Air Force cadet who imaged a time when there would be no borders, or they would be manned differently.

Is there too great a divergence in our gifts and talents? Are some people simply better than others at doing certain things, better at accomplishing different tasks, better at responding to our wants and needs? Certainly, there is an enormously rich diversity in gifts and talents among the human population.

So...

A Final Set of Questions About the Extraordinary

- What would it look like if we organized ourselves to manifest the extraordinary in each of us, the talents we all possess, the gifts which our spirit yearns for us to give away, but for which we have a hard time finding receivers?

    How else can this be put?

- What does a culture of the person **and** the organization look like? One that does not deny our spiritual health? One that cherishes an open and nurturing response to our disparate callings? One that energizes the flowering of the human spirit? One that gives to our spirit the space to manifest itself?

    What a great invitation to you to do some deep imaging in search of your response.

    The organizational crisis is that there is a rising demand for that space for spirit to be created. Our organizational culture and its creatures do not know how to respond. The space is simply not there.

That space is seen as simply chaotic unless parceled, demarcated, bounded, organized. That space is seen as a swamp of people, six billion of us, running around at their wit's end, bumping into each other, getting in each other's way, hurting each other, being unfair if not murderous. Can we live together, two of us or six billion, in ways that subordinate rules, categories, labels and laid-out tasks to human creativity? Can we organize our creativity to still produce the goods and services that are compatible with the expression of the human spirit?

Yet without boundaries, there is no freedom. Freedom is not empty space. It is not homogenous hydrogen atoms filling the infinite universe. Freedom comes from the articulation of our spirit's project, working through our very human circumstances, confronting the limitations of our social biographies, in conjunction, in enspiriting dialogue, in collaboration, in loving discourse founded on presence, vulnerability, intimacy with other human spirit.

Believe me, when that happens, new boundaries—or as I like to say, gathering junctures—will emerge. There will be enough of them and enough difference among them for each of us to seek our fully human beingness, to learn what that is, and to support the search and the articulation of the other in our multiple communities of learners.

In a way, all of these spiritual archetypes call us, each differently, to create a new space for our human spirit to flourish on the planet.

The organizational spirit is called to bring all of these manifestations together; to discover how they might nurture each other in the space between and among us. In a new organizational mode? Perhaps. Perhaps beyond organization to something new.

9

The Enlivening Spirit

BRINGING THE HUMAN SPIRIT TO LIFE

The Call

At the surface, the call of the enlivening spirit is straightforward: to bring the human spirit itself back to life; to give life to the human spirit in us; to enliven it. For everyone? In principle, yes. The enlivener does not prejudge who is ready and who is not.

Is your biography ready to receive its spirit? She invites with hope, but no expectations.

Is your spirit ready to come out of the closet? She asks, with a loving affirmation but no expectations.

The enlivener's call from her own spirit is to give life to the human spirit in others, to bring it back into the world of action, decision, choice, and commitment.

Like the loving and caring archetype, she works with us one-by-one. Her call is not to enliven the world in abstract. She does not try to convince the group, association, institution, organization, or community to "spiritualize" its members and their activities. The focus of the enlivener's work, as well as the loving and caring spirit's, is the individual person.

Her call is clear, pristine, and direct. If you feel it, if you have it, there is no question about its meaning and purport. The criteria and standards by which we humans judge success don't matter too much to her. She cannot help herself, irrespective of the results of her work. Whether or not she learns to do it better, she will always do it, once she uncovers her calling.

Enliven, this archetype calls out. Bring people's spirit back to life in them, so it can work its wonders, big or little, for the whole world or for the individual person. Success does not matter. What matters is that the person's spirit is freed to speak its piece, and that she, eventually, will listen to and enact its invitation.

Yes, but how?

The "How" of It

This is where the surface simplicity of the invitation gives way to a large degree of complexity. How to enliven, how to bring spirit back to life in the person and in the world is no easy piece of work. The de-spiritualized culture, the KBVAF encased in our social biographies, the fear of being open and vulnerable to the human spirit, being out of control: these conspire to make the path of enspiriting difficult, at first, to follow. The enlivener is always confronted with this most practical question of all: How do I offer the gift of the human spirit in such a way that it will be received?

In a way, the question lies at the heart of this book and its method. Does this book, its approach, its concepts, its practices, its invitations, speak to you and help you to call out your own spirit and to respond to its invitation? Or is it light reading on a rainy afternoon? You judge.

In another way, is not this question of how to enliven the human spirit directed to all of us who have responded to our own spirit? For clearly, your own how-to questions (how to mend, how to render just governance, how to create new partnerings, for example) involve engaging with the spirit of others. This means engaging not only their biographies, but also with their spirit.

The Biographical Factor

Now we shall probe further into the so-called biographical factor. It has a great deal to do with the mechanics of enlivening, the "how" of it.

Elsewhere, I have stated quite explicitly that your own spirit comes to life in you and works its magic through you, in the biographical complexity that intermixes heredity and genetic dispositions, on the one hand, and environmental determinants, on the other. To use my vocabulary, your spirit lives in you and comes to life through your biography, both inner and outer. That means it acts in and through your personality, your character,[19] and your life circumstances, good, bad, or indifferent. It matters not to your spirit if you were born into an urban slum, licking leaded paint off the wall, born into a cattle-herding culture and killing a lion single-handed as your rite-of-passage, born into nobility surrounded by servants, or born into a middle-class civilization of false plenty. Nor does it matter to the enlivening spirit. Her project, her reason for being enfleshed in you, has to move forward. But the different circumstances of each person are crucial because they construe the mechanics, the practices of enspiriting.

The Physics of It

After all, the human spirit is not a will-o'-the wisp, ephemeral, smoke and mirrors, untouchable. To the contrary, it is palpable. Its presence is lodged within the infinite complexity of the brain, perhaps one of the inner brains or perhaps in the cortex. Someday, neurobiological research will find out where and how $E=Mc^2$ processes the human spirit within, from energy to mass, and when, under an inner program I have called creating the space for spirit, that mass converts back to spirit energy, a kind of a quantum shift from particle to wave. For then, the human spirit floods through the person's entire being and multiple systems, moving back and forth among the chakras. And, as spirit-energy, it emerges into a social space where it converses lovingly with the spirit of other persons through their biographies, though sometimes directly, spirit to spirit, in an ecstatic epiphany.

That "flooding of the human system" by the conversion of spirit's mass to spirit-energy also plays a part in miracle cures, the remission of terminal diseases which medical science cannot yet explain, and in the reappearance of the human spirit when it is thought to have departed to another world or sphere of existence. In the enormous complexity of our neurobiological, chemical, and physical systems in the human being, and in the enormous complexity of their interplay, what is the trigger? My deepest sense is that the human spirit is not yet ready to leave its body because of some project, some piece of work, some possibility not yet finished.

My own story goes like this. When I was in my late 40s and this work of enspiriting was just beginning to come of age in my own person, my aunt, then in her 70s, was nearly killed in a fire in her apartment. Her husband, my uncle, bedridden, died of smoke inhalation. And she almost did. The doctors were discouraging about the prospects of survival for her. The day after, I sat by her bedside in the hospital, watching this dear aunt scarcely able to breathe, her lungs just about finished off. I said to her out loud that she was free to go, to leave the earth, and that she should know that both my brother and I loved her dearly.

She recovered.

A couple of months later, as I again sat by her bedside late one night in her New York apartment, as she was slowly recovering, she said to me: "Warren, do you remember that afternoon in the hospital when you thought I was dead? Well, I was on the ceiling, hovering, looking through a long tunnel at the end of which your mother, dressed in white and smiling, was beckoning me. Then I looked down at you, sitting beside my body, and realized that my work was not yet done. You needed me. So I returned to my body."

The human spirit is not omniscient, is not omnipresent, is not God. But it is there. Once born into us, the human spirit has an offer to make, a call, an invitation. You will respond, deny it, negotiate with it, capitulate to it. Or, like me, you will work with it to reintegrate it into your entire presence, along with the totality of your biographies, in a dance of discovery and learning, a dance that is full of surprises rather than expectations, adventures rather than guarantees, and road signs pointing in this direction or that.

THE ENLIVENERS AMONG US

Self-research

How did I come to the idea of a spiritual archetype named the enlivening spirit?

I am sure there were many influences in my life that gave credence to my inner biography and placed my social biography into a self-questioning mode. The details need not bore you. Except to remind you that my stories of my spirit's speaking to me, some of which I have shared with you in this book, are told in order to call you to your stories of your spirit's speaking to you.

Your Own Stories

Review your stories. Bring forth more, if you would like. Take a look at these stories and images in your journal. Seek to burrow beneath them, as I did with my own. Uncover the criticals and go to the fundamentals.

Do you detect, in any of that material, a tendency to bring out another person's spirit for its own sake, as Aristotle would say of the final end, and not for the sake of anything else?

With the enlivening spirit, enspiriting with others is done for its own sake. As I have said, the enlivener can't help herself. She is called to emancipate the spirit in herself and in the other.

The Start-up

Throughout my life, I have known persons who called me to myself, starting with my mother. They pushed, teased, and sought to call out my spirit. At first, of course, I didn't know what that was about. Part of me fought them off; not the person so much as the invitation, though often the two are co-mingled. We have a hard time distinguishing the invitation from the person. I was busy getting on with my life... college, marriage, career, family, mortgage, and all the rest.

But occasionally, my spirit would erupt, calling me to its own purposes and standards, and even in my childhood, calling others to theirs. I didn't do it well, of course. Spirit itself had to learn how to work through my biography, had to learn to make its call clearer and more compelling, to cut through my biographical defenses thrown up by my KBVAF.

But, like yours, my spirit bides its time. It never gives up.

So, in my middle years, I began to enact my spirit's enlivening call in a more professional way, learning, developing, testing out the work and methods of futures-invention. Unlike most futurists who saw the future as the domain of knowledge, to be postulated and cemented in through forecasts and predictions, from the very start I understood the future as a metaphor for hope, vision, intention, and action.

Hope, vision, intention, and action: these are the ways the human spirit speaks through the human biography.

The Participant-facilitator

Coming to accept my own enlivening spirit was greatly influenced by seeing spirit's action and presence in others. Years ago, when I began this work with graduate students at Syracuse University, I noticed that a few of the "participants" were more interested in emancipating the social inventions and creativity of their fellow participants than they were in focusing in on their own work. When I also did the envisioning work with community and organizational people far removed from a university setting, I noticed the same activity.

Some persons, a very few, gave their energy to helping other participants come to their vision rather than generating their own. They were facilitating, to be sure, but in a special way which only years later did I come to realize was part of the enlivening process. Untutored in the enspiriting disciplines, nevertheless, they sought in their own ways to become midwives, to help give birth to the true images and ideas of others. That's what they wanted to do. They were called to it. In that activity, they found their own focus. And it was fun for them. They enjoyed it.

Right from the beginning of the work, some of these "participant-facilitators" said to me: Warren, this community we are forming in your envisioning process is a clue to what communities will be in the future; of how we will relate to each other; of how we will acknowledge our learning of ourselves and of each other and of the world, and build our institutions and ways of life on that.

I nodded wisely... or smiled foolishly. They were way ahead of me. They were proto-enliveners. They had discovered that these new envisioning methods and practices appealed to them in a way different from the majority of participants in futures-invention. These were the people I invited for self-training and to prepare themselves to do this work. They were my teachers, though they probably didn't know that, teaching me about the enlivening spirit long before I met her in myself.

But what of you?

Have you ever met, seen, worked with such persons? They are the ones who give attention to the individual, be it at a business meeting, workshop, or group activity of any kind. The proto-enlivener listens deeply and long, with her entire being. She watches carefully. And at some point, perhaps through a public question all can hear, perhaps in a private way where only she and the other person are engaged, she asks questions like:

- Who in our midst is not being heard?
- Who has something to offer which is not yet received because we are not ready for it?
- Who can get underneath the verbiage, the cant, the self-promotion to uncover the deeper issues and concerns?

And then, if in a public gathering, she invites silence, and waiting, and the encouragement of creating that space of stillness where someone's spirit will enter.

And if in a private one-with-one, she'll ask, she'll listen, and she'll wait.

Perhaps, if you have met or seen such a person, it is you meeting yourself coming around the corner.

Let's find out.

WHO SPEAKS THE QUESTION?

The Hard Questions, the Deep Questions, the Generic Questions

If these questions have been addressed to you, and if you have somehow accepted them and not run away, then you are on the path to a self-discovery of your own spirit, perhaps the enlivening one.

- What of your spirit, woman?
- What of your spirit, man?
  Sharp. Direct. Final.
- What's going on here?
- What does your spirit say about this?

These are deep questions, to be sure. In a way, they are perhaps the deepest questions because they come from the enlivener's spirit and are asked of another person's spirit, bypassing the ordinary discourse with the social biography, perhaps even seeking what lies underneath the inner biography.

Have you heard these questions addressed to you? Have you ever asked them of yourself or of others? I think most of us ask them, once in a while, perhaps silently, so only we can hear them.

When are they asked?

Are these questions asked in times of stress? Are they asked in moments of blatant wrongdoing, when you know in your bones that your spirit does not condone such action?

I've asked these questions of a person's spirit. In no uncertain terms, I've been told to shut up. It is none of my business. This, of course, means that it is none of their business, because their business is not yet of the spirit, it is of the biography. Okay. Some are ready. Some are not. Perhaps some will never be.

That is of no concern to the enlivener, for she is called to bring out the other person's spirit in all circumstances where her own spirit is so moved and so discerns. In a way, the enlivening spirit cannot help herself, so strong is this call. Once she has agreed that this is her genius, it is always in action, whether or not the circumstances call for it. She does not direct her spirit-energy to contexts. She directs it to the person. She offers her own spirit, she nurtures the other's spirit in such a way that it can be received, a gift which is not always easy to receive. The loving and caring spirit loves the individual person in all of her totality, including her biography and irrespective of her faults, deficits, idiosyncracies, and misspent possibilities.

The enlivening spirit loves a person's spirit. Basically, that person's biography is irrelevant.

The enlivening spirit does not ask, Are you ready? She assumes and asserts that everyone is ready to listen to the voice of their spirit.

Proven wrong much of the time is of no matter. She cannot help herself, so strong is the call.

But... other voices too?

Am I suggesting, by these generic questions, a universal morality? Are these questions to be addressed to all of us on the planet? Is this a new moral code of enspiriting to supplant the planet's multitudinous moralities, expressed in the many religious, ideological, and ethical systems imbedded in the historic cultures out of which they have emerged?

Not at all. These deep questions to self and to others, these disciplines of the human spirit are no more captured by the world's religions than they are by ideologies or social movements, though the "silent" forms of worship of some of the Friends (Quakers) tend to be more expressive of the human spirit because, simply put, they encourage more listening and less preaching.

But does enspiriting—its disciplines, its practices, its calls— relieve you of your fully human obligation to consider your spirit's relationship with God's? Ask your spirit!

The Call of the Question

Whence these questions? Why do I say we all think of them, if not speak them? Why, using different words, do we ask:

What are you up to, woman?

What are you up to, man?

Why are you doing that, saying that, feeling that, thinking that, being that?

I am talking about calling a person to herself. Don't most of us do that, from time-to-time, or want to?

Calling a person to herself has a common meaning in many languages because of the very human need to remind ourselves that much of who we are and what we do is at a surface of behavior that does not pass the scrutiny of our spirit. Of course, for most the vocabulary of enspiriting is absent. No matter. The asker may well not be aware that these are questions from her spirit. Still, the human spirit breaks out of its silence, and announces itself in a variety of expressions. It is a call, a plea, a reminder to that other person that the behavior in question transgresses not just the culture, laws, social biography, or role definition, but the person's own spirit.

The call is there. There is no doubt about that. Each of us has a little piece of it because we are all of the human spirit. But because it is so much easier to accept the social norms of the situation, that call too seldom nourishes a response except with this spiritual archetype named the enlivening spirit. She does it all the time, persistently, consistently, as part of her being and doing on the planet.

Is the enlivening spirit loving?

Because these deep questions are so tough, we have to ask, "Is the enlivening spirit loving?"

Yes, very much so, but in a special way. She loves the reality of the human spirit, in, of, and for itself. She lives in that space wherein spirit dialogues with spirit, and spirit and biography dance together in that never-ending quest for integrity, unity, and wholeness. She understands the inner turmoil, sometimes the pain that burns within, but does not use that as an excuse to stop enspiriting... she feels it. And too, she shares in the ecstasy when spirit comes out.

She never backs off if there is still a chance, even with the person who is most recalcitrant. Tough love is the way we name it. This is the school teacher in the slum school who will not give up. To hell with expectations, the enlivener says metaphorically. What are you up to, young person? And, as with the loving and caring spirit, she always holds the image of the fully human person in sight of both of them, the teacher and the learner.

With the tough love go its contra points, empathy and compassion. Sometimes there is sadness, when the enlivener sees how the vast potential in the other is misspent or misdirected. And there is anger. Not violence. They are not the same. Violence diminishes the personhood of the other. Anger says that the conflict, the issue, the question, the behavior is too important to let go. It is to be confronted. This anger of the human spirit is a sudden burst of spirit-energy, when the enlivener's project is denied or prevented by those who know her invitation, and refuse its admission into the halls of human conversation, civility, and action.

So with that enlivening compassion for the other person's spirit, the enlivening spirit is prepared to confront as well as to hug; to insist on a response, but to wait a very long time for its coming forth; to offer her spirit as a refuge when the other's inner quest transposes into turmoil, tears, pain, self-violence, and despair.

The Refuge

Refuge is the key to unlock the door so that the person can enter, however tentatively, her own space for spirit. The enlivening spirit offers her own space as a refuge! I think this is the basis of that act of grace we commonly call "nurturing." This lies at the center of her practice, however she comes to be a refuge from the onslaughts of the social biography.

She does not stand back and objectify the other's inner turmoil, self-conflict, or delusion in a clinical mode of study, objectification, or noninvolvement. To the contrary, she offers her spirit-energy and its space to the other person. One-with-one enspiriting is the modus operandi of the enlivening spirit. Gradually, the two, working together, learn to enspirit with each other in enspiriting dialogue, where intimacy, vulnerability, and presence prevail. That is one reason I have insisted that deep listening and deep questioning are not mainly counseling, therapy, problem-solving, or advice-giving.

Whose emotions?

Love and tough love, compassion and empathy, sadness and, occasionally, anger: these are human emotions. Am I now stipulating that the human spirit also has feelings at its disposal? Are these part of its panoply of expressions, of its coming into conscious awareness, emotions that go beyond the activity of the human limbic system whose neurobiological antecedents are buried in millions of years of evolution?[20]

Yes. Of course, I am using a human-invented language to describe a spiritual phenomenon, a presence in us which defies so much of current human understanding, whether or not the proposed insights come from theology, ethics, psychology, linguistics, or sociology as they are now generally understood and practiced. Our language of a de-spiritualized age gives us huge problems not only of explanation but also of sheer description of the enspiriting disciplines and these spiritual archetypes. One of my colleagues in Sweden said to me, "Our language so objectifies. So that vision and spirit are outside of us, when in fact they are of us in the deepest, truest, most sacred way possible."

I ask myself, how does she know this? And why is it sensed everywhere, in every culture, in every linguistic expression, in every person? Because of the immediacy and presence of the lived experience when spirit speaks out and we listen! But that immediacy is frightening to many of us. We deny it happened. Yet it compels us. So we look to the scientific activity to relieve us of choice in the matter, to deny—because we cannot prove—that the human spirit exists.

Yet every culture, every language, every civilization, and even "Lucy" in some early way, acknowledges the human spirit, has its words, settings, and idioms for it. My invitation here is just to acknowledge that spirit within yourself by learning to listen to it. And that is the invitation of the enlivening spirit.

A new morality of the fully human?

Is a new morality birthing, a new religion of which the enlivening spirit is the advance spokesperson?

This is a good question. It reminds me of what I have said before: that there is a popular propensity of human beings to kid themselves, to so spin the ideas and images, that we no longer know which end is up, and don't think it matters too much anyway.

I have said that the enlivening spirit is the one called to invite the human spirit to its active stance in each and every one of us. Does she do this all the time?

Well, pretty much all the time, as a primary condition of being fully human.

But that transposes the focus and gives us a new question. When and why are we supposed to be fully human? Again, all of the time? Some of the time? Rarely?

The hypothesis is that fully human learning is forever pro-active, seeking an exchange between the human learner and that which is learned. Fully human learning, then, is singularly and always hermeneutic, (seeking to interpret or make clear) and heuristic (seeking to discover, to come to the next question). Between the learner and that which is learned is a reciprocating effect so that the learner impacts on that which is learned, so as to change it... and vice versa.

Fully human learning is the work of the human spirit in you. It is not only neurobiological curiosity, pseudopods sent out to explore if the outside environment is dangerous or welcoming. Of course, we sniff and smell and taste and look and touch and do all of those marvelous activities which are not special to humans but found in all living organisms at some level. And like the earth itself and all that it encompasses, we are self-organizing systems, capable of interacting with and modifying our environment in the interest of maintaining, through shifting, its life-sustaining qualities.

But fully human learning involves your own spirit coming to, and creating, that which has not existed. This is transformation, of which we can give no account once we are in it except to say that it is both a process and result of deep learning.

That is a universal possibility in each and every human being. For it to happen, your own spirit has to be enticed out of hiding. That is the invitation of the enlivening spirit. If you have not yet met one, you are in for a great treat. You can deny her invitation. You can try to negotiate it so that it sits more pleasantly with your social biography. Or you can learn to receive the enlivening spirit's gift to you, which is to enter the space for spirit.

Let us find out, together, if this is your call.

THE FOUR DIMENSIONS OF SELF-RESEARCH

The Template

The basic method of this book is to look to your life experience to find your own spirit's call and invitation. Each spiritual archetype is revealed by the questions directed to your inner biography, to your social biography, to your inner action and experience, and to your outer action and experience with others.

These questions differ in content from one archetype to another. Your responses need not be in writing, generated only from your intellect. Perhaps your truest responses will be in your body, in your feelings, in some intuition or sense that comes to you absent of meditation or of sophisticated analysis, perhaps like a surge of feeling that tells you this is right, this is me, this is what I am.

Still, despite these important variations of content and modes of response, there are four kinds or dimensions of self-research. I make these explicit now because querying the enlivening spirit in your self, discerning if it is there, brings these dimensions out into the open. They form a template that you can apply in many ways throughout your life about many issues. They're very helpful in uncovering the call of your own spirit.

The First Dimension—Questions From the Other

This is a marvelous way to initiate the search because right from the beginning it shifts the focus away from you and into the hands of other persons. Sometimes, they are the ones to sense in you who you are and what you have to offer to the world.

243

Often, this begins in childhood, with a parent or sibling, someone close to you, who senses from her own spirit what you are called to, and says so to you. Oh, perhaps not in so many words, not directly. But she shares her hope, even her conviction, that in you is something extraordinary, something unique.

Who could this person be? A teacher? A close friend? Often, it is an adult; though do not discount the young person, who looks at you quizzically because she knows out of her own totality that you are being called in some special way, though probably she can't name it. Sometimes, though, she can describe some of your spirit's characteristics.

In ruminating on the call of my spirit, my memory lifted up a grammar school clue. It was about a girl who, by her presence, called me to my spirit in a small and suggestive but nevertheless lasting way. I remembered this when, out of the blue, she wrote to me and we began a little correspondence 60 years later. We had been classmates, but not close in any way except in music and theater that, in my school, we did a lot of. She was different than the others; a little fey; more quiet than effusive; a question always in her look, not quite accepting herself, me, or the world around us. By conventional standards, she did not stand out except in height, for she was a tall girl. Her presence, I think now her untutored spirit, said to me, Look, Warren, there's more to life, to being alive, than just growing up. Give attention to yourself in the world. Seize the unfamiliar, don't run from it.

And so I got another reminder that I had embarked on a long journey to learn to accept the call of my own spirit within the confusions of my social biography and my fear of my inner biography to which my spirit increasingly spoke... and still does!

This first dimension of self-research need not always be articulated in words or in explicit or obvious behaviors. Sometimes it is, sometimes it isn't. But this preliminary recognition by the other person is always there, the person who may not know you too well but knows your spirit, who queries your potential, who may well sense that to which you are called... before you do!

The First Set of Questions

- Who has asked you about yourself? Who now asks you?
- Did anyone suggest, by word or action, what you might be and do?
- Did you get a new, a different, a clearer, a more challenging sense of your self from anyone? When? How? What was that sense? Describe it as best you can.
- Did anyone, by words or actions, tell you that there was more to you than you knew or thought possible? In the past? Even now?
- And did she or he name it?

As you respond, open up, relax, breathe deeply, yield, and listen for these memories. Invite the images of your past to enter your conscious awareness. Listen for your spirit to speak out. It will remind you of those occasions when other persons saw or felt your spirit working in you.

Of course, these questions fit everyone querying their archetypes, not only the enlivening spirit. But this first set begins to bring out the very presence of your own spirit: that something in you abides; that others "see" it; that you had better begin to give attention.

The Second Dimension—Questions for the Other

This second dimension is the mirror image of the first dimension. Here, you are sensitive to the uniqueness in others, adult or child. Here, you have watched, listened, acted thoughtfully toward another person because you have sensed in him or her a way of being that is somehow outside the norm.

I think we all have this "sense" capacity. But I think we submerge this as part of growing up, of learning how to behave. So when we sense this "something special" in the other, we either deride it or ignore it. More often than not, we seek to put it out of sight and mind so that what we sense in her is not reciprocated.

I knew two classmates, one in grammar school and one in prep school, who turned out to be geniuses in their adult years. My classmates and I either derided or ignored them, but I didn't do this quite as much as the others because I sensed that in these two was something unique and special that challenged my peer-rating quotient and secretly invited me to look and listen again more carefully.

Well, I have learned. Some of my peers sensed my emerging sensitivity to spirit in others, to their spirit, and so began to keep me out of their biographical space. When I reached my 20s, I had learned to accept the differences among us. By the time I was in my 30s, I had begun to learn to invite it out. By my 40s, I was learning how to celebrate and embrace that uniqueness in other persons; to accept it in myself, and to seek to emancipate the underlying themes and calls of my spirit.

Spirit-time knows no chronological imperatives. It comes when biography is ready. Is yours ready?

Herding

The peer pressure to conform is obvious. We all know about it. Most of the time, we let it hold sway over our own judgment. It is the herd instinct at work. Not rocking the boat is a very powerful glue. It binds us together (which in many ways is good). Too many of us, however, become secretive in the presence of peer pressure. We hide our feelings. We hesitate to express our ideas. Our very spirit becomes secretive, as the prevailing KBVAF, like water, flows first into every low-lying place in our biography and social life and eventually, like a rising tide, sweeps all before it, filling the interstices of every neuron, axon, and synapse in our brain, body, and social institutions 'til there is no space left for spirit.

When this herd instinct, as I call it, comes to the fore in political life and civic action, the consequences are intolerable at best, the death knell of just governance, and devastating at worst.

The enlivening spirit, from the onset of its enfleshing in you, seeks out that which is unique in each of us. It will not subvert its call to the demands of uniformity.

Your Sensitivity as a Clue

Am I making too strongly a case about conformity? Is it not true that there are plenty of differences among people, differences of character, belief, and behavior? But so often and too much, we subdue those differences, emphasizing the uniqueness as difference rather than as something special, perhaps even to be celebrated.

It's a mixed picture for all of us. Within that conforming behavior, many seek to give some special sign of their personhood, perhaps no more than a different color tie or a pin on the blouse.

You can choose from among all of the makes, models, styles, and colors of automobiles one that is just you, simply you. And don't the advertisers and auto manufacturers know that? It is the basis of niche marketing.

May I remind you that in this Chapter Nine, *The Enlivening Spirit,* I am inviting you to search out your response to this calling, which is to bring out, nurture, and support the spirit of the other person, to enliven her spirit so that she can enact its call, whatever that is. At issue here is not my amateur social-psychology on the "herd instinct." It is your sensitivity to the other people, to their uniqueness, differences, specialness. That is a clue that perhaps you are seeking openings in their KBVAF, openings to their inner paths that lead through the rich, subterranean corridors of their inner biography to their spirit.

Ask yourself if this is true of you. Here are some questions to help give this second dimension specificity and concreteness.

The Second Set of Questions

These questions are the reverse of the first set. They are questions about your own awareness of spirit's presence in others as distinguished from their sensitivity to spirit's presence in you. Your "awareness" may not, initially, have been at the conscious level. Your query and your memory may now bring these things into conscious awareness, but the full emergence of the enlivening spirit in you may not have happened all at once, if at all. Still, pieces, bits, and clues of this sensitivity to others' spirit may climb the internal ladder into your conscious awareness as you recall the events, relationships, and occasions that you celebrated, or sought to deal with, or perhaps even tried to suppress as your social biography asserted itself.

- Are you sensitive to other persons' uniqueness or specialness?
- Does it upset you? Or do you cherish it?
- When did you become aware of this disposition? Will you not now recall instances of that sensitivity?

These are not meant to be "win-lose" questions. Your responses have nothing to prove, least of all to me. They are signs to search for in order to discern if you have ever been traveling the path of the enlivening spirit.

The empathic mode of deep listening is a way that you may have come to that sensitivity. Sensitivity here means no more than "picking up" the signals that the other person sends out.

- Do you—did you ever—pick up such signals? Become aware of them?
- Do you—did you ever—hide from these signals, dismiss them?
- Perhaps, deep inside yourself, did you nurture and warm them, keep them alive in the space where your own spirit lives?

A Resting Point

In your journal, perhaps jot down a word, a phrase, a little story in response to one or more of these questions. Record the experiences in your life that might attest to the possibility that this archetype of the enlivening spirit has been speaking to you and you have begun to accept its invitation, even though you may not have known it as such.

But by now, you may have dismissed this archetype. No, this is not me.

Okay. Nothing gained, nothing lost. Move on to Chapter Ten on the Reflective Spirit and Chapter Eleven on the Poetic Spirit. Or move back to one of the spiritual archetypes described earlier in the book. Perhaps it is time again to revisit the chapter on your gifts and talents. That section was at the beginning of this long journey to the heart of your own spirit, and you may now bring to it fresh insights about who you are, who you were, who you might yet be. Perhaps there awaits a very special discovery for you, in which you uncover your special calling, your spirit's invitation to you which nobody else on the planet has received.

But if these questions in the first two dimensions have helped you to recall your spirit's action, then move on to the third dimension, for now you definitely have a foundation on which to build.

The third dimension: is this me?

Are you prepared to bring out the spirit of others? Have you discerned the risks? Are you strong enough inside to accept and withstand the negative reactions of those to whom your invitation, your deep questions, the ways you solicit their spirit's presence draws out not their spirit but its denial?

How can you, the enlivening spirit, discern this strength? It is the strength of your spirit. And you come to know it by its action in you, as it has confronted your biography, your KBVAF, your life experiences... and refused to be denied.

What this means is just this. You, the social you, the biographical you, the result of the enormously interactive complex of genes and environment (nature and nurture) may have fought off your spirit and put it back in hiding. It happens to the best of us. There is no shame here, only invitation. Or, right from the beginning your spirit's enlivening spoke out so strongly that it shaped your biography despite the best efforts of others, perhaps even those who loved you the most, to curtail the enlivening spirit in you and to give you a shape and a script the world could more readily accept.

The Third Set of Questions

- Is this me?
- Is my archetype the enlivening one?
- Am I devoted to bringing out, emancipating the spirit of the other person?

These questions focus you on your own inner dynamic, on how, why, and when the enlivening spirit entered your space and began to shape it.

It is from the experiencing of that inner dynamic that you learned what it means to be an enlivening spirit, to listen to its call and respond affirmatively. The experiencing of that inner dynamic, what actually happened to you as you learned your spirit, teaches you how to enliven the spirit of others. As you bring that dynamic into conscious awareness, you learn how, why, and when to invite, to support and nurture, indeed to cherish that dynamic in others. You become skilled at enlivening with others because you became skilled at your own enlivening. You have learned how to be a refuge for others' enspiriting because your spirit, in its refuge for you, taught you how. As we are wont to say, experience is the best teacher, to which I would add, if you query it!

The Skills

What does all of this mean? What are these skills? For as you develop them internally, you prepare yourself to exercise them externally with others.

Of course, they are the skills of enspiriting, particularly becoming enskilled in the practices of deep imaging, deep listening, and deep questioning:

You learned to empty of your biography and to listen to the voice of your own spirit.

You learned to ask deep questions of your spirit and invite its deep questions of you, the biographical person.

You learned to deep image what it would be like to emancipate the spirit in others by trying it on for size yourself.

This "inner dynamic" need not be a situation of inner turmoil, strident conflict, or sharpening pain. The dynamic may be a joyful one, occasioned by self-recognition and self-acceptance: by golly, this enlivening spirit is me!

I am talking about a flash of self-recognition, about a great biographical moment in your life when you see it all come together, the social biography, the inner biography, and the spirit, into a wholeness wherein the enlivening spirit in you has found its home.

Explore this dynamic. This is where the journaling, the storytelling comes to the fore. Recount some of the stories of your inner dynamic, the high points and the low points, what actually happened inside, perhaps which you have never shared with anybody. Perhaps it is time for you to begin to write your own book or talk into a tape recorder.

These stories are about how your enlivening spirit enlivened itself, with or without the help of your biography. How, indeed, your spirit shaped your inner biography, not only to withstand the onslaught of your social biography but, in turn, to begin to shape it.

I don't think the enlivening spirit has yet populated the planet. But the enlivening spirits among us are harbingers of a world, someday, when the human spirit will be present in all we are and do.

What will we call these enliveners? Perhaps... enliveners.

The Fourth Dimension—Enlivening the Other

Let us recapitulate this story of self-questioning to discern if your spiritual archetype is the enlivening one.

The first dimension's questions sought to attune you to what other persons—family, friends, strangers—have seen in you as an enspiritor.

The second dimension's questions invited you to recall to what extent, perhaps even at an early age, you became sensitive to awakening the spirit in others. You saw through their social biography to their inner struggle to emancipate their spirit.

The third dimension's questions directed your attention to your own inner awakening, to the inner dynamic between your spirit's invitation and your biography's response. If you have been able to listen to your spirit's voice and call, you have learned how to do this with yourself and thus may have clues about and competence in how to do this with others.

Of course, the inner dynamic applies to each and every person who somehow enters her space for spirit and hears her spirit's call, whatever the archetype in question. But it applies particularly to the enlivening spirit because her call is the enlivening itself: how to bring out the spirit in others so that they may better enact their spirit's call, whatever that turns out to be.

The Fourth Set of Questions

- Have you so enacted?
- Have you sought to draw out another person's spirit?
- Have you been able to create that space for spirit where the other's spirit will enter?
- Have you provided a safe refuge of nurture and support while the other person lives her own inner dynamic?
- Have you been able to take the heat when people, institutions, and situations attempt to thwart your invitation?

For each of these questions, the most interesting part in your response is:

- How were, and are, you able to do this?

Leading to...

- What are the competencies of the enlivening spirit?

Note them. List them. Give attention to how you can and do emancipate the human spirit. Thus do you begin to demonstrate that this particular call is not an idealistic mirage, but a very practical calling which you profess, which means that you are on the way to becoming a professional in this remarkable endeavor.

Someday, we will know what to name it.

My friend, mentor, and master from olden times, Aristotle, said that we know the end by the means we select to achieve it. Thus did he connect principle with practice, the end with the competence to let it be realized.

You will know of and be with the call of the enlivening spirit when, in the final analysis, you know how and why to enliven the spirit in others.

I am still learning.

10

The Reflective Spirit

A STORY ABOUT STORIES

"Look Before You Leap"

Have you heard that admonition before? I suspect other cautions like this one exist in many languages and cultures. Its antecedents remind us that we humans, despite our enormous mental apparatus, are still part of the animal kingdom. The enfleshment of our human spirit is glorious, but it has by no means conquered our physiology. We still "look." It is a survival mechanism in which the time between the outward event and the inward firing of our neurons to respond is measured in a nanosecond.

We possess a large variety of survival mechanisms that are part of our autonomic nervous system conditioned and evolved over the eons. During that evolution, enter the human spirit from some source other than our biological, geological, and ecological determinants.

We are a species, one among the multitude. Whether or not we are a species out-of-control is a good, or a not-so-good, question. India gave the world the spirit of Gandhi. Peter and Paul give the world the spirit of Jesus. And India, Tibet, and China give the world the spirit of the Buddha. Yet so far, species proclivities have ruled, rather than spirit. Will the historic and enduring calls of the spiritual archetypes enfleshed in our species lead to different results?

My, do we humans just have to have the final say, to convince each other that I am right and you aren't, whether it's about religions, morals, cultures, governmental systems, personal power, or breakfast cereals. At the higher level, we call it dialogue in search of truth. At the lower level, we call it competition in search of survival. But what is our ecological purpose? Is it to generate a cooperative, collaborative, indeed sociable and nonviolent way of life among us that being fully human calls for?

As I have come to understand it, the human spirit is not of biological, geological, or ecological origin. Yet it operates within these systems even as it seeks to shape them according to its project, which is first to enliven spirit throughout this species, one person at a time... and then we'll see what happens. Will justice reign? Sustainability? Shalom? What about harnessing of our vast collective or world brain, to some purposes other than sheer technology, for some purposes other than replenishing the coffers of crass commercialism? Would that we humans could learn to become as fascinated with our spiritual and psychic possibilities as we are with every technological innovation and invention. Millions of people have mastered the electronic information and communications processing devices, from Univac through the worldwide web to e-commerce, in just 50 years.

Enter the reflective spirit. That archetype, like the rest, speaks from our spirit, not our physiology. It builds upon the "look before you leap" response, molding the survival "instinct" to the domain of the human spirit far beyond the species history of biological, geological, and ecological antecedents.

Rethinking the Story

The call of the reflective spirit is to "rethink" the story; to ponder it; to take it apart and put it back together again, quite possibly in a different way.

What story? All stories, about anything and everything. Any way you cut it, life is a story, with characters, themes, local color, sometimes a beginning, middle, and end, and often surprises. And there is continuity to it as well as systems breaks. The whole nine yards. More on this later.

The reflective spirit accepts nothing at face value. Everything is to be queried. That upsets a lot of people. The last things they want are deep questions, like:

- Is that what you want to say?
- Is that what it means?
- Is that what you want to do?
- Is that what it is?
- How do you know this?
- What are you assuming?
- What's going on here?
- Where's the evidence?

And in one form or another, always going back to

- What are you trying to say? What are you trying to do? What are you trying to be?

Your Life as a Story

You can't tell a story without saying it, sometimes in words; or speaking it, sometimes without words. Uncovering the criticals and going to the fundamentals is the way the reflective spirit tells the story. But what have these questions, and many more besides, to do with the story? What story? Whose story? What is that proposition about, that life is a story?

Perhaps by now you realize a central premise of my work: that everything is story, including your life. It may not exclusively be a story, but it is always a story, and not just a literary vehicle. Everything is story, including this book about listening to the voice of your spirit and uncovering your spiritual archetype. Your marriage, your family, and your career are stories about you and your relationships. You can write and live another one from your spirit if you don't like the story the world has given you!

What is the theme of your story? Perhaps you have more than one theme? I have several. The chief one, for me, is about how long it has taken me to let my enlivening spirit speak out. Another part of my story has been not to accept things the way they are just because they are. A third theme has been about justice's call to me. That third theme has been with me for a very long time, like the enlivening theme, and I'm still not quite sure what to do about it because its questions dig much deeper than any response I have been able to generate.

Of course, I'm simplifying. As you look through your journal, you might begin to search out your story.

Who are the characters? Sometimes they are persons with whom you live and sometimes they are not. Sometimes they are individuals who enter your life, perhaps even briefly, and show you a path not yet taken that, upon its appearance, beckons strongly. Sometimes you don't realize their importance in your story until they have died. A good and old friend with whom I worked, on and off, for 30 years, recently died unexpectedly. Only after his death have I come to realize that he was one of perhaps two or three persons in my entire life with whom I entered into deep dialogue almost all the time about what was most important to each of us and, as we discovered over the years, both of us.

How influential, how important, is the local color? Here, I am speaking of the culture, the subgroup, the social environment, the village, city, or countryside into which you were born. Did you accept yours unthinkingly? Did you revolt against it? Did you seek a culture quite different?

How is it all turning out? What have been the challenges, the conflicts, and the coming together of important story lines in your biography? On your deathbed, are you going to be satisfied that you lived a good life or a wasted life, a partial life or a full life, one of abundance replete with the expression of your gifts and talents?

This is all very well, you might say. This is not a bad story about life's being a story. But what about the real stuff, the hard stuff? What about science and technology, about knowledge and truth, about reality, for heaven's sake, about the really real? Are they just stories? Aren't there "objective criteria," separate from our stories, that make one "truer" than another, or "better"?

Stories change with time, including our understanding of "objective criteria." That change is imbedded in the history of science, the history of philosophy, and, most important, the (his)story of human experience.

"Yes, but aren't there some universals?" you might ask. "Some constants? Some unvarying variables?" that belong in all stories?

Well, there may or may not be universals. What is a basic part of the human experience is the search for universals. It has proven useful and satisfying to think-up, investigate, and discover a story with some constants that you hold are always there, were always there, and will always be there. Is the story about uncovering your own spiritual archetype one of them?

The constant that interests me in my story is the never-ending search for the call of my spirit, and the ways that I have sought to express and enact that call.

The reflective spirit asks:

What is your story about?

THE REFLECTIVE SPIRIT—HAVE YOU EVER MET ONE?

The Posture of Thoughtfulness

The true reflective spirit, one who has answered her call since childhood, knows herself, knows whereof she has responded to that posture of thoughtfulness which distinguishes her from the rest of us by the qualities of intellectual probing that will leave nothing alone.

Please be clear that I am not using the word "intellectual" as a substitute for "academic" or "scholarly." These latter refer to institutional and professional roles and behaviors, some of which are enacted by reflective spirits, and some not. I have met and worked with academics who are primarily salesmen. I'm talking about a mind-set that construes a probing type of cognition and carries with it certain characteristics like a readiness to think through an idea, a problem, or an observation until nothing is left untouched. Some people with a modest schooling, a narrow literary interest, and a restricted vocabulary nevertheless exhibit a true intellectual spirit. They constantly use their intellect in support of their actions. When I was a teenager working on a farm in Vermont, the farmer would mumble, purse his lips, even roll his eyes a bit when confronted with a piece of broken farm equipment. He would stand there, working the piece in his hand, thinking it over for minutes at a time before he would finally come to his conclusion and go to work on it. He did the same thing with the pea pods in the garden and the corn maturing in his fields. He would finger the tassels, pinch the cob, and feel the pods, ruminating for minutes on end until he had it right in his mind. I scarcely saw him read a book or offer an opinion on anything but his family, work, cows and horses, the tractor, why the chickens weren't laying so good, and, of course, the weather.

But when asked for an opinion, it would emerge, finally, from a thoughtfulness so silent and deep that I just waited until the gestation was completed. No rushing anything.

"What should I do now?" I might ask, this city boy working a farm during the war years. He'd just shake his head, slightly, and chew a lip, slightly. I learned to be silent, and wait.

I think he was a true reflective spirit, focused through his biography and his upbringing, his history, to put it all to work in his way of life called farming.

When do you know what you know about your spirit's call?

Many of us respond slowly to our spirit's invitation. Sometimes we don't respond at all. Then we may feel an inner unease, the source of which may remain forever unknown. Some of us come to our inner realization reluctantly, so that it is only later in life that our unique spirit finally flourishes in our actions toward ourselves and others. Other people spin about all of their lives, like a top trying to find its center of balance, eventually losing speed and toppling over because that inner invitation has not been clarified.

I say this because, like other spiritual archetypes, the reflective spirit may be initially more visible in others before it is seen, felt, or acknowledged by yourself. For example, I have learned much about myself, and not just the inner call, by listening to and watching others act in ways that I never dreamed of or thought possible. Of course, the infant soaks up the little behaviors of others, reading all the clues to learn how to behave in the world into which he was born. So, in moments of upset or discontent, we say to our child, "Behave yourself," or just plain, "Behave!" But we don't say, "Act." Isn't accommodating and learned behavior called for about most things throughout our lives? This is the survival, the herd instinct at work again, the "bandwagon" effect as some call it. In short, I learned to act by watching others act, mostly by mother, as she simply would not bend to anyone or anything just because it was the correct behavior. She made up her own mind, often by listening to the voice of her spirit rather than the admonitions of the other folks. Her spirit led her on a merry chase, over rocky roads as well as smooth paths, but I'm sure she loved the adventure because she used her adventures as harbingers for mine yet to come.

The Intellectual as a Reflective Spirit

In my early twenties, I learned the arts and craft of inquiry and dialogue at the deepest literary, linguistic, and cognitive levels from a professor at the University of Chicago. He had that unusual knack all the time of uncovering the criticals and going to the fundamentals.

"What is this about? What is he (the author) trying to say? Why does he say it this way? Are his style and methods accidental, or deliberately essayed, and to what purpose?"

Questions like these he would ask of any passage, any chapter, any book we were reading. Like a dog with his teeth in the squirrel's neck, he would not let go, shaking you, shaking the idea, until you had gone into it as far as you could at that point in your own intellectual life. In that classroom, he orchestrated a great concert, day after day, in the life of the mind. And all of his students played as tunefully as they could, varying considerably from person to person, to be sure, but all of us getting at least a sense of the reflective spirit at work in front of us and, as he was a teacher, with us.

What is the point? This man was a trained scientist by profession, with his advanced degree in physics. Yet he neither taught nor did research in physics. Rather, he played in the field of ideas, their philosophy, how you came to know them, what you were to do with them. His material, the "subject-matter," was chapters out of great philosophical works. His method was a prolonged, conjugal relationship with the ideas, a steadfast inquiry into their meanings, their parts, how they were put together, digging and digging until he—and you, if you were lucky enough to work with him—came to the solidest ground on which he and you could stand, which was always another question!

The Maker as Reflective Spirit

Not to be outdone was a foreman: grizzled, pot-bellied, a lover of his breaks and his beer, at a helicopter plant in which I once worked. I was a sheet metal assembler, working at putting together the body of the aircraft. All of the skills needed to do this were foreign to me. I had to learn how to rivet carefully, drill precise holes in aluminum sheeting, cut the parts to specifications, and read blueprints. Of course this foreman had those skills excellently, but so much more than that. When we confronted a tricky problem in assembling the shell of the aircraft, or had already made an error which needed a fix, this foreman would appear on the scene out of nowhere, sound a "tsk tsk," and begin to talk softly about the problem at hand, until he had uncovered all of its elements and solved it. And as we, the sheet metal assemblers and mechanics, watched this, day after day, we learned to emulate him. We learned not to rush but to unpack the entire job, from beginning to end, until we thought we had it right. Then we would call him over for his "tsk tsk," his thoughtful review, his thorough-going analysis. Because, he would always remind us, we don't send this aircraft up until it's 100% ready.

I'd be surprised if this foreman had a high school education. He came from a working class family and social environment that, in the 1920s of his youth, often did not send their kids through high school. In the United States, it wasn't until after the Second World War that we graduated as much as 50% of the age cohort from 12th grade.

How come he could and would think everything through to its end result? Intellectual probing, prolonged thinking, and sustained analysis are not purely academic qualities. They do not depend on your profession or level of educational attainment. They are some of the outward manifestations of a reflective spirit. As you query your own spirit, do not let a social biography that has perhaps denied this capacity in you, this talent, stand in the way.

Is the reflective spirit creative?

In Chapter Eleven, the next section, we will find that creativity is a quality more closely associated with the poetic spirit rather than the reflective.

Perhaps the simplest way to know the creator is to know the maker. Creating is making something, bringing into existence something that was not in existence, lifting the curtain of the universe's holographic shield and shifting its livingness from the implicate to the explicate order (the latter order of which most of us humans consider reality).

All enspiritors, those who respond to the call of their spirit, or are in process of so doing, are creative. By no means are all uniquely reflective. Their spiritual archetype is calling them to be and do some-thing they have perhaps not yet been and done. I have no problem in calling that an act of creativity, as it involves both will and imagination. So we all have a piece of it. Perhaps your own self-reflection on your gifts and talents in Chapter Two showed you that.

But the reflective spirit does not make things. She takes them apart. Sometimes, she puts them back together the way they were, satisfied that the making was good. Sometimes she puts them back together another way. All of the ingredients were there. After unpacking, she offers alternatives—ideas, images, schemes, programs, ways of being and doing—by reshuffling the deck. She has not created the deck. Still, by virtue of that reflection, it is a new deck.

Copernicus and Galileo reshuffled the deck, and the world has never been the same. From John Locke to Tom Paine, reflective spirits reshuffled the deck of 17th and 18th century political thought, and we in the West are still trying to live out that new deck of self-governance. Einstein reshuffled the deck of mass, energy, light, time, and space and no one yet quite knows where that will lead.

Have you reshuffled yours, someone else's, the world's? Let's find out.

How many reflective spirits are there?

Actually, there are quite a few reflective spirits around and about. One out of a hundred? Perhaps. More than that? I think more potential reflective spirits would respond to their call were our culture not so practical, so pragmatic, so grounded in the "hardware" of living.

Thinking is okay, just not too much of it. "You think too much." "Get on with it." "Oh boy, are you a procrastinator." "Time waits for no man." "The production line is moving. Your life is moving. Do something with it. Don't waste it."

You see, the reflective spirit has a leg up on many of the spiritual archetypes because it does its work primarily in collaboration with the human cerebral cortex, that enormous expansion of brain cells which overrides, sometimes, our inner brains and glands whose evolutionary history goes back to the beginning of organic life on our planet. Thus did some universal beingness of spirit become enfleshed in us at the point that we, the human species, could handle it. We've been learning how, but also repressing and forgetting, ever since. The enspiriting disciplines and practices are centered in deep learning that is an antidote to despiritualization, which characterizes the era of modernity.

I have seen the reflective spirit at work in many of the workshops and seminars I have conducted over the years. But the reflective spirit's practices, like those of most spiritual archetypes, are much of the time not welcome. Often, they are anti-institutional because, to achieve their purposes, their projects, they have to unpack the institutions and start all over again.

These are the people who will simply not be rushed to produce before they are ready. Not on an automobile assembly line, and also not in a lockstep schooling curriculum. One is not invited to reflect too much or too often. The assembly line, in the 1950s, was the crown jewel of the factory system whose mentality pervaded most of the management of organizations, including the administration of our public schools. One did not pry loose that jewel from the crown of efficiency, except in a labor strike or by dropping out of school.

It took me some years before I realized that these reflective spirits who participated in my own programs of envisioning and enspiriting, who took their time, were not being too slow. They were being thoughtful. My participants wanted a larger space for their own reflection about the concerns that brought them to the envisioning work, about their images of a future in which their concerns were well-addressed, about their emerging vision and their subsequent compelling action.

While the reflective spirits among us may be noticed first by their slowing things down so that there are time and space to think things through, it is not chronological time that is the main indicator of their presence. Sometimes the mind works at post computer speed, something like the speed of light, and the onlooker might not even notice it. What are the indicators of their presence? Reflective spirits take things apart to see how they work. It may be an idea that is dissected in the classroom or a frog in the high school laboratory. It may be unscrewing the plastic cover to your first radio, to begin the patient task of figuring out how its components work together to produce sound.

How does this work? Why is it this way? What would happen if we changed this around a bit? The reflective spirit asks such questions about anything and everything, about mechanical things, about human relations, about the way society is organized, or any one of the infinite number of questions about nature, a star system, a grain of sand, a jelly fish. Any and all things can enter its domain. One's biography gives focus to the reflective spirit but not the impetus. Which is why we find it in any and all endeavors.

REFLECTING ON REFLECTING—QUESTIONS TO SELF

Impulsive to reflective—where are you on this scale?

I hope you have been able to maintain a dispassionate appraisal of how and whether you have responded to the call of your spiritual archetype. I hope you have been able to refrain from self-judging your worth as you have read these pages and responded to the questions. Is one spiritual archetype better than another, more useful, morally superior, or easier to uncover, to respond to more fully, and to enact more easily? Not in any experience or evidence to which I can turn.

These archetypes are not part of a moralistic scheme, so many of which have led to judgments of superiority and subordination. My strong sense is that we are all needed. One archetype, one call, one invitation is no better than another, and they are all vital to themselves, to you, to us, and to our world, else why would they have been enfleshed?

Thus, the questions that follow are for search, not preference judgments; for authenticity, not for self-games; for seeking truth in your experience, getting underneath it, not molding yourself to some arbitrary scheme of who you are and what you're supposed to be and do.

If your own spirit does not partake of the reflective archetype, that is a conclusion for you to draw from the sources of your own inner truth and sense of yourself. To be sure, we all think in one way or another, so have some reflective qualities, just as most from time to time do love and care, do mend, do seek to sustain ourselves and others, do cry out at unjust events, and do act in ways that personify the other archetypes. After all, our subculture, those families and groups into which we were born and brought up, does exhibit a range of KBVAF which is the consequence of the spiritual essences groping their way into the world to make their offer. To this, over the aeons, we humans have sought to listen.

So we all do think. That is a virtue of the human species. But some of us are called to the reflective mode by our spirit, and cannot do otherwise.

But we can hide from that call, suppress it, not listen to our spirit's voice. So the reflective spirit's invitation, to uncover the criticals and go to the fundamentals will stand you in a good stead even if, especially if, you uncover little inclination of the reflective kind.

Questions About the Story—the Content

A first set of questions takes us to the reflective content, opening the door to that room where the reflective spirit feels so much at home.

The first set of self-questions are these:

- Do you understand, deep inside, that life is a story?
- Do you ask of anything or everything: what story is this?
- Do you query: what is this story about?
- Do you sense that the world—the event, the person, the situation, the idea, the image, the physical object, the experience (cultural, interpersonal, private)—is a story and you want to hear it, acknowledge it, unpack it?

To the reflective spirit, the many pieces of human experiencing come to it as a story. The tree in the forest or the forest itself: what is this? The person seen acting in a specific way and situation, or the totality of that person: who is this? The specific metaphor, phrase, or set of descriptive words in the poem, speech, or news report, or in their totality: what is this about? The broken piece of machinery, the new kitchen gadget you don't know how to make work, the phantasmagoria of icons in the great painting or the multitude of stars overhead: why and how are they put together this way and not that?

What is this about?

What is it trying to tell me?

What are you trying to tell me?

As you look at the empty lines and spaces in your journal, tell your story. Remember, if you will. Search back to find that reflective quality.

Source material may be found in any of the other searches and responses already brought forth into your conscious awareness any place in the book. Here, I think you are looking less for illustrative, concrete episodes than for how you have addressed concrete episodes of any kind.

Unpacking the Story

Now, you've entered the space, the room of the reflective spirit. You have brought into that room whatever is to be queried. Is it the story of human civilizations and cultures, of the universe and its galaxies, of your marriage, your family and its generations, of why your teacher said this, told this, explained this… and not that?

The reflective spirit is looking for reasons, causes, accounts, the way things work. And it is rarely satisfied with the first account.

You recognize this inner state of affairs in yourself, and welcome it in others when you find yourself or them unpacking the story, which means taking it apart in a deliberate and constructive way, not by accident but by choice, not finding it distasteful, time-consuming, off center and out of focus, but delightful.

This second set of questions, then, refer to your dissecting proclivities.

- Do you remove the cover to the story, probing beneath the "cover story"?
- Do you look down the street to see what's there before you take too many steps? Do you look at the mountain peak in the distance as you take the initial stride onto the trail?
- Do you pull things apart, first to see what are the elements or components, then how they fit together?
- And have you taken one of the pieces of the larger story, one of its components, and examined it closely to find the larger whole inherent in the fragment?

Once again, try for a story or two in your journal, what you actually did in some concrete situation if it turns out, upon reflection, that you're an unpacker.

Alternatives

The person who responds positively to the reflective spirit's call is always open to alternatives, even energetically seeking them out, promoting that search in others, and listening for the results.

Thus, a third set of questions goes like this:

- Do you look and listen for alternatives?

  Once again, you ask reflectively:

- What are the other ways of saying, or doing, this?

- Do you not accept the cover story, the traditional account, the tried and true, the past legitimations, the solutions or directives offered by someone else until they are examined in their meanings, their assumptions, their consequences, and their implications?

Is this relativism?

The fourth set of questions invites a probe of other people's response to your reflective qualities if, as your self-query proceeds, these prove to be part of your deepest tenor. The querying mode of the reflective spirit is ongoing and continuous. Sometimes it is not easily received in a culture whose members want quick responses and quick action.

One of my closest colleagues, a powerful facilitator of the enspiriting practices, gets tired of and a bit upset at the continuous inquiry by me about the very enspiriting practices I have so far uncovered. Too often, I ask of my own work: Is this true? Does it make sense? What are we assuming here? Where is the evidence? To what experience do we appeal? Is there another way? But my faith is in dialogue, not belief.

Like many people, at some point in the work, she wants to get on with it, to stand on a firm surface rather than to dig deeper in order to uncover the criticals and go to the fundamentals.

A negative response to lifting up alternatives takes many forms. One way the reflective spirit knows these negatives is when the other person becomes angry, frustrated, or critical, sometimes even in a personal way or a moralistic way. Often, the other persons want to get on with the task rather than assessing and unpacking it first. Accusations of relativism are moral claims stemming from some ground that brooks no counterclaim and certainly no ongoing exploration characteristic of the reflective spirit.

This last set of questions goes like this:

- Do people say to you in a critical way: Don't you believe in anything? Or
- Don't you have faith in anything? Or
- Why are you always changing things around? Or
- Don't you get tired of questioning everything?

The American language has a slang way of saying this: Can't you let sleeping dogs lie?

I think the reflective spirit is not out to win a popularity contest.

Of course, all of the spiritual archetypes I have so far uncovered seek their expression in the biographical person. Their aim is not to be loved, acclaimed, or approved in any superficial sense. Their aim is to be enacted in the person and in the world.

The reflective spirit receives and accepts that negative response.

So also did Socrates in his dialogue circle.

So also did Aristotle in his academy.

So also did Adlai Stevenson in his first presidential campaign.

And so might you—if the reflective archetype is lodged within—experience some negative reactions in your family, circle of friends, fellow workers and colleagues, or in the government in which you search and ask rather than give in to public pressure or go along with political correctness.

Even the reflective spirit acting through the persona of scientist or scholar is challenged by the princes and principalities of her profession.

But the reflective spirit need not reside only or even mainly in the university or "think-tank." It extends its invitation to all in whom it is born: the farmer, the mechanic, the bus driver, the nurse, whomever.

Perhaps in you?

11

The Poetic Spirit

ITS ORIGINS

A Special Slant on Creativity

What of the creators? Is creativity expressive of a spiritual essence? Are those who bring into existence something new and different unique among us? Are they responding to a special spiritual call? What of the tinkerers and the revolutionists? And what about the builders of a better mousetrap and the Founding Fathers of the United States Constitution? Do homeowners who design a second story addition to their home and the children who build sand castles on the beach have something in common? How about those who add a new seasoning to their spaghetti sauce or egousi soup and those who create new computer programs?

There are degrees and qualities of difference, of course, among these people. Some differences are even dramatic. But they are all expressions of our tinkering, problem-solving, "let's try something new" capacity. Perhaps this creative capacity is generic to our species, a next step beyond but rooted in the tool-making and tool-using capacity that we share with other primates. So we look, we listen, we probe, we inquire, and we discover at a very early age that we can change things and that we construct our own realities as we learn them.

That creativity, bringing into existence something new, is shared by all of us in varying ways and degrees by virtue of being human. It is closely tied to our capacity to learn and to change that which we learn because of the proactive quality of human learning. Each of the spiritual archetypes invites that universal creativity in its own expression. Bringing into the world something new lies close to the heart of the enactments of each archetype's call.

So what's the difference? Why have I identified from among the envisioners and enspiritors with whom I've worked the "poetic spirit"? What is there about this archetype that deserves a special name, a description of its special call and invitation that is discovered in some of us but by no means all?

Drawing Pictures

Don't we all, at some point in our day, draw pictures? Doodling? Copying? Imagining on paper, especially when we are youngsters?

Yes, and you would think most people would know that even though they dismiss it as unimportant in their lives. But imagine my surprise when I discovered that some of my envisioning partners, persons from all walks of life, preferred to draw their images of the future with colored crayons on flip chart paper rather than write them in words! They were literate. But when invited to reflect on and then share in a plenary session their visions of a future, they chose to draw pictures of their deepest thoughts and feelings.

Sometimes the pictures were well-drawn, sometimes poorly, and sometimes you couldn't tell what was depicted. There were strange symbols and diagrams as well as identifiable houses, trees and people. They drew pictures of loving human relationships, of sustainability, of justice, of work skills, of living and sharing in a community qualified by plenty for all and unique opportunity for all, of economic development and new urban configurations. Here were hundreds, indeed, over the years, thousands of proto-visions, of compelling images, of senses of the future drawn out from their spirit. And some put them into pictures!

At first, when a few participants began to share their images this way, I was surprised and a bit perturbed. I had been trained in intellectualized pursuits in a university setting. I had been taught to embrace the "word," logos, out of the Judaic-Greek traditions which undergird the modus operandi of our Western educational culture. Logos is a mysterious ship. Like the Flying Dutchman, it is built to withstand the stormy seas of the mind's intellectual journey, but not the travels of feelings, of body senses, of images, and of spirit.

What were these people doing to express their vision of the future in pictures instead of words? I would ask: How can anyone understand you? What does that picture mean? How do you expect to share? How will your fellow envisioners know what you mean? Why don't you write it and speak it? Maybe this belongs in a museum, but does it belong in a workshop?

I had not yet come to realize that to speak true about your deepest insights and feelings, to image a future that calls to you in a compelling way invites the widest array of human expression which includes but goes far beyond spoken and written language.

What's going on here?

What brings the "picture-drawers" to their kind of expression, one in which they speak in picture-forms their truths and their yearnings for a better world? Why are they reconfiguring their worlds, their realities, and their situations literally in pictures, rather than in the common spoken language? Somehow, that spoken and written language is not enough for what they want to express. Why?

When people use the words of a common language, they believe that the meaning is clear and shared. When people draw pictures to express their meanings, often the viewers don't know what the pictures are conveying or what the pictures stand for. What are they trying to say, to convey, to establish as they come to their vision? We onlookers have to ask questions of the picture which might never be asked of the words. We can no longer assume meanings. We can no longer assume a common language of pictures.

In the early years of schooling and pre-schooling, children draw lots of pictures. They also sing and dance. Sometimes, they learn the rudiments of musical instruments like drums and cymbals, the timing and the beat. They even gesticulate broadly, embrace, use all of their bodies and all of their senses as natural ways of expression and enactment until the socialization process in the Western styles takes hold and firmly guides the youngster into the culture of logos—

and now, the culture of the computer in front of which we sit and connect our neurological system to the electronic system through our eyes and our fingertips, and more recently, voice commands. And when we figure out exactly how to insert electronic chips into our bloods streams, where they may move inexorably to specific locations in our brains, and spinal chords, what is the next step? Is it that children, expressing the totality of their emerging humanness, will become, as adults, electronic cyborgs, devoid of feelings, empty of spirit, but remarkably adept at commands of the word?

Gradually, with the help of participants and co-facilitators, some of whom were true enliveners, I learned first to relax, yield, and accept these alternative forms; then, indeed, to invite envisioners to their own best ways of expression. Some invariably did that in drawing pictures, diagrams, symbols, and portrayals of their intended and desired futures. Sometimes their renditions were quite striking, sometimes obtuse, until I learned to let the pictures speak through their own medium, through their own language. Then, I could nod, hesitantly perhaps, and say, Yes. Maybe I've got it.

At first, I was a reluctant learner. My educated social biography stood in the way. But if I was to learn to be a better enlivener, I had better renegotiate the interplay of my own spirit with my social biography. I had better acquire the competencies that would facilitate the expression of their spirit in whatever ways their spirit chose to express itself.

"STAND-FORS"

From Pictures to Metaphors

These pictures, diagrams, symbols, and other visual renditions, well or poorly drawn, were what I call "stand-fors."

What is a "stand for"? It is something important that comes from a range of inner experience, from feelings, thoughts, and imaginings that are tinged with spirit's call, yet difficult, perhaps impossible, for some to articulate in conversation.

In my work, starting in 1970 at Syracuse University, I have always invited that: the personal, the experiential, and the deep-seated.

A vogue among futurists of the 1950s and 1960s was the gedank experiment—thought experiment—called simulation-gaming. Even now, it is still used in military circles and among think-tanks that construct scenarios to see "what would happen if... " It is also in use at the "commanding heights" of political parties, corporations, and governments. Simulation-gaming seeks to help people answer the question: What can we get away with? Almost all public relations, advertising, and image-spinning start with that practical and ubiquitous question. That question is at the cutting edge of marketing. It is the oil that smooths the rough-running engines of global economics and a civilization of false plenty that has overtaken the rich nations and left the poor nations kicking in the dust.

But, contrary to those simulation-games so popular among the ostensible wielders of political, economic, and military power, I always and no doubt naively asked this:

- Among the possible alternative futures you might generate in your imagination, which one or ones speak to your deepest sense of yourself? Which one or ones are compelling? Which one is that which you **cannot not be** and **cannot not do**?

- This is an invitation for your human spirit to speak out through your biography.
- But how do you speak out?
- For this spiritual archetype, the poetic spirit, it is through metaphor.

Drawings, like any form of artistic expression, are stand-fors. Some participants found that expressing their visions in pictures rather than words was more congenial. The pictures stood for that which they had come to in their deep imaging which they wanted to display. When invited to share their images with other envisioners, they chose to draw pictures on flip-chart paper rather than to write words. We left that choice up to them.

But why did they find pictures more congenial? Why did they make that choice?

Because these persons, some of them at least, are of the poetic spirit.

Who is the poetic spirit?

The poetic spirit is the one who speaks out in metaphors, whether the metaphors come in sounds, pictures, clay, wood, dance, song, or a reassembling of words outside the confinement of logic: all of the ways we humans express and share our realities so as to open up the horizon of understanding rather than to close it down.

Creative? Of course. But most of us are creative in all kinds of ways about all kinds of things.

What of the poet, per se? I mean, if you are called by your spiritual archetype to the poetic way of interacting with and impacting your experience, creating your reality, does this mean that you are, or have to be, a "poet," writing poems? Not to my way of thinking about the poetic archetype. I use the naming poetic because central to poetry is the metaphor: that which stands for something else, and so casts a new light on that something so that we see it, feel it, hear it, touch it differently. A metaphor calls out some aspect of the something else so that it comes to us, our sensibilities and our understandings, in a new way, challenging us to a newer or different response.

The "stand for" is a product of the human imagination that eschews logic and the scientific frame of mind for poetic forms. I am speaking of all forms of what we call "art," to include music, painting, sculpture, doodling, drawing, in some ways architecture, certainly storytelling in all of its forms and traditions, oral as well as literary.

The human language, taken in its totality of how we communicate, is rich in the forms of expression I call "stand-fors." That must include the ubiquitous human capacity to generate symbols. Symbols capture and assign meanings from immediate experience in such a way as to transfer those meanings from one setting to another, from one person to another even though the immediacy of the experience is not transferred.

So, of course, there is a piece of this creative capacity in all of us. But the poetic archetype is supremely unique, for it calls its inheritors to transpose and transform everyday "reality" into something new.

Are you one of them?

One way to tell, in addition to the deep probing you will undertake in the next section, is to recall situations where you have said to yourself some things like:

- I wish I could tell her, but I can't. She wouldn't understand.

  Perhaps leading to,

- I just can't describe to her what this is like. I can't find the words for it.

  Perhaps leading to,

- Silence.

  Or to,

- This situation... or my feelings... or my vision... or my spirit's call... simply defies description. There's no way I can speak it.

  But speak it I must. How?

Are these naive questions, naive feelings? Is it that you weren't trying hard enough? Were you too awkward, too inept, not well-enough steeped in the vocabulary and mechanics of your spoken language? Perhaps these are the case. But perhaps it's something else that gets in the way of words, but doesn't get in the way of music, poetry, painting, sculpture, dance, depictions and symbolizations of all kinds.

Music? Isn't that pushing "stand-fors" far beyond the domain of metaphor?

Music as a Stand-for

I think music is a great way to help you think about the archetype of the poetic spirit. It is the extreme case. Its domain is so distant from intellectual meaning, from cognitive understanding, from verbal symbolization, and from "poetic" metaphor as we have come to understand these in the lexicon of the human language.

Music? But haven't you hummed a tune, whistled a tune, sung along with one of the pop singer's renditions of your favorite song, or conducted the orchestra (in privacy, of course) when the radio or the disc player was sounding forth Tchaikovsky's 1812 Overture, Beethoven's Fifth, or Mozart's Jupiter symphony?

Children do this all the time. The spoken language is such a marvelous invention, perhaps a gift given to us gradually as we were learning to become human. But it has some inadequacies. One deficit is that it constrains our other forms of communication to very special occasions and very special people. But children are not so inhibited until their socialization is well underway. Children create and express their "stand-fors" all the time until an adult asks, as I originally did with the envisioners who drew pictures, What does it (do you) mean?

Music speaks to our species through a multitude of ways and forms. Tribal groups gather to sing their history, their traditions, and their stories, but without written music (or any writing, for that matter). Music is a way of interacting with one's realities, social as well as personal, outer as well as inner, about any aspect of experience. Music shifts that reality to a new domain. Music stands for the other reality but is expressed in this different domain. See how the poetic spirit creates Gregorian chant as well as the soaring sonorities of Hildegaard von Bingen, the harp or flute music of the ancient Greeks, the rock and roll, heavy metal, jazz and swing of the Twentieth Century, or the Riga called forth by the sitar.

Certainly, this is not the only way to talk about music. Professionals in music have their own ways of talking about music. I'm talking about it now, using the common English language of speaking, writing, and reading. But underneath my "talking" is something much deeper. Even for the non-musician, the non-music-lover, the nonprofessional, music responds to and expresses a range of experience that is deep within us. It stands for a vast range of human experiencing. Its sounds convey the widest array of feelings, both individual and shared in a group. It is a series of metaphors for experiencing those feelings.

The poetic spirit, lodged in some of us, creates many different kinds of metaphors that, like the music-maker's, constitute her lock on reality.

Is all human experience a metaphor, a "stand-for?"

The "formal" arts use metaphor as their lingua franca in multiple ways. That which we now call "art" is a formalization and a conceptualization of an ancient, pre-literate past, where people drew, painted, sculpted, made music, told legends and constructed myths to describe, share, celebrate, or bemoan their experiencing of life through these metaphorical languages, communicating through "stand-fors."

Some special ones among us are called by their spiritual archetype to realize, which means to bring into their own realities, that all of human experience is a metaphor, a "stand-for." These poetic spirits seek to fix, to glue that human experience by attaching it to whatever metaphors they find conducive to their gifts and talents.

Some of us are caught up in the scientific, empirical, techno-logical, practical and pragmatic linear, analytic culture of recent centuries—no doubt, a great contribution to the creativity of our species in its own right. So we don't quite know what to do with others of us called by this poetic archetype. Music, art, and mul-tiple nonlinguistic forms of creativity are last in-first out in school budgets when they come under the pressures of rising costs and taxpayer skepticism, at least in the United States. Learn the intel-lectualized pursuits in all of their forms, in schools and colleges, but don't give much time or effort to the "poetic" pursuits. For that spiritual archetype's call, were it to be given its due, would shift how we look at the world, how we look at ourselves, how we understand, feel about, and act in and upon our realities, our conformities, our uniformities. It invites us to create others.

The Crux of It

That is the crux of it. The call of the poetic spirit is to create new meanings for human experience by expressing them in the multiple languages of "stand-fors." It is to get beyond the conversation of the ordinary and to uncover alternatives still lying in the hologram of the implicate order, until a poetic spirit brings an alternative to the explicate order. She lifts the curtain and helps our universal imaginative capacity bring into existence that which is not yet in existence.

All humans share in a capacity to respond to the images, the new meanings, and the new "stand-fors." So too do all of the persons I have encountered who have responded to their spiritual archetype needs and who use whatever creative disposition is available to them.

But the poetic spirit is very special indeed. The ones who respond to that call create anew and differently our human experiencing of anything and everything. By their acts, they assign different meanings to the ordinary, making it sometimes extraordinary. By their acts, they invent new meanings in one form or another, sometimes meanings so powerful that they enter into spoken discourse, into our common mental life, and so show us what might have been, and what still might be.

I KNOW I'M CREATIVE.
AM I POETIC?

What is obvious... is obvious.

Readers who have gotten this far, who have felt the inspiration of their poetic spirit's call to them, might be having a good laugh by now. Certainly that would include some of the artists among them. Painters, sculptors, dancers, wood carvers, poets and dramatists, and composers, for example, don't need to be reminded that their spirit has been calling to them, through their talents and gifts, to "do their thing." They have been, and they know it. That's the first and most obvious case.

What of those who feel their spirit's call is to be a creative artist, but for one reason or the other, it hasn't panned out? It may be lack of training or lack of financial backing. There may be lack of institutional support within the domain they have chosen, or their approach or product may be too distant from the popular path to be promoted by those with influence or acceptance by the public. This is the second case and, I'm afraid, prevalent among too many of us.

How about not believing in yourself, or not trusting yourself? How about thinking you don't have the talent that is called for? What about being unwilling to give away that which has been given to you, your gift, because you don't think people are ready for it? Here, your spirit weeps.

This third case is the one that we might now begin to search out. For the poetic spirit calls us to a range of opportunity, challenge, and action far beyond the artistic domain. It calls us to turn things upside down, to stand reality on its head, to find the metaphor that brings into existence a new perspective, a new point of view, a new way of understanding that opens up the space for all of us to participate in our transformation.

Is that you? Might it be you? How would you know? How might you find out?

Entering Your Futures Room

Peel away the shell of your social biography. Uncover the call of your spirit lurking within.

That is the offer throughout this book. Entering your futures room is an act of deep learning. Once again, I invite you to enter, to ask yourself these questions.

- What would it be like if I were called to be poetic in my life, my work, my relationships, my understanding of how the world works and why it works that way?

As you sit and reflect, perhaps first for only a few minutes, put the question deep inside you, into your Tant'ien, the center of your vital life energy within which your spirit glows and warms itself. Then let the images emerge: the pictures, ideas, words, smells, voices, feelings—all the ways that images announce themselves to your conscious awareness.

Jot down some of these in words, or draw some pictures, symbols, diagrams, some doodles that represent these images.

As you reflect, yielding to that which is inside, other questions might suddenly seize upon you like a freshet of rain coming out of what you thought was clear, blue sky.

- But haven't I been poetic all my life? Haven't I always seen, felt, and known people, settings, situations, and organizations in ways that they haven't seen, felt, or known themselves?

If this is the case, you will know it and remember it. You will be able to think of a myriad of examples: the way a person seemed to you, different from other peoples' perceptions; the way a conflict struck you; the way a joy came to you; the way an idea was harboring something underneath it which people were reluctant to talk about, but you saw it instantly; the way some description or understanding of a situation didn't match your description or understanding.

Here, take a bit more time. Don't push for responses. Don't try to force anything. Just yield to the coming together of your memory and your imagination. Listen for what's there. Deep listen. Journaling this can be quite delightful if you don't suppress.

And finally, create the metaphors, the "stand-fors," for the ways you see, feel, think about, understand, describe and act towards and with your realities, the very ways you name them, that are unlike the customary ways of seeing, feeling, thinking about, understanding, describing and acting towards.

- Does this happen to you? Perhaps only within, which you keep to yourself? Perhaps also without, so that other people look at you and sense the differences?

These questions will draw a heartfelt sigh of relief from a person whose call is poetry no matter what may be her life circumstance.

Ah-hah, you will then say. This is me. This is my project: to shift the realities of the world by opening up the space for change and transformation, by naming them differently, by describing them differently, by seeing them through the eyes of my own spirit... fresh, unique, often misunderstood.

Many of us will find these words, these questions, this invitation, these chapters on the poetic spirit archetype absolutely unintelligible.

Okay. Some of us, more than you would think in the presence of a culture which most of us did not invent, are now just standing on the cusp of self-recognition.

My heart goes out to you. Among all of the archetypes of the human spirit, yours is the most unique because it offers us a different language to understand and deal with not only who we are but also who we might be. You are not schizophrenic, though you may live in more than one world. You are not paranoiac, though people may laugh at you, point at you, or persecute you. You dance with your dogs and see the Commander-in-Chief as a spoiled brat rather than a great leader. You talk to your cats as if they were lions, you feel your organization as the fabled centaur blindly felt his labyrinth as he ran this way and that seeking what had always eluded him, his freedom. You fold yourself flat against a tree or lie down in a mountain meadow of soft, virgin grass, ready to receive their gifts just as you deep listen to the genius of the neglected, the despondent, the poor, the recalcitrant. You embrace your own constitution of body, mind, and spirit, sacred and solid enough to hold you as you transform yourself every second of your life. You sense the spirit of the trees, the animals, the mountains and oceans in you because you know they have accepted your spirit in them. You understand that the universe is also your universe, a tabula rasa until you fill it with what your spirit and the Hubble scope call you to, and vice-versa, for the universe, your universe, is waiting for that declaration.

The poetic spirit understands these words, these examples, these metaphors, these "stand-fors." No doubt, for the rest of us, it's a bit of a stretch. Yet we all need this archetype, the poetic one, to remind us of what we might have been and what we yet might be in the becoming of our future on this planet.

The Symphony of the Human Spirit

Using words, I have sought to create in these pages a symphony of the human spirit, in which the poetic spirit plays its own part and creates its own music. We need the music of the other archetypes, too, else the symphony sounds the wrong music. The entrepreneurial spirit—what do we dare? The sustaining spirit—how do we learn to partner together and with our Earth? The loving and caring spirit— can we yet learn to become fully human persons to each other? The mending spirit—let us bind up so we can begin to heal. The just spirit—inviting us to live together without violating each other's spirit. The organizational spirit—how might we create the space between us for each person's spirit energy to be given to all of us, and all of our spirit-energy to be given to each of us. The enlivening spirit—to bring each person's spirit into the world. The reflective spirit—going to the criticals and uncovering the fundamentals.

And now the Poetic Spirit—re-conceiving our realities by helping us to explore the alternative offers the universe makes to us.

The Search Continues

I hope by now you have explored your calls and your invitations. No doubt, some of you have found or have reconfirmed your project in this world, that which you **cannot not be** and **cannot not do**. Others are still questioning. Perhaps none of these archetypes is your call, yet you desperately seek that which is unique to you and which you can share because spirit—your spirit—loves to share, is sociable, needs and wants to create that space where we are together in a community of human spirit. Perhaps still others of you feel drawn to more than one archetype, not because of its popularity or singularity but because your inner biography, the stories of yourself that only you know, are grounded in the marvelous push and pull between your human spirit, your very own, and your social biography.

In Chapter Twelve, *Discerning and Living Your Call*, my intention is to fashion the space wherein you can find a response to these practical, or operational, or living alternatives that will lead you into a full life, a right life, an abundant life. Who among us deserves less?

PART THREE

12

Discerning and Living Your Call

NAMING YOURSELF

Who names whom?

Some of you may have come to clarity about that to which your spirit calls you. Responding fully to that call is to name your spiritual self. For example: I am of a sustaining spirit, seeking a way of partnership with all things; or, I am an enjusting spirit who is called to seek justice throughout; or, I am of a reflective spirit, always uncovering the criticals and going to the fundamentals.

What you name yourself in your life is another matter. You have to make the translation into a reconstituted biography. You have to find or invent the ways in which you can put into practice that to which your spirit calls and how you have decided to respond. For many of us, this is no easy undertaking. The nine spiritual archetypes recount the search and vision of thousands of persons who decided to invent their futures, to generate alternatives, and to come to a vision which would give direction to their lives, their work, and their relationships.

So I have fashioned in Chapter Twelve some discerning practices which go to the heart of your self-naming. First, I invite you to review and discern the essence of your spirit's call; second, to reflect on how and to what extent your spirit's call has been expressed and enacted in your life, your work, your relationships, and the world; and third, to envision what it will be like when you have learned to offer your spirit's gifts to your world in the fullness of their promise.

For some of you, the call of your spirit has been strong since birth. Perhaps you are one of those who has known this at an early age, perhaps even in early childhood. Perhaps you have not only heard her call but have also responded to it. I have met young children who enact a loving and caring spirit as if that archetype were invented just for them. I have seen that in the playground and the classroom. I have no doubt that children of that same spirit offer their loving and caring in the tin-roofed huts of the São Paolo slums as well as on the plains where the Mongols dwell.

That archetype, like all the rest, is not culture-bound. But, like all the rest, it is translated through cultural forms into ways of expression that make it both relevant and challenging to that particular culture.

Sometimes, we humans can sense an archetypical call in another person, and so marvel at the unique ways it comes to be expressed. Recently, I saw on television an ornithologist offering a wildlife program about birds. He was talking about birds and their varied behaviors appropriate to their habitats and total ecologies. But this was more than talk, for he was standing in a field near a copse of trees. As he described and sometimes explained about particular subspecies, he acted the part of the birds, birds of all kinds, shapes, and sizes. He ran through the field, emulating the take off, flight, and soaring of the birds he was describing, his arms flapping, head and neck gesticulating, hips and back and legs somehow integrated into this mimicry that made you see bird, not man. This was more than his profession, his university degree, his training. It was clear that he and the birds were partners at some level of spirit. They sustained each other. He could not exist without his birds. They sustained him so that he could give to the rest of us a sense of birddom, what it is to live and be as a bird lives and exists.

How are any of these archetypes expressed in you?

I can only offer the description of their essences, as these have been revealed to me. You have to decide for yourself. I cannot call you to your spirit. Your spirit calls you. At best, we invite each other to the deep listening, the deep questioning, and the deep learning.

That means that neither I nor anyone else is to name your archetype, the one that calls to you. Neither psychologists nor career counselors can do that for you. You have to do that for yourself. If others do it for you, be suspicious. Skilled enliveners can invite you to that naming by their own deep listening and deep questioning, thus "walking the talk" with you in deep dialogue.

But only you can name yourself.

How do I name myself?

Most of us don't name ourselves. That is the secret of the social biography. Now it is out.

Throughout our countless interactions with others, throughout the ebb and flow of our lives, from birth to death, each of us is named by others. In many ways, this is not a "bad" thing, for as a species, we are social animals. Of course, that is not all that we are. But for most of historic time, our species has accumulated vast experience in living the groups and cultures that are the story of our beingness on this planet. Those who have loved you, cared for you, taught you, played with and disciplined you are also creatures of their social biographies.

But, this is a main point; they too have been called by their spirit, though they perhaps have not heard its call. You are not alone in this. The invitation comes in many ways, some so mysterious that we discount them, some so discombobulating that we dismiss them. Well or poorly, they too have sought to fight their way through the morass of social culture interred in their social biography, sought to discover that which is unique to each of them so they can make their contribution to the larger whole. Perhaps you have known or met one or two whose self-striving has overcome the barriers created by the group into which he or she was born.

Each of the spiritual archetypes constitutes a call to transcend the social biography. Your social biography is not mainly of your own making. That much is clear. To name yourself is to search out your gifts and talents, to acknowledge your inner biography, and to enter the inner space where your spirit will speak out. You have listened to the invitation of each of the nine spiritual archetypes

I have uncovered. Which speaks your name? One of them? More than one? Still another, yet unnamed, which is special to you? Which spiritual archetype sounds the clarion call to which your spirit responds? Perhaps it comes through as a whisper, a hint here or there, a clue that gives direction to your search.

Each spiritual archetype is bred into a human who can then respond in the unique way which gives her her special project on the planet; to contribute, as her spirit calls her, to the survival of all of us in loving, generous, just, creative, beautiful ways.

Now it is your turn to go as far as you choose in this self-exploration. What are your search tools?

YOUR SEARCH TOOLS—THE ARCHETYPES

First, the Archetypes Themselves

The first set of search tools is the descriptions of the nine spiritual archetypes set forth in the preceding pages. I have sought to describe their qualities and characteristics so as to reveal and convey their essences. Let me name them again, as they have come to me through the envisioning and enspiriting work with which I have been associated.

These nine archetypes are conceptual frames that seek to make sense of the enormous array of experience of thousands of folks doing envisioning and enspiriting around the world in the last 30 years. These nine spiritual archetypes have shown themselves through their deep work: first, their concerns about what is truly important to them; second, their compelling images of a future in which those concerns are well-addressed; and third, their enactments which seek to actualize the new realities their spirit calls them to.

The Entrepreneurial Spirit
(Chapter Three)

If lodged in you, it propels you to risk-taking, to shaping the curve, to making breakthroughs, to seeking and enacting new ways of being and doing in any or all arenas of your life and work. For persons of this cast, its realm of expression covers the waterfront of human activity. It is not restricted to starting up new businesses. It includes any arena of human activity where the risk is equal to the invention. Those of the entrepreneurial spirit often work with other people who try for the invention, the creation, even the transcendence of the ordinary, but who do not know how to take the risks.

The Sustaining Spirit
(Chapter Four)

This calls us to create partnerships with any or all of the entities on the planet without discrimination; with human beings who may be close to us, certainly, but also those who may be distant by virtue of biography, social class, ethnicity, heritage, physical location, or culture. These sustaining partnerships are not only with persons. They include the other ecologies of our dear earth; its rocks, forests, fish, deserts, elephants, and the entire biosphere, so that each sustains the other in an ineluctable spiral of giving and receiving, birthing and dying, while they hold each other close and celebrate their unique contributions to that partnering which keeps our very earth alive.

The Loving and Caring Spirit
(Chapter Five)

This spiritual archetype is so enfleshed in you that each individual you meet, for a brief moment or over your lifetime, is a person to you in her wholeness and in her potential, a person whom you are called to love, to nourish, and to nurture in and through the totality of her personhood. This includes her social biography, her inner stories and, of course, her very own spirit. In the loving person, loving and caring is offered regardless of the roles or categories by which we differentiate and discriminate among human beings. Labels mean absolutely nothing to the person in whom this call is fulfilled, because she is called to love and to nurture each person in the fullness of her promise and potential. By her offer, the gift of her spirit, she invites us to be fully human.

The Mending Spirit
(Chapter Six)

This archetype gives the unique invitation to enter into those situations of fragmentation and conflict which tear us asunder, both within a person and in our group lives; to "bind up the wounds"; to bring together, cleanse, and sew up the ragged edges of antagonisms, raw emotions, splits and tears so that, over time, healing might take place. True peacemakers are menders. Most of us stand in want of mending, inner or outer, so we must search for those of the mending spirit who are called to enter into our predicaments of fragmentation and conflicts. They join with us in our continuing search for wholeness.

The Just Spirit
(Chapter Seven)

This archetype's call is difficult to enact because at this stage in the world, its call is expressed mainly though asking questions rather than providing answers. Its essence is constantly to question how best might we live together (govern ourselves) on this planet, so that our spirit is not denied. How are we to govern ourselves, both inside and out, so that our human spirit flourishes? How can we be fair to ourselves and at the same time fair to others? How can we respond fruitfully to our inner demands and at the same time participate creatively (which means contribute) in the social experience? The just spirit seeks to balance the inner claims and the outer claims. It calls for acts of governance of self and with others that place these questions and criteria at the center of our living together as a human species on this planet.

The Organizational Spirit
(Chapter Eight)

Those called by it push at the boundaries of our ubiquitous organizational structures in order to create a space between and among us that promotes our creativity, our humanness, and above all, our spiritual possibilities. The organizational spirit invites us to reach beyond the roles, entitlements, obligations, systems of sanctions and rewards, hierarchies, labels, missions, loyalties, and levels of superiority and subordination that bind us to organizational purposes few of us have participated in establishing. Why? So as to emancipate the spirit of each member, and thus her unique contribution, in the interests of all members, and all members' spirits for the sake of each. She seeks to create a coalition of spirit-energy that translates into new purposes and shapes the space between us in new ways of being and doing together.

The Enlivening Spirit
(Chapter Nine)

Enliveners seek to bring the human spirit back to life, in the particular person and her world, which might be the whole world or her own, very unique, intimate setting. That scope matters not to the enlivener, because her call is to animate the human spirit and its action person-by-person, through deep dialogue. When confronted, as she continually is, by persons who suppress their spirit, her own spirit feels this as a loving challenge to open up the other to her own human spirit. She of this archetype can't help herself, so powerful is this calling. Her metier, perhaps more than any other, is deep listening.

The Reflective Spirit
(Chapter Ten)

Its reality is expressed in a constant questioning of everything. The person so called takes nothing for granted. She lives in a continuous search for understanding what's going on. She is compelled to go underneath the surface events, accounts, explanations, and excuses to the foundations on which all claims about what is real and true rest. How? By uncovering the criticals and going to the fundamentals, whether the occasion is repairing automobiles (the auto mechanic), repairing ideas (the philosopher), or repairing emotional imbalances (the psychiatrist). The call is to discern clearly and to question deeply as her primary method of inquiry.

The Poetic Spirit
(Chapter Eleven)

She is of the metaphor. That is her life. Her call is to create a language that places any or all realities—events, things, people, processes, ideas—in new configurations so as to uncover their alternative meanings. Her life is an ongoing "stands-for," as she creates and uncovers new ways for understanding, appreciating, and enacting who and what we might be and not yet are.

The Multiplicity of Our Responses

How do you take these archetypes to your bosom, internalize them, test them out, and discern the strength of their call to and within your spirit? While this self-research is serious and demanding, be sure that your spirit welcomes it. Know that these nine spiritual archetypes lie on a never-ending spiral that is open, revealing, and always in the process of your becoming. This means that:

- Some persons clearly respond to their spirit in such a way that they name themselves.

- Some persons, if they could find a clarity of call and response, would bring sense and meaning to a lot of what they do which hasn't worked, which hasn't flourished, which has been a bit of this and a bit of that, always seeking their true call. This is a source of enormous frustration and self-seeking among so many creative people.

- Some of us respond to a mixed call. This person's spirit accepts the fuzziness, ambiguity, uncertainty, and general messiness in the world of institutions we have invented and created. We name them "realists." But the best of them know inside what they are called to be and do as they too seek to change, to invent, to transcend the very realities in which they are immersed.

Discerning if and to what extent more than one archetype calls to and within your spirit (the mixed call) is no game for neophytes, because the spiritual archetypes possess a powerful surface appeal. Who wouldn't like to be known as loving and caring, mending, sustaining, entrepreneurial, reflective, poetic, and all the rest? Would we not like to discover or to confirm that in us exists a character and intention that answers all or most of the calls described in this book? That is why the disciplines and practices of enspiriting are so crucial to your search. Deep listening and deep questioning are important tools to help you get underneath this surface attractiveness so as to discern the essence of your spirit's call. If necessary, return to the discerning questions posed at the end of each section. Some persons may have listed a lot of surface data in response to all of the questions, but my experience is that the attractiveness of these nine spiritual archetypes, as well as their importance to our world, is not the same as uncovering and hearing your special call, that which is your own spirit's essence.

- And some of us are not yet ready to listen to our spirit. Whatever its call, it goes unheard, unheeded, unrequited. If this is your case, do not get down on yourself. Your spirit will speak out when it feels you are ready, and it doesn't much matter if you are two years old or seventy. The enspiriting practices, like deep listening and deep imaging, are ready for you when you are ready for them. Walking the spiral is a grand and ultimately joyous adventure. Searching your spirit is not a task. It is a self-invitation. Guilt, anxiety, preference judgments, and value judgments are simply not applicable in this search. They are wrong strategies that get in the way of deep listening and deep questioning. They are roadblocks, even barriers to discovering your spirit's path.

The Logic of the Search for Your Archetype

Yes, but what is the logic of the search?

Keep in mind that the spiritual archetypes are templates. But they are not your reality until you discover that!

The invitation of this book, ultimately a self-invitation, is to listen to the voice of your spirit, to hear its call, and to seek to respond as best you can.

I have discerned nine basic calls in the envisioning and enspiriting work of thousands of individuals. Why these nine and not some others? My response has to do with where we find ourselves, right now, on this planet. Here-and-now reality is a dynamic rendition and summary of the history of our species. Where we are now calls out, cries out, shouts out for transformation of ourselves and how we choose to live together. The specific invitations for that transformation are to be undertaken in different ways because of the complexity and the richness of that transformation. One way will not do it: not one policy, not one ideology or belief system, not one single issue-advocate. Many ways together just might do it. Our human spirit knows this. And this is why God, the Universal Spirit, has sent us the entrepreneurs, the sustainers, those of loving and caring, the menders, the enjusters, the organizers, the enliveners, the reflectives, and the poets.

For some of us, then, the call is clear. Some persons are of a particular spiritual archetype, and they know it. They act it out.

Others are also of a particular spiritual archetype, but for one reason or another, they have not yet learned that. Their life relationships, their work, their position in their world are a source of frustration, discontent, and imbalance, for they don't yet understand what they are called to be and do. By searching through the panoply of their experience, by uncovering their gifts and talents, they may come to clarity about their projects in this lifetime.

Others of us may be attracted to enacting the calls of more than one archetype. We see ourselves—our lives, our actions, our relationships, our work—as exemplifying more than one singular approach. We hear a multiple call, perhaps varying by the particular situation in which we find ourselves at a particular time in our history. That "overlap" and "mix" appear in the multiple ways we humans choose to enact our lives.

In the application of how we are called and to what we are called, the nine spiritual archetypes have "leaky margins." The dynamic of our lives is to experience being fragmented into roles and perceptions. These just don't fit together into a harmonious inner integration of spirit, body, feelings, and mind and an outer integration and appreciation of the remarkable and wonderful differences among us.

By listening to the voice of your spirit (the practices and disciplines of enspiriting), you seek to uncover your particular essence, that to which you are called, your project, your potential, and your promise. The spiritual archetypes help us to understand the call and invitation that so many of us have too long subdued or dismissed.

One spiritual archetype supports, nurtures, even helps create the other archetypes' expressions in "real life." How they support and interact with each other is understood only in their enactment.

These archetypes, standing as templates, as prisms, and as spiritual essences, are not simply my inventions or anyone else's. We humans have not created them, as we like to think we create our worlds. We have not invented them, as we invent our cultures. These archetypes constitute a special language for understanding the call of our spirit. That language is not only a language of words but also of feelings, of the body, and of the spirit itself. Like all new languages, you certainly can choose not to learn it.

We have invented our languages, borrowed from one to the other, appropriated, used, and added to. The language of the electronic media has blossomed to a wealthy vocabulary unheard of 50 years ago, and now in a universal usage among a sizeable portion of the human population. Computers work, and we have learned to talk about them, and to them.

What of the language of the human spirit, with its archetypes? What of the vocabulary of enspiriting, with its disciplines and practices? Shall we dismiss these? Some will, because our modern cultures have neglected the human spirit within. But those persons responding to the calls of their spirit no longer dismiss. Through the ages, we can speak their names. Now, shall we not seek to name ourselves as our spirit seeks to constitute us?

THE OTHER SEARCH TOOLS—
ENSPIRITING, THE QUESTIONS, YOUR RESPONSES

The Enspiriting Practices and Disciplines

The second set of search tools is yours.

Try them, appropriate them, own them.

Enspiriting is not a perceived reality lying somewhere out there. Its tools are yours, in you. Learning to enspirit is the new curriculum of change, invention, and transformation. First, learn to create the space inside. Later, create it outside with others, where your spirit will speak out.

This is deep listening to that part which too many of us neglect: the voice of our human spirit. When well shaped, that space takes on its own reality, its own qualities of yielding, nurturing, and being empty so that your social biography does not erect insurmountable barriers. Your inner biography, yours alone, and your spirit, yours alone, confront each other. Perhaps, they embrace. Then the inner dialogue ensues, characterized by the vulnerability, the intimacy, and the presence of each to the other. That deep dialogue puts you and your spirit in the same space.

When that comes to pass, a mending begins, far surpassing the words to describe it. If we were mended, if we were whole, if we human beings had not so fragmented ourselves, we would not have to talk about it and this book would never have been written. But talk about it we do because the discord has become a dissonance, a noise of self-violence and other-violence. We humans seek respite.

Listening to the voice of your spirit is one such respite.

The Questions

As you now know, for each of the archetypes I have forged a set of questions designed to help you to discern your response to their call and invitation. And I have invited you to uncover and describe your gifts and talents (Chapter Two). I have also invited you to test them in the crucible of your inner as well as your outer experience, both those gifts and talents which are acknowledged by others as part of your social biography, and those which only you know in the deep reaches of your inner biography. Laying these out begins to map the territory to explore as you search to uncover your spiritual archetype.

The record of this search is collected in your journal. It recounts your voyage through the archipelago of the spiritual archetypes to see where your gifts and talents might have taken you... and might yet take you.

What if these questions have not been helpful? Perhaps you have already fashioned your own self-questions to discern how, why, and when you respond to the voice of your spirit. Through these questions, I have sought to uncover the criticals and go to the fundamentals. Fashioning the questions and fashioning the responses are no easy tasks. I have invited you to look at your own inner life and your outer life; your inner biography of hopes, dreams, images, alternatives, a sense of yourself from your own perspective; and your outer biography, your social biography that joins you to the world of other people because they share the same expectations and meanings. Each question has invited your response.

Your Responses

Now is the time to review your journal. Revisit the experiences on which they draw and revisit your conclusions. You are certainly not locked in. The winds and seas of your voyage may shift and change as you visit one island, stay a while, then sail on to the next. New ideas, insights, and images may emerge. The process is much like sitting in front of the fireplace, or taking a walk, and remembering a trip you once took, perhaps recently, perhaps long ago. As you remember, you relive the trip. The events, places, and people take on the vibrancy of your experiencing that memory.

You can sail through the archipelago again, letting your spirit take you through calm seas or stormy wind and waves as your inner biography steers, your outer or social biography sets the sails, and you listen to the sound of your spirit-energy propelling you to this island or that. You may choose to revisit islands you particularly liked, those spiritual archetypes that invited you to call out: Is this me? Some of the islands in the archipelago of human spirit may be so unfamiliar to your life experience that you want to visit them again.

I thought the journey was finished, you might be saying to yourself by now. I've read the book. My journal is filled with notes, images, responses. What now? What more?

This is now where you are. As you look at the responses to the questions—whichever ones caught your attention, one or many, one archetype or all—how do you feel about them? Here is a bit of a spiritual challenge, which encompasses your intellect and your body as well as your mind. You are invited to uncover the criticals. How do you feel about your responses? What are they saying to you? Do they generate new questions? Do you want to revisit the islands of the archetypes in the ocean of your spirit? Did you miss some, and now want to take another look?

Sometimes this self-reflection is a relaxed meandering through the inner events of the journey I have invited, and sometimes there is an urgency. Let be what will be. There is no test here, no grades. There is not even success or failure.

There is the search. Do it. The spirit—your spirit—is with you.

CREATING YOUR BENESTROPHES

Years ago, I learned from Robert Theobald to name some of our happenings and creations benestrophes—those events, discoveries, and inventions which are good, beautiful, advantageous, helpful to all of us—as distinguished from catastrophes.

Is that not what our transformation is all about? Is that not what our human spirit invites? To create benestrophes?

The Vision Thing

One of America's recent presidents disparagingly named our hopes for the future, our heartbeat intentions toward the future, and the richness of our human potential and possibilities "the vision thing," thereby not only admitting his own lack of vision—though he was a very good politician—but also relegating it to a fairly unimportant place in presidential leadership and the making of public policy. And too often, organizations have equated vision with the "bottom line," whether that's measured in dividends, successful outcomes, or the number of "hits" on the Internet.

None of these is vision. Vision is that sense, usually quite specific and concrete, of what we humans are called to be and do which is worthwhile and which we are not yet being and doing. So it is a future state that describes only our potential and our promise, and is also compelling. It is a new way of being that starts now, even though its completion may be in the decades ahead. It is rarely final—we always have more to learn about ourselves, which is both blessing and burden—but it will not let go. One way to assess the truth of your own vision is to understand that vision is that which we **cannot not be** and which we **cannot not do**.

And it comes from your spirit. To be sure, it is announced and expressed most frequently through your biography, so it is colored by your life experience and your "values." But underlying these, giving a foundation solid enough to build a new sense of what is both possible and desirable in your life, is the call of your spirit.

Imaging That Call

To this point, you have addressed what that call is. You have sought out the strength of this or that archetype in your spirit, perhaps even uncovered a different or unexpected call. You have looked at your life and asked to what extent you have been living and enacting your spirit's invitation.

Through the enspiriting disciplines and practices, you have listened to the voice of your spirit and entered into dialogue with it.

Is that enough? Is there no further to go on the path you have been exploring?

I think there is one additional, exciting question, one next step which involves "the vision thing," and which places you squarely on the cusp of action to bring into being your spirit's call. It is described by your response to this question:

- What would it be like—in my life, my relationships, my work, my world—if I expressed and enacted this call? Not waiting around for the "right time." Not hoping that the stars will align themselves in a more propitious configuration. Not waiting for "permission" to be given by my own social biography, by the "authorities," by "cultural correctness" as defined by my group, my society, the fads and styles of the times, the media and on the Internet.

The key question here is "What would it be like if... "

The key response, as you probe your alternatives, your projects, your new way of being and doing, is to live that new state of affairs enacting your call in your imagination. Give it so strong a sense of inner reality that you realize you can do no other; that it is your spirit's call to action on behalf of that which you **cannot not do** and that which you **cannot not be**.

Thus, to the Deep Imaging

Perhaps you now realize that in several of the exercises and questions posed in this book, you have all along been trying out the deep imaging approach as a strong way to test whether this or that spiritual archetype indeed speaks to you through the voice of your spirit.

But this is no longer testing time. It is more "rehearsing." Rehearsing is what we humans do on many important occasions: before the important interview; before the wedding; before the contest of wills; sometimes even before the loving, the birthing, and the dying. Before most important events and challenges in our lives, we "try out" our actions and our responses. Thank God for that great capacity of our human imagination to rehearse.

Put that now to use on behalf of your spirit's voice. At first, you did deep imaging when you imagined what it would be like if you listened to the voice of your spirit, and indeed remembered what is was like when your spirit did speak to you.

But now you have more precise and clear material. For in one way or another, you have been listening and you have heard, perhaps not all at once, perhaps still with some doubts, some questions. Asking this question—what would it be like if—may very well help you to greater clarity about that call, its meaning and its strength, even as you describe in concrete and specific terms what it would be like.

- What might, could, would you do differently?
- What would you continue doing over the course of your life, because that longevity too is expressive of your spirit's call?
- How would you be? With yourself? With other people? A new presence in you? How expressed and articulated? With whom? When? Why?
- What might be the consequences? There are always consequences. That is another name for human action. Without consequences, there is no action. Sometimes negative, perhaps for yourself, perhaps for others. What negative? How negative? By whose criteria and standards? Your spirit's? Your biography's? The other person's in the setting or situation?

- But sometimes, I hope often, there are positive consequences in which you and other persons experience benestrophes, those experiences and events that are beneficial, advantageous, good in and of themselves, worthwhile, perhaps even important, perhaps with some longer-lasting significances. Again, by whose criteria and standards?
- Spell out all of your imagined, heartfelt, deep responses. Be specific and concrete. At the same time, be open as new and different images come to you.
- And how would you know that you were living out your spirit's call? What would you look for that would tell you that? What changes in yourself, what changes in other people, what

changes in the world? We call these indicators. But now, you have to choose them, you may even have to invent them, as you rehearse the advent of your spiritual archetype in you. For the old behavioral and social indicators may no longer suffice.

Why do this?

That is a question you might best answer for yourself. The actual inner action of deep imaging is certainly within your skill area if you have gotten to the end of this book. Your self-research, your probing, your deep listening, deep questioning, and deep learning have brought you to the point of this next step. I have said all along, in different ways, that if you will invite, love, nurture, and warm your spirit, it will do the same with you. As it reintegrates into your very beingness, it will afford you an enormous amount of spirit-energy to do this work in the face of whatever barriers you or others have thrown up over your lifetime.

Now comes the action: first, through deep imaging your response to the questions above. That is your inner action. Then comes the outer action: about who you will become, what you will be and do, in very specific and concrete ways, that constitute the presence of your spirit in you and in the world. First the rehearsal. Then the opening act.

How I wish I could be present with each and every one of you as you bring your spirit's call to fruition, whether it is in one little thing or in dramatic ways, whether it is over your lifetime or tomorrow, whether it is acknowledged by others or only by yourself.

And my spirit says to yours, in its welcome and support:

BE OF GOOD SPIRIT!

Acknowledgements

Books like this don't see the light of day as unaccompanied solos, absent of friends who are colleagues, who comment on the work in progress, and who give their own spirit-energy when mine wanes. Among them during the course of this writing, and to whom go in return the affection of my own spirit are Steffie Allen, Dave Barr, John Brennan, Kathy Buchenauer, Donna Cardinal, Wes Denison, Gordon Dveirin, Eva Grundelius, Melanie Mulhall and Jeanine Ransom. Some of them journeyed from Canada and Sweden to participate in the enspiriting work to which this book constitutes a contribution, and all have been part of the ongoing dialogue about how and why the enspiriting disciplines and practices have engaged their own lives.

Warren Ziegler
1927 – 2004

There are several people to whom I will be forever grateful for supporting the publishing of this second edition. To my editor, Dorsey Moore, for the many hours she spent in making this book more accessible and readable. The insights she has into Warren's thoughts and spirit as she fine-tuned the content is an acknowledgment of her gifts and talents. To Sheila Hentges, a special thank you for her artistic graphic design and production of this book. Her knowledge and constant efforts made this book a reality. To my book shepherd, Dr. Judith Briles, who has tremendous knowledge of the publishing world and who taught me so much about the dos and don'ts of marketing this book. To my attorney, Jon Tandler and my CPA, Steve Hittesdorf, I am grateful for their professional and personal guidance through some very dark days. If not for all of these people, I don't believe I would have accomplished this work.

To many members of my family and Warren's family, I extend my love and gratitude for their encouragement, support, advice, and all the times they spent listening to my plans and exasperations. Jerry Ziegler and Kathy Buchenaur were always available to ask for their advice and to listen to my tales of woe and to my hopes. To Pat and Jerry Ziegler, Cate Ziegler, Warren's daughter and to my sister, Gretchen Cooper, I am grateful for their support and their interest in the success of this book. A loving thank you goes to my son, Zachariah, who was always there with a hug and words of encouragement whenever I needed it.

And to Warren for teaching me how to discover my spiritual voice, I owe my loving and unending gratitude.

Mandy Ziegler
NOVEMBER 2008

About the Author
1927–2004

An international futurist, researcher, teacher, author, and enspirited envisioner, Warren Ziegler was born in New York City. He served in the U.S. Navy in World War II and completed postgraduate work at the University of Chicago. He served as Director of Eastern Nigeria for the Peace Corps and Director of the Educational Policy Research Center at Syracuse University. He was a senior fellow at the Center for Discovery and Invention at Long Island University and to the Learning Center for Creative Change at Rhodes College in Memphis, Tennessee.

Warren also held a senior position with the U.S. Agency for International Development in Washington, D.C. He taught at the university level in the U.S., Canada, Denmark, England, Venezuela and Yugoslavia.

Published extensively in the fields of lifelong learning, post-secondary education, civic literacy, leadership and policy planning, futures work, creative conflict and enspirited envisioning, Warren inspired others towards a vision of world peace and the fulfillment of human potential. He pioneered enspiriting techniques and is the author of *Ways of Enspiriting, Transformative Practices of the Twenty-First Century; When Your Spirit Calls, In Search of Your Spiritual Voice (Second Edition, Revised); Enspiriting Tapes; Legends of Red Planet,* and numerous workbooks and papers.

Endnotes

PART ONE
Chapter One

1   The nature of our de-spiritualized age is described in an earlier book of mine, *Ways of Enspiriting: Transformative Practices for the Twenty-First Century.*

2   My first writing on deep listening took the form of a guidebook, *Deep Listening the Empty Vessel Way.* When I began my work on it, I realized that a brand new way of listening to each other was required because the material of their dialogue, in its best mode, was an expression of their spirit. How does spirit listen? It is not an act of communication as we have come to understand that. It is beyond the theories, practices, and research in that field. It is to participate in that space where the human spirit is the chief actor.

3   Sometimes, I have had to coin a new word to convey the active voice, the doing of it, rather than that which is done. So *enspiriting* is the active voice of the human spirit, intentioning is coming to your own intentions, the very action which produces your intentions. Enjusting is what we do when we called to bring about justice in this world.

4   Fritjof Capra, *The Web of Life,* Anchor Books Doubleday, 1966.

5   Mary Watkins, *Waking Dreams,* Dallas. Spring Publications, Inc. 1994.

6   The *Tant'ien* is the Chinese word for the center of your being, of your vital life force, which I learned many years ago from a T'ai Chi master at the same time that I began my study of Lao Tse's *Tao Te Cning* and Chuang Tzu's *Inner Chapters.* From these I came to the basic enspiriting practice of deep listening, which is an emptying so that nothing but your spirit is left to listen.

Chapter Two

7   Hannah Arendt, *The Human Condition,* The University of Chicago Press, 1958.

8   In an earlier book, *Ways of Enspiriting* (Ibid), I coined the acronym *KBVAF* to stand for "knowledge," "beliefs," "values," "attitudes," and "faiths," taken all together, as an interlocking system of mental phenomena which are external to us but which become internal to us, part of our inner working of thinking and feeling as a result of the socialization process. Each of these mental phenomena is the separate

focus of a multitude of scientific, philosophical, theological, and behavioral fields of study. Rarely are they all put together into one interlocking system that comes from the outside and is internalized into our social biography as we grow up in and accommodate ourselves to the society, the culture, the group in which we live. On the one hand, the *KBVAF* is the binding glue of society. On the other, it takes substantial courage to break free of it and chart a course more conductive to the call of your spirit.

9   James Hillman, *The Soul's Code. In Search of Character and Calling.* Random House, 1996.

10   *Deep Learning* is another enspiriting practice, a discipline of the spirit in which you shed your protections, your habits, and your personal culture to create the space for both you and your spirit to learn from each other, sometimes after a long absence.

PART TWO
Chapter Four

11   Do read Susan Sharpe's remarkable report, essay, and analysis *Restorative Justice: A Vision for Healing and Change,* Edmonton Victim Offender Mediation Society, (#205, 10711-107, Edmonton, Alberta, T5H 0W6), 1998, ISBN 0-9683595-0-7. This crisp treatise exemplifies how the sustaining spirit's modality of partnering is at the very center of a transformative relationship among victim, perpetrator, and community.

12   The enspiriting dialogue, sometimes called deep dialogue, is the ultimate discipline of the spirit. Its qualities and practices are fully discussed in Ibid, *Ways of Enspiriting.* We tend to think of dialogue solely, or at least mainly, as an intellectual exchange, always verbal, between two persons or within a small group. But we have learned that its inner counterpart is also truly dialogue, and that it can also take place among a very large number of persons when they have learned its practices and their social biographies are ready for it. Spirit is always ready for it. Its chief characteristics are intimacy, vulnerability, and presence. The words come later, if at all.

13   Intentioning is a discipline of the spirit. Often, it comes into conscious awareness as a compelling image that gives direction, sustenance and compellingness to your actions. The discipline and its enspiriting practices are described in *Ways of Enspiriting*, Ibid, and in the *Enspiriting Tapes.*

14   Sam Keen, *Learning to Fly—Trapeze-Reflections on Fear, Trust, and the Joy of Letting Go,* Broadway Books, New York, 1999.

Chapter Six

15 As quoted in Chang Chung-yuan, *Tao: A New Way of Thinking, a translation of the Tao Te Ching with an introduction and commentaries,* Harper and Row, New York, 1975. Chang Chung-yuan goes on to comment page 208: *What Lao Tzu has in mind is an ideal society in which the great Tao prevails... When people are really able to enjoy their lives, their being and their thinking are totally identified. It is through this deep, underlying harmony that people are freed from the intention of war... In their harmonious lives, the people grasp the reality of things, not merely their appearances... their spiritual lives are harmonized.*

16 This work is described in Linda Ryan, *How the Women of Belfast Envision Peace: Exploring the Use of Visioning in Analyzing a Conflict,* Nova Southeastern University, 1998. This is a remarkable, empirical study of what these women envisioned, a future state of affairs in very specific and concrete terms which, when actualized and enacted, would bring not only the absence of violence but a range of positive conditions and behaviors whose absence has rent asunder their lives, their families, their communities, and the very possibility of being mended.

Chapter Eight

17 This is also the title of an essay I wrote in 1983, so impressed was I by this call to free human learning from the prison walls of our educational systems.

18 *The Challenge of Imaging Peace in Wartime,* in "Futures, the journal of forecasting, planning and policy," Volume 23, No. 5, Butterworth-Heinemann, Ltd., Oxford, 1991.

Chapter Nine

19 Character is not the same as personality. The latter is a relatively modern term, taking its meaning from psychology. Character is an ancient word, meaning your virtues, your assemblage of strengths, competencies and dispositions that are your presence in the world, not to be analyzed but to be offered and accepted.

20 See Daniel Goldman, *Emotional Intelligence,* Bantam Books, 1995. As I said earlier, spirit enters into that extraordinary development in the human being when its neuro-biological mechanisms have matured to the point of imagining alternatives to an otherwise inevitable and involuntary biological control. Each spiritual archetype offers its call, its invitation, and its project as that counter-balance.

Index

E
Earth, partnering with, 16, 101–103
ecological purpose, 258
economic themes, malfeasance of, 77
effectiveness, 215
efficiency, 193, 215
Einstein, Albert, 268
Eisenhower, Dwight, 201
emancipation of spirit, 122
emotions, 240–241
empathy, 16, 238–239, 240
    See also loving and caring spirit
employment, 41
emptying, 34–35, 37, 56–57, 79
enlivening spirit, 7, 20, 225–255, 296,
    310
    and the biographical factor, 227–228
    the call to, 253–255
    and deep listening, 20
    and deep questioning, 20
    described, 225–230, 231–234
    and emotions, 240–241
    and enlivening of self, 250–253
    and enlivening the other, 253–255
    and enspiriting, 231, 233, 239–240,
        251
    and herding, 247
    and journaling, 231, 249–250, 252
    as loving, 238–239
    and new morality of the fully human,
        241–242
    physics of human spirit, 228–230
    questions for, 234–238
    and questions for the other, 246–250
    questions from the other, 243–245
    and self-research, 243–255
    and sensitivity, 247–248
    skills for, 252–253
enspirited envisioning, v–viii, 85–86, 150,
    153, 193, 212
    See also envisioning the future
enspirited listening
    See deep listening

enspiriting
    and deep imaging, 65–66
    and deep learning, 198
    and deep listening, 24–26, 33
    and deep questioning, 34–35, 118
    described, 4, 24, 314
    and enlivening spirit, 231, 233, 239–
        240, 251
    and entrepreneurial spirit, 80
    four practices of, 37
    and the inner and outer, 104
    and invitation, 31–32
    and journaling, 25
    and mending spirit, 141–142
    and new moral code, 236–237
    preparation for, 35–37, 40
    vs. psychologizing, 116
    skills of, 252
enspiriting craft, 56
enspiriting dialogue, 101, 209, 212, 214,
    223
enspiriting disciplines and practices, 176,
    269, 312–315, 321
    See also deep imaging; deep learning;
        deep listening; deep questioning;
        discerning; inner dialogue;
        intentioning
enspiriting matrix, 26–27
enspiriting practices and disciplines,
    316–319
enspiritors, 12, 37, 80, 107, 191, 199,
    214, 219, 268
entrepreneurial spirit, 6, 15–16, 75–96,
    296, 307
    and breakthroughs, 78–81, 82–84, 86
    the call to, 75–80
    and deep imaging, 94–96
    and enspiriting, 80
    and the illusion of failure, 88–89
    and malfeasance of economic themes,
        77
    and outer and inner risks, 90–92
    questions for, 82–84, 86–88, 92–93
    and risk-taking, 75–78, 84, 85–88

Printing Notes

Enspiriting Press, LLC has made a commitment to utilize and implement environmentally-friendly standards—not only in theory but in action. The revised printing of this book has been a learning experience, an opportunity for growth and an example for how one seemingly small decision can have such a tremendous impact.

PRINTED WITH 100% VEGETABLE-BASED INKS

Mixed Sources

Cert no. SW-COC-001271
© 1996 FSC

FSC

ENVIRONMENTAL BENEFITS STATEMENT

Enspiriting Press saved the following resources by printing the pages of this book on chlorine free paper made with 100% post-consumer waste.

TREES	WATER	ENERGY	SOLID WASTE	GREENHOUSE GASES
6	2,144	4	275	516
FULLY GROWN	GALLONS	MILLION BTUs	POUNDS	POUNDS

Calculations based on research by Environmental Defense and the Paper Task Force. Manufactured at Friesens Corporation

Friesens Corporation is a Canadian-based printer, founded in 1907. Friesens has been employee-owned since the 1980s and, as of this printing, employs seven US citizens.

QUICK ORDER FORM

Place your order using any of the following methods:

WEBSITE EnspiritingPress.com

EMAIL orders@EnspiritingPress.com

MAIL Enspiriting Press, LLC
3551 S Monaco Pkwy, #291
Denver, CO 80231

TELEPHONE 303/306-1399 **FAX** 303/751-0337

Please include the following information to process your order:

Name

Address

City   State   Zip

Telephone

Email address

When Your Spirit Calls $21.95 US   x _____   = $_____
PER COPY   QUANTITY   SUBTOTAL

+ $_____

SALES TAX
Applicable For Delivery to Colorado Addresses Only
Select ONE OPTION for city of Denver OR all other CO cities.

7.72% SALES TAX
FOR DENVER, CO
ADDRESSES

OR $_____

2.9% SALES TAX
FOR CO ADDRESSES

SHIPPING/HANDLING COSTS
U.S. Orders
$6.00 for the first book plus $3.00 for each additional book.

International Orders
Please contact by phone or email for shipping estimate.

+ $_____
SHIPPING/HANDLING

= $_____
TOTAL

❑ I am enclosing a check payable to *Enspiriting Press, LLC*

❑ Please charge:
   ❑ VISA   ❑ MASTERCARD   ❑ DISCOVER   ❑ AMERICAN EXPRESS

Card #   Expiration Date

Print Name on Card   Signature